Mathematics and Applications of Computer Graphics

Jun Mitani · Kenshi Takayama ·
Yoshinori Dobashi · Tomohiko Mukai ·
Makoto Fujisawa

Mathematics
and Applications
of Computer Graphics

 Springer

Jun Mitani
Graduate School of Science
and Technology
University of Tsukuba
Tsukuba, Ibaraki, Japan

Yoshinori Dobashi
Graduate School of Information Science
and Technology
Hokkaido University
Sapporo, Hokkaido, Japan

Makoto Fujisawa
Institute of Library, Information and Media
Science
University of Tsukuba
Tsukuba, Ibaraki, Japan

Kenshi Takayama
AI Lab
CyberAgent
Shibuya, Tokyo, Japan

Tomohiko Mukai
Faculty of Systems Design
Tokyo Metropolitan University
Hino, Tokyo, Japan

ISBN 978-981-96-2932-9   ISBN 978-981-96-2933-6   (eBook)
https://doi.org/10.1007/978-981-96-2933-6

Translation from the Japanese language edition: "3DCGの数理と応用" by Jun Mitani et al., © Authors 2023. Published by Coronasha. All Rights Reserved.

The original submitted manuscript has been translated into English. The translation was done using artificial intelligence. A subsequent revision was performed by the author(s) to further refine the work and to ensure that the translation is appropriate concerning content and scientific correctness. It may, however, read stylistically different from a conventional translation.

This Springer imprint is published by the registered company Springer Nature Singapore Pte Ltd.
The registered company address is: 152 Beach Road, #21-01/04 Gateway East, Singapore 189721, Singapore

If disposing of this product, please recycle the paper.

Preface

It is said that the origin of computer graphics (CG) dates back to the early 1960s when Ivan Sutherland, an American computer scientist, invented Sketchpad, which was a precursor to the graphical user interface (GUI). For a long time thereafter, computers were primarily used for scientific and technical calculations and back-office tasks. However, with the advent of personal computers and gaming consoles being used in our daily lives, a wide range of applications for entertainment purposes have been developed. As computer performance improved and the demand for creating images as if the real world was expanding on the screen increased, 3D CG became an indispensable technology. Today, various services based on 3D CG have been born in games, movies, advertisements, VR experiences, and more. Furthermore, with the advent of head-mounted displays, the range of applications has expanded due to the possibility of immersive experiences. More than 60 years after the birth of CG, computers have achieved dramatic performance improvements that would have been unimaginable at the time, and with the development of 3D CG technology, images with such realism that they are indistinguishable from live-action can now be generated almost in real time.

Virtual reality, virtual space, cyberspace, metaverse, parallel world, and so on, terms representing activities in virtual spaces created by computers have appeared one after another, and the challenge to create a new world with 3D CG shows no signs of stopping. Perhaps humans inherently have a desire to create a new space with their own hands that is similar to the space they live in. If so, 3D CG will continue to evolve until that is achieved and will continue to be universally needed in the future.

Now, such 3D CG technology did not appear overnight. There was a steady accumulation of technical development over a long period from the birth of computer graphics. We are now reaping the fruits of that effort. However, if you want to master 3D CG technology and contribute to its development, you need to understand the underlying technology. To meet this need, this book was written.

This book explains the technologies that support 3DCG, divided into four chapters: "Geometry Processing with Surface Meshes," "Rendering," "Character Animation," and "Physics Simulation." Each of these is explained in a separate chapter. If we were to express these four technologies in simpler terms, we could say they are about creating shapes, creating images, creating movements, and reproducing the behavior of the natural world. In Chap. 1 (authored by Kenshi Takayama), we explain the theories for describing the shape of an object with a surface mesh and editing and processing it. In Chap. 2 (authored by Yoshinori Dobashi), we focus on the calculation of the appearance of the object's surface and explain global illumination calculation methods for generating realistic images, fast image generation methods using pre-calculation, and physical phenomena such as light scattering necessary for improving realism. In Chap. 3 (authored by Tomohiko Mukai), we introduce the skeleton method, a standard technique in animation production, and explain various animation editing techniques for humanoid character models. Finally, in Chap. 4 (authored by Makoto Fujisawa), we explain methods for calculating the behavior of complex natural phenomena, including not only rigid objects but also fluid like water and air. The four themes mentioned here can indeed be said to be the fundamental elements that support 3DCG. Each chapter was written by researchers who are active at the forefront of each field. All the authors have remarkable achievements and are leading the development of 3DCG technology with their abundant experience and knowledge.

The content covered in this book is the basics of 3DCG, but that does not mean it is simple. Compared to similar books, it contains mathematically advanced content. Specifically, basic knowledge of analysis and linear algebra, which is taught in college science and engineering courses, is required. Also, basic knowledge of continuum mechanics and fluid mechanics, and knowledge of mathematical optimization such as least squares method would make it easier to read. Therefore, the main target readers of this book are senior students in science and engineering courses or graduate students. This book is also recommended for a wide range of people, including high school students and professionals interested in the theory behind 3D computer graphics, engineers working at game development companies, and those considering 3D computer graphics as a research subject.

We hope this book will be useful in understanding the technologies that support 3DCG.

Tsukuba, Ibaraki, Japan   Jun Mitani
October 2024

Contents

Chapter 1
Geometry Processing with Surface Meshes

Kenshi Takayama

Abstract The first thing that is necessary for 3DCG production is to appropriately represent the shape of the object one wants to depict on a computer. If we exclude things like clouds or fur that do not have a clear outline, the shape of an object can be described by its *surface*. Therefore, representing the shape of an object as a surface and further editing and processing it is extremely important in 3DCG production. The theoretical background related to surface shape processing includes various fields of mathematics such as differential geometry, and research has been continuously conducted from the dawn of computer graphics. In this chapter, after introducing basic concepts and data structures for representing surfaces, we will discuss several representative tasks and their basic solutions.

1.1 Introduction

1.1.1 Methods of Representing Surface Geometry

The methods of representing surface geometry on a computer can be broadly classified into implicit and explicit approaches. In the implicit approach, we consider an *implicit function* in 3D space $f : \mathbb{R}^3 \to \mathbb{R}$, and represent the shape as its *isosurface* $\{\mathbf{x} \mid f(\mathbf{x}) = 0\} \subset \mathbb{R}^3$. For example, a sphere with radius r centered at the origin can be represented by the following implicit function

$$f(\mathbf{x}) = \|\mathbf{x}\| - r.$$

In this case, the implicit function is a signed distance from the input 3D position to the sphere (negative inside the object, positive outside), and such functions are specifically called *signed distance functions* (SDFs). Although SDFs are often used as implicit functions, any function that changes sharply from positive to negative near the surface can be used as an implicit function, not just SDFs.

J. Mitani et al., *Mathematics and Applications of Computer Graphics*,
https://doi.org/10.1007/978-981-96-2933-6_1

In the explicit approach, on the other hand, a point $\mathbf{p} \in \mathbb{R}^3$ on a 3D surface is a function of two parameters $(\alpha, \beta) \in \mathbb{R}^2, \mathbf{p} : \mathbb{R}^2 \to \mathbb{R}^3$. For example, the same sphere as above is represented by

$$\mathbf{p}(\alpha, \beta) = \begin{pmatrix} r \cos \alpha \sin \beta \\ r \sin \alpha \sin \beta \\ r \cos \beta \end{pmatrix}, \quad \begin{array}{l} 0 \leq \alpha < 2\pi \\ 0 \leq \beta \leq \pi \end{array}.$$

As another example, a triangle formed by three points $\mathbf{p}_1, \mathbf{p}_2, \mathbf{p}_3 \in \mathbb{R}^3$ is represented by

$$\mathbf{p}(\alpha, \beta) = \alpha \mathbf{p}_1 + \beta \mathbf{p}_2 + (1 - \alpha - \beta)\mathbf{p}_3, \quad \begin{array}{l} \alpha \geq 0 \\ \beta \geq 0 \\ \alpha + \beta \leq 1 \end{array}.$$

By covering the surface of an object with such triangles, in theory, any 3D shape can be represented. Such a representation is specifically called a *triangular mesh*.

Note that in the above, each triangle is described by a linear polynomial in α and β. By expanding this to a second or higher degree polynomial (with the expanded set of points $\{\mathbf{p}_i\}$), it is possible to describe curved surface shapes. This kind of representation is often called a *parametric surface*, but it will not be covered in this chapter.

As shown above, the implicit and explicit approaches are fundamentally different in terms of how they represent shapes, and they have their own strengths and weaknesses. The greatest strength of the implicit representation is that they can easily handle changes in surface topology. Here, surface topology is a concept that distinguishes between a sphere and a donut, for example. A sphere will never become a donut no matter how it is deformed, but a mug cup can become a donut by deformation (Fig. 1.1). To make a donut from a sphere, operations that change the surface topology, not just deformation, such as opening a hole or bridging two points on the surface, are necessary. When using the implicit representation, such operations can be easily implemented simply by changing the values of the implicit functions. On

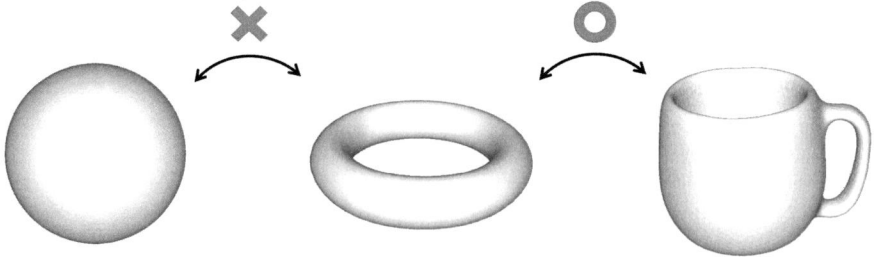

Fig. 1.1 Examples of surfaces of different topologies

the other hand, when using the explicit representation, complex procedures such as appropriately updating the connectivity of triangles are necessary to perform such operations.

The greatest strength of the explicit representation is that they can easily access points on the surface just by giving parameters (α, β). Thanks to this, drawing shapes using real-time graphics APIs such as OpenGL is straightforward. In the case of the implicit representation, because the surface is expressed as a set of roots of the implicit function $f(\mathbf{x})$, it is necessary to solve equations to accurately obtain the position of points on the surface. For this reason, it is difficult to directly draw shapes represented by implicit functions using OpenGL or the like; one must convert them into explicit representations (where the Marching Cubes [1] method is the most popular) before drawing.

In this chapter, we will discuss the processing of surface shapes explicitly represented by triangular meshes. Before moving on to the formulations and algorithms of representative geometry processing tasks for surface meshes, we will explain the basic definitions and data structures of polygonal meshes.

1.1.2 Shape Representation by Polygonal Meshes

A *polygonal mesh* is a structure that can be formed by connecting a set of vertices with polygonal faces. Those in which all faces are triangles are specifically called triangular meshes. The lines that connect the vertices forming a face are called edges. For a given edge, if the number of faces sharing it is one, it is called a boundary edge. If the number is two or more, it is respectively called a manifold or a non-manifold edge. Vertices belonging to boundary edges are called boundary vertices, and those that do not are called internal vertices. For boundary vertices and internal vertices, if the set of faces sharing them forms a semi-circular or disk-shaped surface patch, they are called manifold vertices. If not, they are called non-manifold vertices (Fig. 1.2). We call a mesh that does not include any non-manifold edges or vertices a *manifold mesh*.

A triangle can define a front and back orientation, and conventionally, when the sequence of its vertices appears counterclockwise from a certain viewpoint, we call that visible side the front. For a manifold mesh, when the two faces adjacent to every edge can be consistently oriented, we call that surface mesh *orientable*. Figure 1.3 shows some examples of non-orientable surface meshes. A mesh representing the surface of a 3D object is inherently manifold and orientable. In this chapter, we will assume shapes are represented by manifold and orientable triangular meshes.

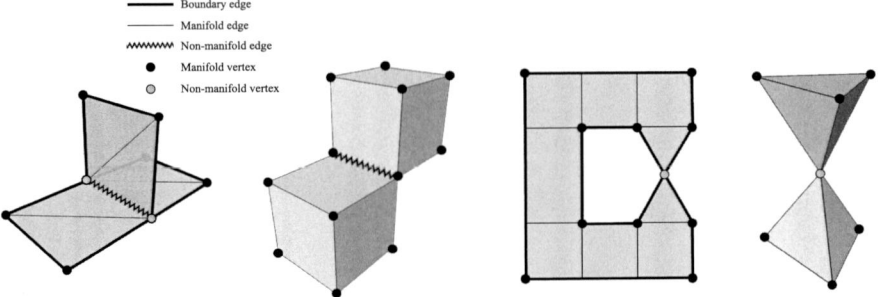

Fig. 1.2 Examples of manifold and non-manifold edges and vertices

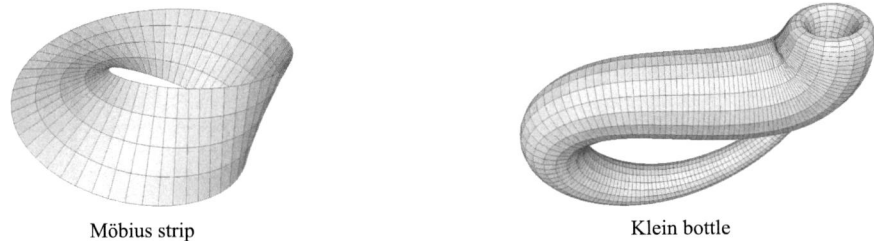

Möbius strip   Klein bottle

Fig. 1.3 Examples of non-orientable surfaces

1.1.3 Data Structures for Polygonal Meshes

1.1.3.1 Array-Based Data Structures

The most basic data structure for polygonal meshes is array-based, consisting of
arrays of vertices and faces. For the array of vertices, each element stores the 3D
coordinates of a vertex. For the array of faces, each element stores a list of indices of
the vertices that form the face. This data structure is very simple and is widely used in
many file formats, such as .obj and .off, because it is convenient for passing data
between different software. An example of a .off format file is shown in Fig. 1.4.
Assuming a triangular mesh, the arrays of vertices and faces can be represented as
$n_V \times 3$ and $n_F \times 3$ matrices respectively (where n_V, n_F are the total number of
vertices and faces), allowing various shape processing algorithms to be described as
matrix operations. A popular geometry processing library based on this approach is
libigl [2].

1.1.3.2 Half-Edge Data Structure

While the array-based data structure has the advantage of being simple and compact,
it has the drawback that it requires costly searches when accessing nearby elements.

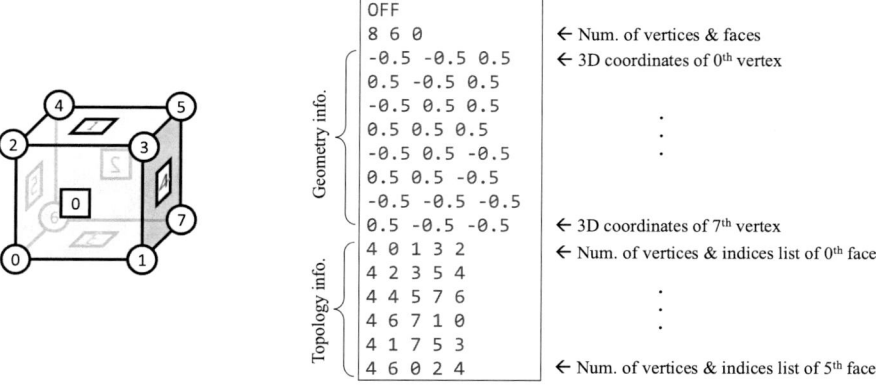

Fig. 1.4 Example of representing a cube in .off file format

For example, to enumerate all faces adjacent to a certain vertex, it is necessary to search all faces in the array that include that vertex. If one wants to sort that set of faces in the order of clockwise walk around the center vertex, one will need to search again within that set.

The *half-edge* data structure is well suited for such purposes (Fig. 1.5). The basic idea is to represent an edge, which originally has no distinction of direction, as a pair of two half-edges that are directed in opposite directions to each other. Each half-edge maintains references to the following four adjacent elements:

a. The destination vertex
b. The next half-edge
c. The opposite half-edge
d. The face to which it belongs

In addition, each vertex maintains (in addition to its 3D coordinates) a reference to one of the half-edges that start from it, and each face maintains a reference to one of the half-edges that constitute it.

This set of additional reference information makes traversing adjacent elements on the mesh easy and efficient. For example, to obtain all the faces adjacent to a certain vertex i in the clockwise order, one proceeds as follows:

1. Obtain the half-edge ij that the vertex i refers to.
2. Obtain the face that the half-edge ij belongs to and add it to the result list.
3. Obtain the opposite half-edge ji of ij.
4. Obtain the next half-edge ik of ji, and repeat 2., 3., and 4. until this matches the first half-edge ij.

Using half-edges, operations that locally alter the mesh structure, such as vertex insertion and edge collapse, can be performed at a constant cost. In contrast, array-based structures incur a cost proportional to the number of elements in the mesh.

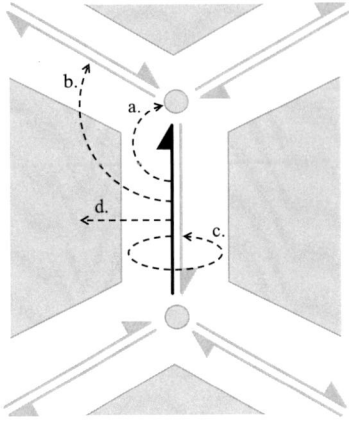

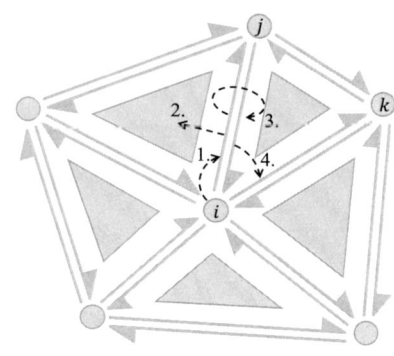

References held by a halfedge   Enumeration of faces adjacent to a vertex

Fig. 1.5 Half-edge data structure

To implement a half-edge data structure, one can either dynamically instantiate an object for each of the elements (using the `new` keyword in C++) and make them refer to each other by pointers, or create a dynamic array in a contiguous memory area and store objects there, and make them refer to each other by indices within the array. Implementing mesh operations correctly and efficiently with half-edge data structures is not as simple as it may seem, so it is recommended to use existing libraries (CGAL [3], OpenMesh [4], Geometry Central [5], pmp-library [6], etc.). Note that the geometry processing algorithms discussed in this chapter can be implemented using either array-based data structures or half-edge data structures.

1.1.4 Structure of This Chapter

In this chapter, we will discuss representative tasks of geometry processing with surface meshes, namely smoothing, parameterization, and deformation. In particular, the notion of *cotangent Laplacian* is repeatedly used throughout these tasks, highlighting its importance in geometry processing.

Topics on geometry processing in 3DCG is extremely diverse. To make this chapter compact and easy to read, we assume the input shape and its triangular mesh representation is already at hand, and we do not cover topics on how to obtain/create 3D shapes (either automatically from images or manually using intuitive authoring tools). Furthermore, there are many other important tasks on surface meshes such as remeshing, simplification, and mesh repair. Readers who want to learn more about these are encouraged to study the excellent book by Botsch et al. [7].

1.2   Smoothing

In this section, we will discuss *smoothing*, one of the most fundamental tasks in geometry processing. Smoothing, in a nutshell, means removing noise, and it is a concept that can be considered for all kinds of data distributed in temporal/spatial domains (such as sound or images). Intuitively, it can be interpreted as a phenomenon where the value present at each point disperses over time and the distribution becomes increasingly smoother. Mathematically, it is described by the following *diffusion equation*:

$$\frac{\partial f}{\partial t} = \lambda \Delta f \tag{1.1}$$

Here, $f : \Omega \to \mathbb{R}$ is a scalar field on domain Ω, t is time, λ is a coefficient representing the speed of diffusion, and Δ is a differential operator called the *Laplacian*. In the case where Ω is an Euclidean space, Laplacian is the sum of the second derivatives in each direction. Specifically, sound and images are 1D and 2D data respectively, and the Laplacian is defined as $\Delta := \frac{\partial^2}{\partial x^2}$ and $\Delta := \frac{\partial^2}{\partial x^2} + \frac{\partial^2}{\partial y^2}$ respectively. Intuitively, the Laplacian can be interpreted as an operation that subtracts the center value from the average value of the surroundings. By repeatedly adding this value to the current value at each location, the distribution becomes smoother over time.

1.2.1   Smoothing by the Uniform Laplacian and the Forward Euler Method

In order to apply the above equation to a 3D surface shape represented as a triangular mesh, it is necessary to provide a definition of the Laplacian for the triangular mesh. Among various definitions, the simplest one is called the *uniform Laplacian*, which literally performs the operation of "subtracting the center value from the average value of the surroundings". With a scalar value f_i given to the vertex i of the triangular mesh, its uniform Laplacian δ_i is defined as

$$\delta_i := \frac{1}{|\mathcal{N}_\star(i)|} \sum_{j \in \mathcal{N}_\star(i)} (f_j - f_i) \tag{1.2}$$

Note that some literature might put the subtraction order the other way around. Here, $\mathcal{N}_\star(i)$ is the set of vertices connected to vertex i by an edge (called a *1-ring neighborhood*), and the operator $|\cdot|$ represents the number of elements in a set. The process of calculating the uniform Laplacian for each vertex can be simply described using vectors and matrices as

$$\delta = \underbrace{\mathbf{M}^{-1}\mathbf{L}}_{\mathbf{K}} \mathbf{f}. \tag{1.3}$$

Here, $\mathbf{f} = (f_1, \ldots, f_{|\mathcal{V}|})^\top$ is a vector containing the scalar values of each vertex (where $\mathcal{V}$ is the set of all vertices), $\boldsymbol{\delta} = (\delta_1, \ldots, \delta_{|\mathcal{V}|})^\top$ is a vector that contains the Laplacian values in the same way, and the square diagonal matrix $\mathbf{M}$ and sparse matrix $\mathbf{L}$ are given by

$$\mathbf{M}_{ii} = |\mathcal{N}_\star(i)| \tag{1.4}$$

$$\mathbf{L}_{ij} = 1, \quad j \in \mathcal{N}_\star(i) \tag{1.5}$$

$$\mathbf{L}_{ii} = - \sum_{j \in \mathcal{N}_\star(i)} \mathbf{L}_{ij}. \tag{1.6}$$

Using the Laplacian defined in this way, we consider numerically solving the diffusion equation (1.1). For this purpose, first, the time is discretized using finite difference as

$$\frac{\partial \mathbf{f}}{\partial t} \approx \frac{\mathbf{f}^{t+1} - \mathbf{f}^t}{h} \tag{1.7}$$

Here, $\mathbf{f}^t$ is the known scalar field at the current time, $\mathbf{f}^{t+1}$ is the unknown scalar field at the next time, and h is the time step parameter. Substituting the above equation into the left-hand side of Eqs. (1.1) and (1.3) into the Laplacian on the right-hand side, we get

$$\frac{\mathbf{f}^{t+1} - \mathbf{f}^t}{h} = \lambda \mathbf{K} \mathbf{f}^t \tag{1.8}$$

$$\Leftrightarrow$$

$$\mathbf{f}^{t+1} = (\mathbf{I} + h\lambda \mathbf{K}) \mathbf{f}^t \tag{1.9}$$

where $\mathbf{I}$ is the identity matrix. This way of calculating changes in time is called the *forward Euler method*. Applying this process not to the scalar field $\mathbf{f} \in \mathbb{R}^{|\mathcal{V}|}$, but to the vertex coordinates themselves $\mathbf{x} \in \mathbb{R}^{|\mathcal{V}| \times 3}$, yields 3D shape smoothing:

$$\mathbf{x}^{t+1} = (\mathbf{I} + h\lambda \mathbf{K}) \mathbf{x}^t \tag{1.10}$$

The result of applying smoothing by the forward Euler method to the triangular mesh shown in Fig. 1.6 is shown in Fig. 1.7.

1.2.2 Numerically Stable Smoothing by the Backward Euler Method

The advantage of the aforementioned forward Euler method is that it is simple to implement and has a low computational cost [8]. The drawback is, however, that it tends to generate oscillations and eventually explode if the parameter $h\lambda$ controlling the speed of change is made large (see Fig. 1.7b). The solution to this is the *backward*

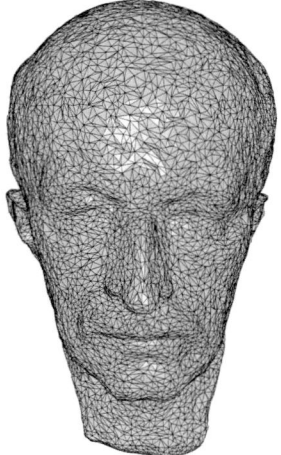

Fig. 1.6 Triangular mesh used in the smoothing experiment

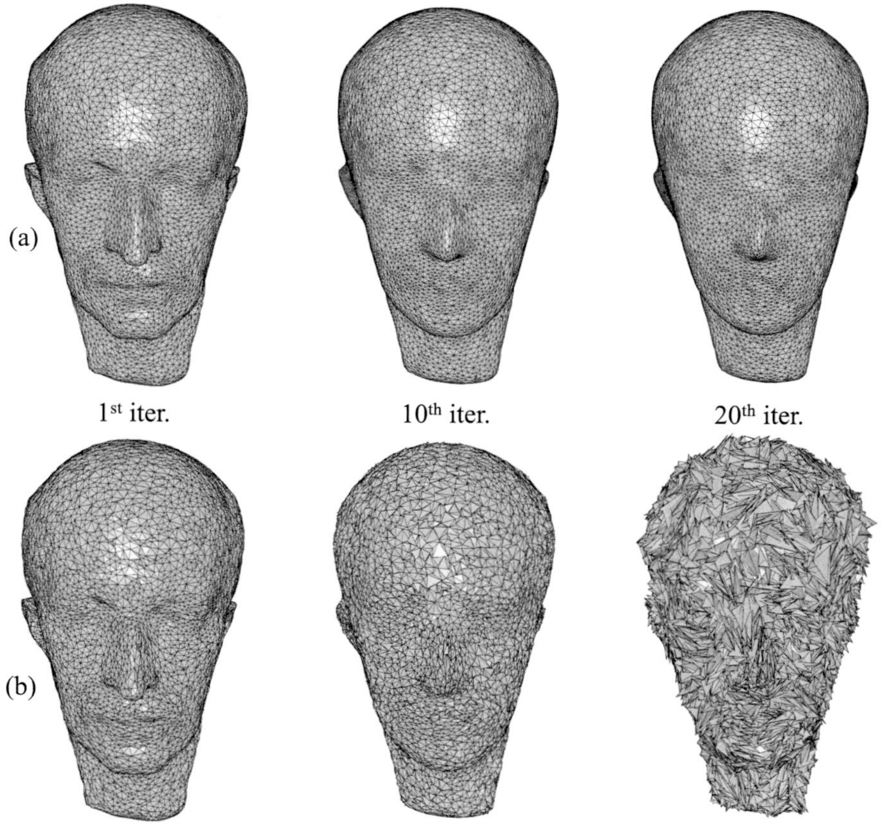

(a)

1st iter.   10th iter.   20th iter.

(b)

Fig. 1.7 Smoothing by the forward Euler method. **a** In the case of $h\lambda = 1$, **b** In the case of $h\lambda = 1.5$

Euler method [9]. Instead of using the Laplacian of the current data as the right-hand side of the diffusion equation (1.1), the backward Euler method uses the Laplacian of the unknown data at the next time step:

$$\frac{\mathbf{x}^{t+1} - \mathbf{x}^t}{h} = \lambda \mathbf{K}\, \mathbf{x}^{t+1} \tag{1.11}$$

$$\Leftrightarrow$$

$$(\mathbf{I} - h\lambda\mathbf{K})\, \mathbf{x}^{t+1} = \mathbf{x}^t \tag{1.12}$$

Because this system of linear equations for the unknown $\mathbf{x}^{t+1}$ needs to be solved, the computational cost per step is higher compared to the forward Euler method. Nevertheless, its unconditional stability even for the larger parameter $h\lambda$ makes it very useful for cases where strong smoothing is to be applied to large triangular meshes.

Note that the coefficient matrix of the linear equation (1.12) $\mathbf{I} - h\lambda\mathbf{K} = \mathbf{I} - h\lambda\mathbf{M}^{-1}\mathbf{L}$ is generally not symmetric, but it can be easily made symmetric by multiplying $\mathbf{M}$ from the left on both sides:

$$(\mathbf{M} - h\lambda\mathbf{L})\, \mathbf{x}^{t+1} = \mathbf{M}\, \mathbf{x}^t \tag{1.13}$$

This coefficient matrix is also positive definite, so it can be solved efficiently using the conjugate gradient method. An example is shown in Fig. 1.8a.

1.2.3 Prevention of Shrinkage by Preserving Surface Area or Volume

If the above-mentioned process of "moving the vertex to the average of the surrounding vertices" is repeated, the shape will inevitably shrink as a whole, and eventually all vertices will collapse to the centroid of the original triangular mesh. A simple method to prevent this is to scale the entire body to preserve the surface area or volume of the original triangular mesh [9]. For the vertex coordinates $\mathbf{x}$, the surface area $\text{Area}(\mathbf{x})$ and volume $\text{Vol}(\mathbf{x})$ of the triangular mesh are respectively given by

$$\text{Area}(\mathbf{x}) := \frac{1}{2} \sum_{\tau_{ijk} \in \mathcal{F}} \left\| (\mathbf{x}_j - \mathbf{x}_i) \times (\mathbf{x}_k - \mathbf{x}_i) \right\| \tag{1.14}$$

$$\text{Vol}(\mathbf{x}) := \frac{1}{6} \sum_{\tau_{ijk} \in \mathcal{F}} \left(\frac{\mathbf{x}_i + \mathbf{x}_j + \mathbf{x}_k}{3} \right) \cdot \left\{ (\mathbf{x}_j - \mathbf{x}_i) \times (\mathbf{x}_k - \mathbf{x}_i) \right\}. \tag{1.15}$$

Here, $\mathcal{F}$ represents the set of all triangular faces, τ_{ijk} represents the triangle formed by vertices i, j, k, $\mathbf{x}_i \in \mathbb{R}^3$ represents the 3D coordinates of vertex i, and $\times$ and $\cdot$ represent the cross and dot products of 3D vectors, respectively. Note that the volume

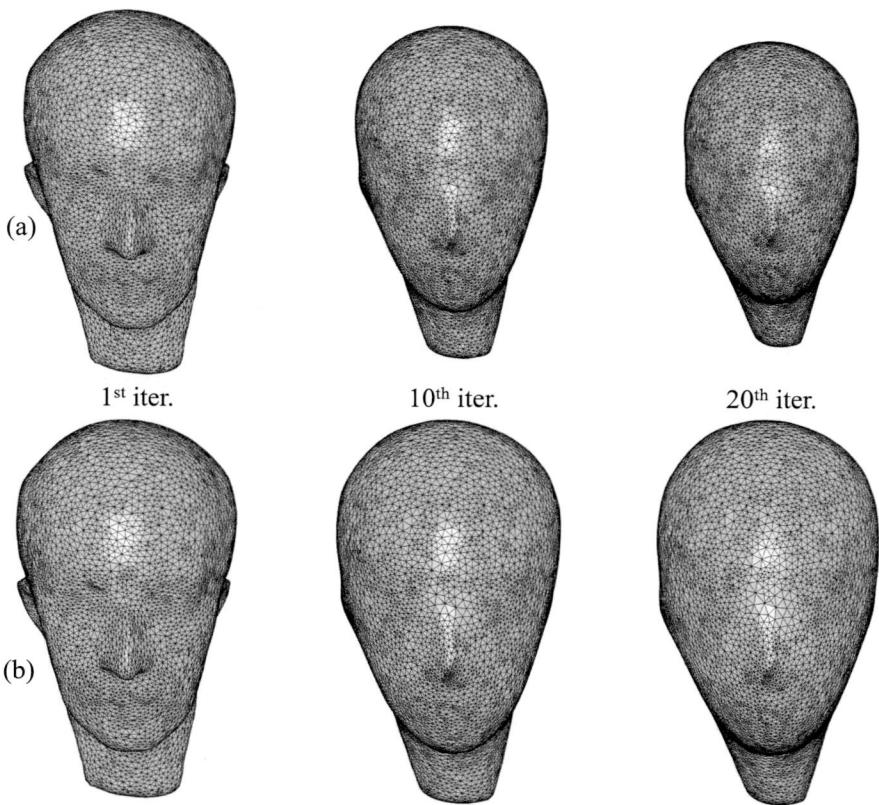

Fig. 1.8 **a** Smoothing by the backward Euler method ($h\lambda = 10$). **b** Prevention of shrinkage by scaling that preserves surface area

can only be correctly calculated when the triangular mesh is closed. After solving the linear equation (1.13) and determining the vertex coordinates $\mathbf{x}^{t+1}$ for the next step, we update the vertex coordinates by

$$\mathbf{x}^{t+1} \leftarrow \sqrt{\frac{\text{Area}(\mathbf{x}^0)}{\text{Area}(\mathbf{x}^{t+1})}}\, \mathbf{x}^{t+1} \tag{1.16}$$

or

$$\mathbf{x}^{t+1} \leftarrow \sqrt[3]{\frac{\text{Vol}(\mathbf{x}^0)}{\text{Vol}(\mathbf{x}^{t+1})}}\, \mathbf{x}^{t+1} \tag{1.17}$$

By doing this, we can preserve the surface area or volume (Fig. 1.8b).

1.2.4 Issues with the Uniform Laplacian

The smoothing using the uniform Laplacian described so far works intuitively when the mesh is uniform as a whole, that is, when the vertices are distributed at almost the same density, all edge lengths are almost the same, and all triangles are close to equilateral. If this is not the case, however, the smoothing result can vary greatly depending on how the triangular mesh representing the surface is made. Figure 1.9a shows an artificial example where the right half of the mesh is made significantly denser than the left half. If smoothing using the uniform Laplacian is applied to such an input, the original left-right symmetry of the shape is lost (Fig. 1.9b).

Figure 1.9d shows another example where the input shape is already mostly smooth (while its vertex distribution is not uniform), so it is intuitively expected that applying smoothing to this shape will not change the vertex positions much. However, when using the uniform Laplacian, the vertices move in the tangent plane direction, resulting in a more uniform distribution of vertices (Fig. 1.9e). This effect can be useful, for example, when one wants to improve the quality of a mesh for finite element methods, but in other cases where one wants to preserve the original triangle shapes after smoothing, a different Laplacian is needed to achieve that goal.

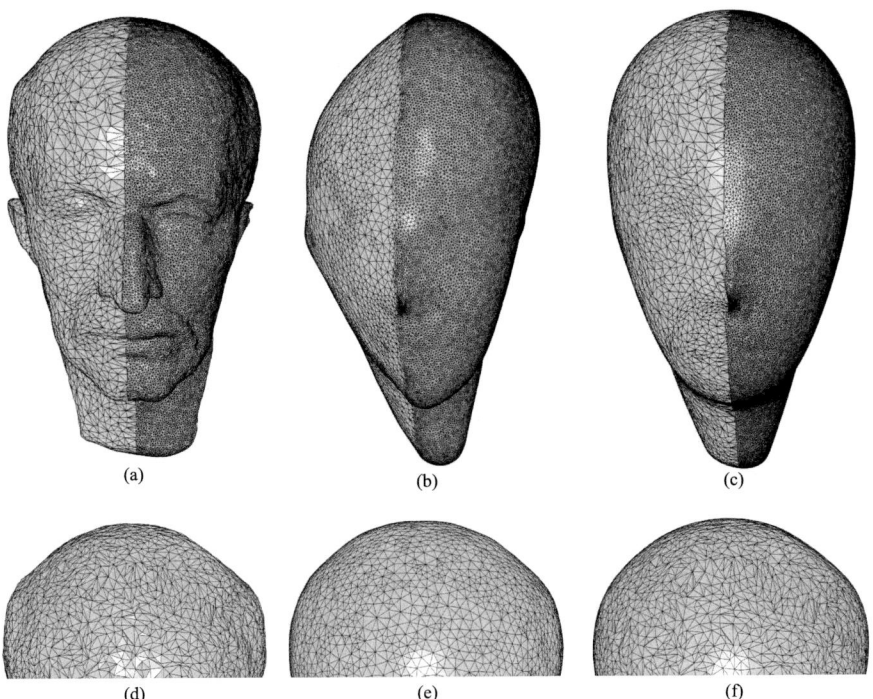

(a)   (b)   (c)

(d)   (e)   (f)

Fig. 1.9 Comparison of smoothing the initial shape (**a, d**) using the uniform Laplacian (**b, e**) and the cotangent Laplacian (**c, f**)

The *cotangent Laplacian*, which is the most commonly used tool in various shape processing tasks, is what we need here. Examples of smoothing using the cotangent Laplacian are shown in Fig. 1.9c, f. In the following section, we will discuss its derivation.

1.2.5 Derivation of the Cotangent Laplacian

First, let's revisit the gradient, divergence, and Laplacian in the 2D Euclidean space for ease of understanding. The gradient of a scalar field $f(x, y) \in \mathbb{R}$ is defined as $\left(\frac{\partial f}{\partial x}, \frac{\partial f}{\partial y}\right) \in \mathbb{R}^2$, which can be written as ∇f using the differential operator $\nabla := \left(\frac{\partial}{\partial x}, \frac{\partial}{\partial y}\right)$ (called nabla). The divergence of a vector field $\mathbf{g}(x, y) := (g_x(x, y), g_y(x, y)) \in \mathbb{R}^2$ is defined as $\frac{\partial g_x}{\partial x} + \frac{\partial g_y}{\partial y} \in \mathbb{R}$, which can be written as the dot product $\nabla \cdot \mathbf{g}$. The Laplacian of a scalar field f is defined as $\frac{\partial^2 f}{\partial x^2} + \frac{\partial^2 f}{\partial y^2} \in \mathbb{R}$, which can be written as the divergence of the gradient:

$$\nabla \cdot (\nabla f) = \left(\frac{\partial}{\partial x}, \frac{\partial}{\partial y}\right) \cdot \left(\frac{\partial f}{\partial x}, \frac{\partial f}{\partial y}\right) \tag{1.18}$$

$$= \frac{\partial^2 f}{\partial x^2} + \frac{\partial^2 f}{\partial y^2} \tag{1.19}$$

$$= \underbrace{\left(\frac{\partial^2}{\partial x^2} + \frac{\partial^2}{\partial y^2}\right)}_{\Delta} f \tag{1.20}$$

If we discretize the scalar field f on a uniform two-dimensional grid and store the scalar value $f_{i,j}$ at each grid point (i, j), the finite difference approximations for the first and second derivatives in the X direction are respectively

$$\frac{\partial f}{\partial x} := \frac{f_{i+1,j} - f_{i,j}}{h} \tag{1.21}$$

$$\frac{\partial^2 f}{\partial x^2} := \frac{\frac{f_{i+1,j} - f_{i,j}}{h} - \frac{f_{i,j} - f_{i-1,j}}{h}}{h}$$

$$= \frac{f_{i+1,j} - 2f_{i,j} + f_{i-1,j}}{h^2} \tag{1.22}$$

where h is the grid width. The Y direction is defined similarly, so we get

$$\Delta f := \frac{4}{h^2} \left(\frac{f_{i+1,j} + f_{i-1,j} + f_{i,j+1} + f_{i,j-1}}{4} - f_{i,j}\right) \tag{1.23}$$

Compared to the uniform Laplacian ("the average of the surrounding values minus the center value"), the difference is the scaling factor $\frac{4}{h^2}$ due to the grid width. In order to accurately approximate the value of the Laplacian, it is necessary to not only calculate the "average of the surrounding values" appropriately, but also to apply the appropriate scaling.

In the following, we first derive the gradient and divergence operators for a triangular mesh, and finally derive the cotangent Laplacian by combining them. Note that this way of computing the Laplacian on a general two-manifold surface is specifically called a *Laplace-Beltrami operator*.

1.2.5.1 Derivation of the Gradient

First, on the triangular mesh $\mathcal{M} = (\mathcal{V}, \mathcal{F})$, we define a scalar field f that returns $f(\mathbf{p}) \in \mathbb{R}$ for each point $\mathbf{p}$ as a combination of *basis functions*:

$$f(\mathbf{p}) = \sum_{i \in \mathcal{V}} f_i B_i(\mathbf{p}) \tag{1.24}$$

Here, $B_i(\mathbf{p})$ is a function that is linear within each triangle, satisfying $B_i(\mathbf{x}_i) = 1$ and $B_i(\mathbf{x}_j) = 0$ for $j \neq i$. Functions defined in this way are called *piecewise linear*. When a point $\mathbf{p}$ exists on a triangle $\tau_{ijk} \in \mathcal{F}$, there are only three basis functions B_i, B_j, B_k that take non-zero values, so the function restricted to this triangle can be written as

$$f(\mathbf{p})|_{\mathbf{p} \in \tau_{ijk}} =: f_{\tau_{ijk}}(\mathbf{p}) = f_i B_i(\mathbf{p}) + f_j B_j(\mathbf{p}) + f_k B_k(\mathbf{p}). \tag{1.25}$$

The gradient of a piecewise linear function is piecewise constant, so the slope of $f_{\tau_{ijk}}(\mathbf{p})$ is constant independent of $\mathbf{p}$:

$$\nabla f_{\tau_{ijk}} = f_i \nabla B_i + f_j \nabla B_j + f_k \nabla B_k. \tag{1.26}$$

The values of the three non-zero basis functions, $B_i(\mathbf{p}), B_j(\mathbf{p}), B_k(\mathbf{p})$ equal to the ratios of the areas of sub-triangles that splits the triangle τ_{ijk} into three (Fig. 1.10a). For this reason, they are also called *barycentric coordinates*. From this property,

$$B_i(\mathbf{p}) + B_j(\mathbf{p}) + B_k(\mathbf{p}) = 1, \quad \forall \mathbf{p} \in \tau_{ijk} \tag{1.27}$$

$$\nabla B_i + \nabla B_j + \nabla B_k = \mathbf{0} \tag{1.28}$$

holds. Substituting $\nabla B_i = -\nabla B_j - \nabla B_k$ from Eq. (1.28) into Eq. (1.26), we get

$$\nabla f_{\tau_{ijk}} = (f_j - f_i) \nabla B_j + (f_k - f_i) \nabla B_k \tag{1.29}$$

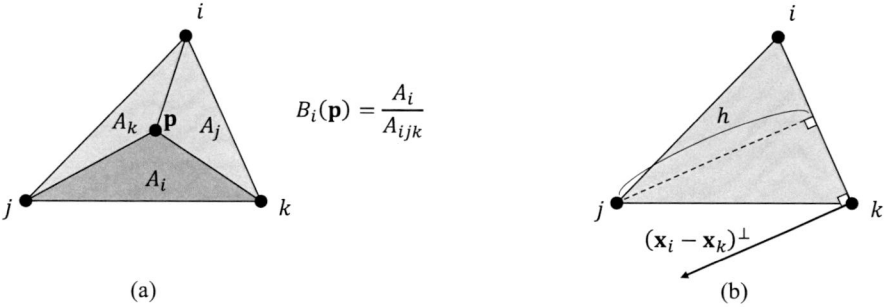

Fig. 1.10 Basis function and its gradient

Next, we derive the specific expression of the vector ∇B_j. B_j is a linear function that satisfies $B_j(\mathbf{x}_j) = 1$, $B_j(\mathbf{x}_i) = B_j(\mathbf{x}_k) = 0$, so the direction of its gradient is obtained by rotating the vector $\mathbf{x}_i - \mathbf{x}_k$ by $90°$ counterclockwise on τ_{ijk} (denoted as $(\mathbf{x}_i - \mathbf{x}_k)^\perp$), see Fig. 1.10b. Also, if we denote the height of τ_{ijk} with respect to the base edge connecting i and k as h, the value of the function increases by 1 when moving by h in the gradient direction, so the magnitude of the gradient is $\frac{1}{h}$. If we denote the area of the triangle as A_{ijk}, since $\|\mathbf{x}_i - \mathbf{x}_k\| h = 2A_{ijk}$, we have $\frac{1}{h} = \frac{\|\mathbf{x}_i - \mathbf{x}_k\|}{2A_{ijk}}$. In summary, we have $\nabla B_j = \frac{(\mathbf{x}_i - \mathbf{x}_k)^\perp}{2A_{ijk}}$. The same derivation applies to B_k, so we have $\nabla B_k = \frac{(\mathbf{x}_j - \mathbf{x}_i)^\perp}{2A_{ijk}}$. Substituting these into Eq. (1.29), we get

$$\nabla f_{\tau_{ijk}} = \frac{(f_j - f_i)(\mathbf{x}_i - \mathbf{x}_k)^\perp + (f_k - f_i)(\mathbf{x}_j - \mathbf{x}_i)^\perp}{2A_{ijk}} \tag{1.30}$$

1.2.5.2 Derivation of the Divergence

Next, let's discuss how to calculate the divergence when a vector field $\mathbf{g}$ is given on the surface. To be consistent with the definition of the gradient which is piecewise constant, we assume that the input vector field is also piecewise constant, given as $\{\mathbf{g}_\tau | \tau \in \mathcal{F}\}$, and the divergence is computed at each vertex. To define the divergence for such a discontinuous vector field, we define a local domain Ω_i around each vertex i and apply the divergence theorem

$$\iint_{\Omega_i} \nabla \cdot \mathbf{g} \, dA = \int_{\partial \Omega_i} \mathbf{g}(s) \cdot \mathbf{n}(s) \, ds \tag{1.31}$$

Here, ∂ is an operation that extracts the boundary line of the domain, and $\mathbf{n}(s)$ is a unit normal vector pointing outward at the point s on the domain boundary. This allows us to replace the surface integral within the domain with the line integral

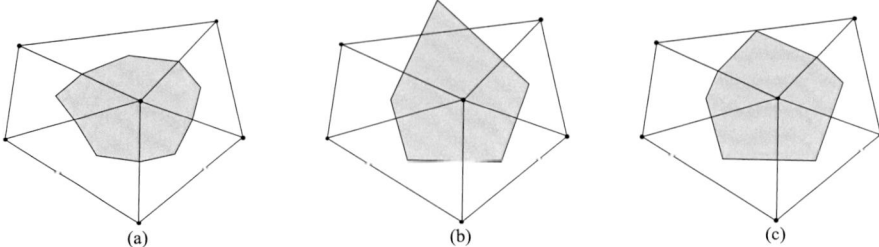

Fig. 1.11 Definition of the local domain around the vertex

on the domain boundary. The simplest definition of the local domain Ω_i is the so-called *barycentric region*, which can be formed by connecting the centroid and the edge midpoints of each triangle (Fig. 1.11a). A better accuracy can be achieved with the *Voronoi region*, which can be formed by connecting the circumcenter and the edge midpoints of each triangle (Fig. 1.11b). If the triangle is obtuse, however, the circumcenter will be outside the triangle, so for such triangles, the region is divided at the edge midpoint of the side opposite the obtuse vertex (Fig. 1.11c) [10].

Once the local domain Ω_i is defined, we can define the divergence. If we denote the set of triangles sharing vertex i as $\mathcal{N}_{\blacktriangle}(i)$, and utilizing the fact that the vector field is piecewise constant, the right side of Eq. (1.31) becomes

$$\int_{\partial\Omega_i} \mathbf{g}(s) \cdot \mathbf{n}(s)ds = \sum_{\tau_{ijk}\in\mathcal{N}_{\blacktriangle}(i)} \int_{\partial\Omega_i\cap\tau_{ijk}} \mathbf{g}_{\tau_{ijk}} \cdot \mathbf{n}(s)ds \qquad (1.32)$$

$$= \sum_{\tau_{ijk}\in\mathcal{N}_{\blacktriangle}(i)} \mathbf{g}_{\tau_{ijk}} \cdot \int_{\partial\Omega_i\cap\tau_{ijk}} \mathbf{n}(s)ds. \qquad (1.33)$$

When using the barycentric region as the local domain, $\partial\Omega_i \cap \tau_{ijk}$ becomes a line sequence connecting three points $\mathbf{q}_1 := \frac{\mathbf{x}_i+\mathbf{x}_j}{2}$, $\mathbf{q}_2 := \frac{\mathbf{x}_i+\mathbf{x}_j+\mathbf{x}_k}{3}$, $\mathbf{q}_3 := \frac{\mathbf{x}_i+\mathbf{x}_k}{2}$ (Fig. 1.12). On the segment connecting $\mathbf{q}_1$ and $\mathbf{q}_2$, the outward normal is constant, its direction coincides with $(\mathbf{q}_1 - \mathbf{q}_2)^\perp$, and the length of the segment is $|\mathbf{q}_1 - \mathbf{q}_2|$. The same applies to the segment connecting $\mathbf{q}_2$ and $\mathbf{q}_3$, and we have

$$\int_{\partial\Omega_i\cap\tau_{ijk}} \mathbf{n}(s)ds = (\mathbf{q}_1 - \mathbf{q}_2)^\perp + (\mathbf{q}_2 - \mathbf{q}_3)^\perp \qquad (1.34)$$

$$= (\mathbf{q}_1 - \mathbf{q}_3)^\perp \qquad (1.35)$$

$$= \frac{(\mathbf{x}_j - \mathbf{x}_k)^\perp}{2}. \qquad (1.36)$$

Note that in the above derivation, $\mathbf{q}_2$ disappears, implying that the quantity is independent of the choice of the local domain (as long as the boundary passes through

Fig. 1.12 Calculation of the divergence

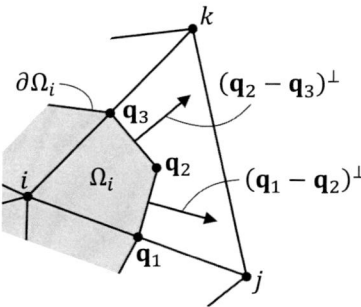

edge midpoints). In summary, the divergence within the local region Ω_i of vertex i is given by

$$\iint_{\Omega_i} \nabla \cdot \mathbf{g} \, dA = \sum_{\tau_{ijk} \in \mathcal{N}_\blacktriangle(i)} \mathbf{g}_{\tau_{ijk}} \cdot \frac{(\mathbf{x}_j - \mathbf{x}_k)^\perp}{2} \tag{1.37}$$

To calculate the *pointwise* amount (i.e., amount per unit area) of divergence, this integral value needs to be divided by the area of the region $|\Omega_i|$.

1.2.5.3 Derivation of the Cotangent Laplacian

Substituting the gradient $\nabla f_{\tau_{ijk}}$ of Eq. (1.30) into the vector field $\mathbf{g}_{\tau_{ijk}}$ of Eq. (1.37), we get

$$\iint_{\Omega_i} \Delta f \, dA = \iint_{\Omega_i} \nabla \cdot (\nabla f) \, dA \tag{1.38}$$

$$= \sum_{\tau_{ijk} \in \mathcal{N}_\blacktriangle(i)} \frac{(f_j - f_i)(\mathbf{x}_i - \mathbf{x}_k)^\perp + (f_k - f_i)(\mathbf{x}_j - \mathbf{x}_i)^\perp}{2A_{ijk}} \cdot \frac{(\mathbf{x}_j - \mathbf{x}_k)^\perp}{2} \tag{1.39}$$

$$= \sum_{\tau_{ijk} \in \mathcal{N}_\blacktriangle(i)} \frac{1}{4A_{ijk}} \Big[(f_j - f_i)\{(\mathbf{x}_i - \mathbf{x}_k) \cdot (\mathbf{x}_j - \mathbf{x}_k)\}$$

$$+ (f_k - f_i)\{(\mathbf{x}_i - \mathbf{x}_j) \cdot (\mathbf{x}_k - \mathbf{x}_j)\} \Big] \tag{1.40}$$

Here, if we denote the angle at vertex k in τ_{ijk} as θ_k, we have

$$\|\mathbf{x}_i - \mathbf{x}_k\| \, \|\mathbf{x}_j - \mathbf{x}_k\| \cos \theta_k = (\mathbf{x}_i - \mathbf{x}_k) \cdot (\mathbf{x}_j - \mathbf{x}_k) \tag{1.41}$$

$$\|\mathbf{x}_i - \mathbf{x}_k\| \, \|\mathbf{x}_j - \mathbf{x}_k\| \sin \theta_k = 2A_{ijk} \tag{1.42}$$

From this, we get

$$\frac{(\mathbf{x}_i - \mathbf{x}_k) \cdot (\mathbf{x}_j - \mathbf{x}_k)}{4A_{ijk}} = \frac{1}{2} \cot \theta_k. \tag{1.43}$$

If we make the same substitution for the second term, we get

$$\iint_{\Omega_i} \Delta f \, dA = \frac{1}{2} \sum_{\tau_{ijk} \in N_\blacktriangle (i)} \{(f_j - f_i) \cot \theta_k + (f_k - f_i) \cot \theta_j\} \qquad (1.44)$$

By replacing the summation over the neighboring triangles with the summation over the neighboring vertices, we finally derive the cotangent Laplacian

$$\iint_{\Omega_i} \Delta f \, dA = \frac{1}{2} \sum_{j \in N_\star(i)} (\cot \alpha_{ij} + \cot \beta_{ij})(f_j - f_i) \qquad (1.45)$$

where α_{ij}, β_{ij} are the angles of the vertices opposite the edge connecting i and j in the two triangles that share the edge.

By changing the Laplacian definition formulas in Eqs. (1.4) and (1.5) as

$$\mathbf{M}_{ii} = |\Omega_i| \qquad (1.46)$$

$$\mathbf{L}_{ij} = \frac{1}{2}(\cot \alpha_{ij} + \cot \beta_{ij}), \quad j \in N_\star(i) \qquad (1.47)$$

one obtains pointwise Laplacian per vertex in the same way as $\mathbf{M}^{-1} \mathbf{L} \mathbf{f}$. The diagonal matrix $\mathbf{M}$ defined in this way is generally called a *mass matrix*.

1.2.6   Mean Curvature Flow

By solving Eq. (1.13) while using the cotangent Laplacian, we can perform smoothing that takes into account the shape of the triangular mesh.

According to the theory of differential geometry, there is a relationship between the Laplacian $\Delta \mathbf{x}$ at a point $\mathbf{x}$ on the surface, the normal $\mathbf{n}$ at that point, and the mean curvature (the average of the maximum and minimum curvatures) H as

$$\Delta \mathbf{x} = -2 H \mathbf{n} \qquad (1.48)$$

The above smoothing process moves each vertex by a distance proportional to the mean curvature along the normal direction of the surface. This particular way of gradual deformation is called *mean curvature flow*, and has the property of changing the shape in a direction that minimizes the surface area. As we saw above, the cotangent Laplacian is dependent on the vertex positions $\mathbf{x}$, so we denote this dependence as $\Delta_\mathbf{x}$, and now the mean curvature flow is formulated as

$$\frac{\partial \mathbf{x}}{\partial t} = \lambda \Delta_\mathbf{x} \mathbf{x}. \qquad (1.49)$$

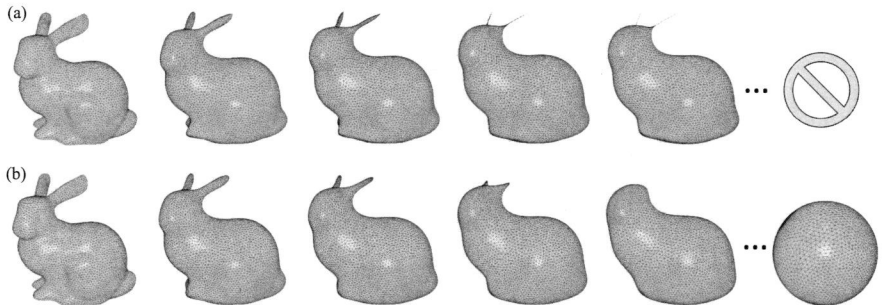

Fig. 1.13 Occurrence of singularity in the mean curvature flow (**a**) and its avoidance by the conformalized mean curvature flow (**b**)

This means that the equation is nonlinear in contrast to the linear diffusion equation (1.1), and its numerical computation is generally unstable.

If the initial shape is mostly spherical and the parameter $h\lambda$ is taken sufficiently small, the flow according to Eq. (1.49) will converge to a sphere. If this is not the case, however, some triangles will shrink, and the computation of the cotangent Laplacian will hit a *singularity* (Fig. 1.13a), causing the computation to break down. Kazhdan et al. [11] pointed out that this phenomenon is due to the triangles undergoing anisotropic deformation (stretching in one direction and shrinking in a direction perpendicular to it) during the flow process. Their proposed solution is to only recalculate the mass matrix $\mathbf{M}$ from $\mathbf{x}^t$ when solving Eq. (1.13) at each step of the flow, and simply reuse the cotangent Laplacian $\mathbf{L}$ calculated at the initial state $\mathbf{x}^0$. This modified flow is called the *conformalized mean curvature flow*, and while its convergence and other properties are still unproven, it is known to empirically converge to a sphere very robustly while maintaining the aspect ratio of the original triangles (Fig. 1.13b). This method can also be used as a way to map surfaces onto a sphere.

1.3   Parameterization

Parameterization (also known as UV mapping/unwrapping or flattening) is the process of assigning 2D coordinates $\mathbf{u}_i = (u_i, v_i) \in \mathbb{R}^2$ to each vertex $i \in \mathcal{V}$ of a triangular mesh $\mathcal{M} = (\mathcal{V}, \mathcal{F})$ which has 3D coordinates $\mathbf{x}_i = (x_i, y_i, z_i) \in \mathbb{R}^3$. These 2D coordinates are commonly referred to as the UV space.

For a point $\mathbf{p} \in \mathbb{R}^3$ inside the triangle $\tau_{ijk} \in \mathcal{F}$ of the mesh, the corresponding 2D coordinates can be calculated using the barycentric coordinates B_i, B_j, B_k described in Sect. 1.2.5 as

$$\mathbf{u}(\mathbf{p}) := B_i(\mathbf{p})\mathbf{u}_i + B_j(\mathbf{p})\mathbf{u}_j + B_k(\mathbf{p})\mathbf{u}_k \qquad \in \mathbb{R}^2$$

| 3D shape | UV flattening & texture image | Texture mapping result |

Fig. 1.14 Example of texture mapping

The uses of parameterization in 3DCG are diverse among which the most representative is texture mapping (Fig. 1.14). Texture mapping applies a 2D image onto a 3D shape so that the visual detail is significantly enriched while the 3D shape is approximated with a small number of polygons, a technique indispensable for various 3DCG applications, both real time and offline.

In the literature of differential geometry, a field in mathematics, it is common to define a 3D surface as an image from 2D parameter space to 3D space, and this is why the process of finding unknown UV coordinates for a known 3D shape surface mesh is referred to as parameterization.

Any closed surface needs to be cut somehow into a disk topology before it can be flattened onto a plane. Furthermore, if the entire 3D shape is cut into a single disk-topology surface and is flattened at once, the resulting distortion will likely become too large. Therefore, it is common to cut the mesh along some geometric features, producing many disk-topology patches, and unfold each patch separately. This task of appropriately cutting surfaces into patches is called *segmentation*, and it is a field of study in its own right. Here, we assume that the mesh has already been cut into disk-topology patches, and discuss a method for parameterizing a single patch.

1.3.1 Method with Fixed Boundary

The simplest method for parameterization is to fix the UV coordinates of all the boundary vertices. The intuition is as follows: if each edge of the mesh is considered as a spring with zero rest length, fixing the boundary vertices to a certain convex shape (such as a circle) will determine the UV coordinates of the internal vertices as an equilibrium of the spring tension. The energy generated by the spring tension is

$$E_{\text{Tutte}}(\{\mathbf{u}_i\}_{i\in\mathcal{V}}) := \frac{1}{2}\sum_{(i,j)\in\mathcal{E}}\|\mathbf{u}_i - \mathbf{u}_j\|^2 \qquad (1.50)$$

where $\mathcal{E}$ represents the set of edges of the mesh. If we arrange the U coordinates and V coordinates into vectors respectively as $\mathbf{u} := (u_1, \ldots, u_{|\mathcal{V}|})^\top$, $\mathbf{v} := (v_1, \ldots, v_{|\mathcal{V}|})^\top$, the above energy can be written simply using the uniform Laplacian $\mathbf{L}$ described in the previous Sect. 1.2.1 as

$$E_{\text{Tutte}}(\mathbf{u}, \mathbf{v}) = -\frac{1}{2}\left(\mathbf{u}^\top \mathbf{L}\,\mathbf{u} + \mathbf{v}^\top \mathbf{L}\,\mathbf{v}\right). \tag{1.51}$$

This energy can be minimized by a $\mathbf{u}$ that satisfies the condition of its derivative being zero:

$$\frac{\partial E_{\text{Tutte}}}{\partial \mathbf{u}} = -\mathbf{L}\,\mathbf{u} = \mathbf{0} \tag{1.52}$$

The same applies to the V coordinates. If no boundary conditions are given, the constant vector $\mathbf{u} = (c, \ldots, c)^\top$, $c \in \mathbb{R}$ is the trivial solution, but in the problem setting mentioned above, the UV coordinates of the boundary vertices are fixed, so by giving that as a boundary condition, a meaningful solution can be obtained.

Rearrange the order of the variables to $\mathbf{u} = (\mathbf{u}_{\text{int}}^\top\ \mathbf{u}_{\text{bnd}}^\top)^\top$, so that the values corresponding to the internal vertices come in the first half, and the values corresponding to the boundary vertices come in the second half. If we partition the Laplacian matrix accordingly, the above equation can be rewritten as

$$\begin{pmatrix} \mathbf{L}_{\text{int,int}} & \mathbf{L}_{\text{int,bnd}} \\ \mathbf{L}_{\text{bnd,int}} & \mathbf{L}_{\text{bnd,bnd}} \end{pmatrix} \begin{pmatrix} \mathbf{u}_{\text{int}} \\ \mathbf{u}_{\text{bnd}} \end{pmatrix} = \mathbf{0}. \tag{1.53}$$

The values of the boundary vertices $\mathbf{u}_{\text{bnd}}$ are known, so the lower half of the equation can be ignored. If we rearrange the upper half of the equation, we get

$$\mathbf{L}_{\text{int,int}}\,\mathbf{u}_{\text{int}} = -\mathbf{L}_{\text{int,bnd}}\,\mathbf{u}_{\text{bnd}} \tag{1.54}$$

By solving this, we can find the UV coordinates of the internal vertices. This method, proposed by Tutte in 1963, is now widely known as the Tutte embedding [12]. It guarantees that if the boundary shape is convex, the resulting map will be bijective (in other words, no triangle flipping occurs in the UV space), a property very important in many applications. Therefore, despite being very classical, Tutte embedding is frequently used as a component of more advanced algorithms in various shape processing research to this day.

As discussed in the previous Sect. 1.2.4, using a uniform Laplacian does not take into account the shape of the input mesh triangles at all, which can easily result in unwanted jaggies in the resulting image (Fig. 1.15a). By using the cotangent Laplacian instead, a more reasonable image can be obtained (Fig. 1.15b).

The energy defined by the cotangent Laplacian $\mathbf{L}$ for a piecewise linear scalar function $f(\mathbf{p})$ defined by a set of scalar values assigned to the mesh vertices $\mathbf{f} := (f_1, \ldots, f_{|\mathcal{V}|})^\top$,

$$E_{\text{Dirichlet}}(\mathbf{f}) := -\frac{1}{2}\mathbf{f}^\top \mathbf{L}\,\mathbf{f} \tag{1.55}$$

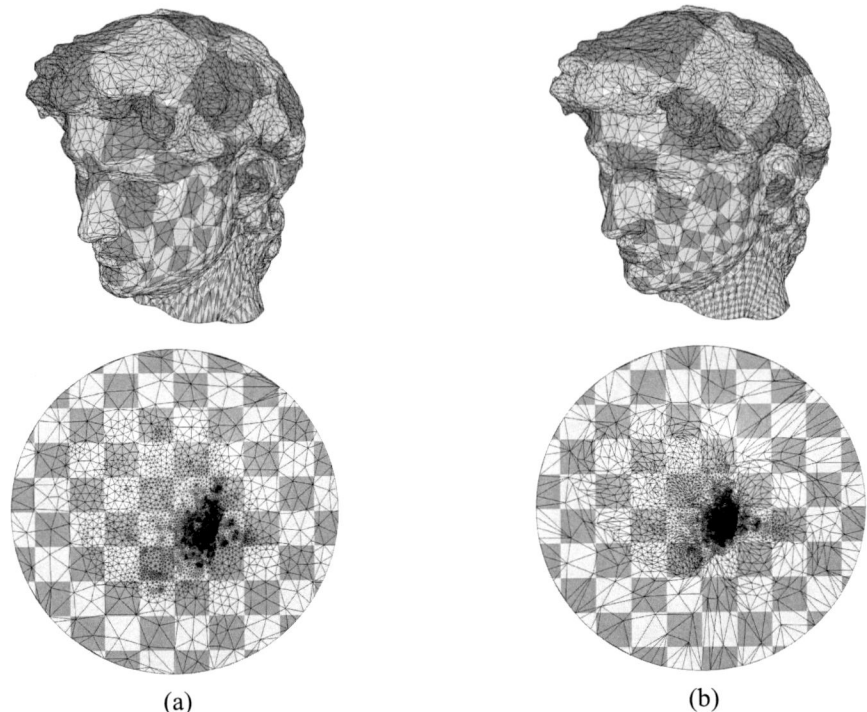

Fig. 1.15 Example of parameterization with fixed boundaries

is called the *Dirichlet energy*, and it equals to

$$E_{\text{Dirichlet}}(f) = \frac{1}{2} \iint_{\mathcal{M}} \|\nabla f(\mathbf{p})\|^2 \, dA = \frac{1}{2} \sum_{\tau \in \mathcal{F}} \|\nabla f_\tau\|^2 \, A_\tau. \qquad (1.56)$$

That is, the Dirichlet energy is a measure of the total magnitude of the function's gradient, or more intuitively, a measure of the degree of change in the function. Specifically, when the function does not change at all (i.e., constant), its Dirichlet energy is zero. The function f that minimizes the Dirichlet energy under given boundary conditions is obtained by solving the *Laplace equation*

$$\Delta f = 0. \qquad (1.57)$$

under the boundary conditions, and its solution strictly satisfies $(\mathbf{Lf})_i = 0$ at every internal vertex i. Such a function that has zero second derivative at all points inside the domain is specifically called *harmonic*. The fixed-boundary parameterization method described above finds harmonic functions for the U and V coordinates, so the method is often called *harmonic parameterization*.

When using the cotangent Laplacian, one must pay attention to the fact that the off-diagonal elements $\mathbf{L}_{ij} = \frac{1}{2}(\cot \alpha_{ij} + \cot \beta_{ij})$ may become negative when the mesh triangles contain very obtuse angles (specifically, when $\alpha_{ij} + \beta_{ij} > \pi$). Floater [13] demonstrated that the bijectivity guarantee of Tutte embedding is maintained when using other Laplacians, as long as all off-diagonal elements are positive. If some of the off-diagonal elements are negative, it is not always the case that bijectivity is lost, but the guarantee of bijectivity is lost.

As a replacement for the cotangent Laplacian that can take negative off-diagonals, Floater [14] proposed a method called the *mean value coordinate*, which sets the off-diagonal elements of the Laplacian as

$$\mathbf{L}_{ij} = \frac{\tan \frac{\angle \mathbf{x}_k \mathbf{x}_i \mathbf{x}_j}{2} + \tan \frac{\angle \mathbf{x}_j \mathbf{x}_i \mathbf{x}_l}{2}}{\left\| \mathbf{x}_i - \mathbf{x}_j \right\|} \qquad \tau_{ijk}, \tau_{jil} \in \mathcal{N}_{\blacktriangle}(i). \tag{1.58}$$

This method, like the Tutte embedding, guarantees bijectivity while considering the shape of the mesh triangle, and is widely used.

Another solution to this problem is a technique called *intrinsic triangulation* [15]. The key insight is that the cotangent Laplacian can be constructed solely from the edge lengths, i.e., the knowledge of the 3D coordinates of the mesh vertices is not needed. The idea then is to alter the mesh connectivity without changing the surface geometry by applying *intrinsic edge flips* to the mesh such that the resulting cotangent Laplacian has only positive off-diagonals. This approach has been actively researched in recent years, and further progress is expected [16, 17].

1.3.2 Methods with Free Boundary

1.3.2.1 Distortion of the Map

To discuss the quality of parameterization, let's consider the distortion of the map. There are two types of distortion: *area distortion* and *angle distortion*. A map with no area distortion is called an *authalic mapping*, a map with no angle distortion is called a *conformal mapping*, and a map with neither area nor angle distortion is called an *isometric mapping*. An isometric mapping is ideal in the sense that it has no distortion at all, but this is only possible if the original 3D shape is a *developable surface*, that is, a shape that can be made by folding or bending a piece of paper. For general 3D shapes, some kind of distortion is inevitable. A familiar example is a world map. The only way to represent the geography of the world without any distortion is to use a three-dimensional globe, and as soon as one tries to draw a world map on a flat surface, some distortion will inevitably occur. Depending on which distortion is acceptable, various types of world maps have been considered and are used (Fig. 1.16).

In the harmonic parameterization method described in Sect. 1.3.1, no consideration is given to the distortion of the map. In the actual uses of parameterization in

Equirectangular projection   Lambert conformal conic projection   Goode homolosine projection

Fig. 1.16 Various types of world maps. In the Goode method, the distortion is reduced by introducing many cuts in the map

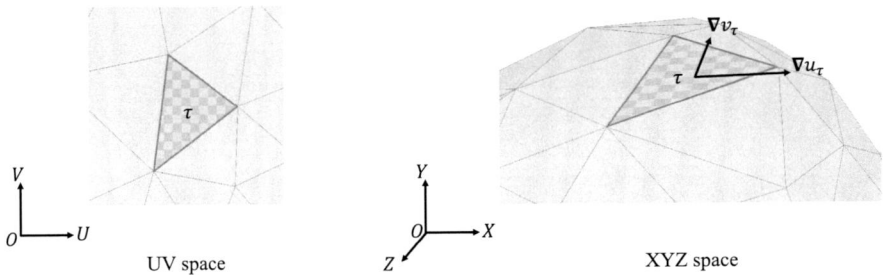

UV space   XYZ space

Fig. 1.17 The relationship between the gradients of the functions u, v defined on the triangular mesh in the XYZ space and the unit vectors in the coordinate axis directions of the UV space

3DCG, it is desirable to have smaller map distortions, so in that sense, harmonic parameterization is not a very practical method, and methods that minimize map distortion are being extensively researched.

Assigning U and V coordinates to the vertices of a triangular mesh is equivalent to defining a pair of piecewise linear functions over the mesh corresponding to these two coordinates, and the map distortion can be quantified by using their gradients. The gradient vector ∇u_τ of the U coordinate for a certain triangle $\tau \in \mathcal{F}$ corresponds to the unit U-axis vector when the XYZ space is mapped to the UV space, and the same applies to the V coordinate (Fig. 1.17). The parallelogram in the XYZ space formed by these two vectors ∇u_τ and ∇v_τ corresponds to the unit square formed by the unit vectors $(1, 0)$, $(0, 1)$ in the UV space.

If this parallelogram is a square with unit area, the linear map defined on the triangle τ is isometric, if it is a parallelogram with unit area, the map is authalic, and if it is a square with non-unit area, the map is conformal.

1.3.2.2 Minimization of Area Distortion

First, let's consider the area distortion. Let the angle between ∇u_τ and ∇v_τ be θ. Then, the area of the parallelogram formed by these two vectors is

$$\|\nabla u_\tau\| \, \|\nabla v_\tau\| \sin\theta \; = \; \|\nabla u_\tau\| \, \|\nabla v_\tau\| \sqrt{1 - \cos^2\theta}$$

$$=\sqrt{\|\nabla u_\tau\|^2 \, \|\nabla v_\tau\|^2 - (\nabla u_\tau \cdot \nabla v_\tau)^2}$$

Optimizing this value to approach 1 is nonlinear, making it difficult to solve numerically. Generally, minimizing the area distortion is computationally expensive.

1.3.2.3 Minimization of Angle Distortion

On the other hand, the angle distortion can be simply formulated. If the vector ∇u_τ rotated by $90°$ counterclockwise on the triangle τ (denoted as $\nabla u_\tau^\perp$) coincides with ∇v_τ, the quadrilateral formed by ∇u_τ and ∇v_τ is a square, hence the map is conformal. Therefore, by summing how far each triangle's map is from being conformal, we can define the minimization objective (or energy function) as

$$E_{\text{LSCM}}(u, v) := \frac{1}{2} \sum_{\tau \in \mathcal{F}} \left\| \nabla u_\tau^\perp - \nabla v_\tau \right\|^2 A_\tau. \tag{1.59}$$

This energy is quadratic in **u** and **v**, and its minimizer can readily be obtained by solving a linear system of equations. This method is called the *Least Squares Conformal Mapping* (LSCM).

1.3.2.4 Details of LSCM

Expanding Eq. (1.59), we get

$$E_{\text{LSCM}}(u, v) = \frac{1}{2} \sum_{\tau \in \mathcal{F}} (\nabla u_\tau^\perp - \nabla v_\tau) \cdot (\nabla u_\tau^\perp - \nabla v_\tau) A_\tau$$

$$= \frac{1}{2} \sum_{\tau \in \mathcal{F}} (\|\nabla u_\tau\|^2 + \|\nabla v_\tau\|^2 - 2\nabla u_\tau^\perp \cdot \nabla v_\tau) A_\tau$$

where the first two terms are the Dirichlet energy of the U and V coordinates. To examine the last term $\nabla u_\tau^\perp \cdot \nabla v_\tau$, we substitute actual values for the triangle $\tau_{ijk} \in \mathcal{F}$. Substituting the U and V coordinates into Eq. (1.30) and noting that for any vector $\mathbf{d}$, $(\mathbf{d}^\perp)^\perp = -\mathbf{d}$, we get

$$\nabla u_{\tau_{ijk}}^\perp = \frac{-(u_j - u_i)(\mathbf{x}_i - \mathbf{x}_k) - (u_k - u_i)(\mathbf{x}_j - \mathbf{x}_i)}{2A_{ijk}}$$

$$\nabla v_{\tau_{ijk}} = \frac{(v_j - v_i)(\mathbf{x}_i - \mathbf{x}_k)^\perp + (v_k - v_i)(\mathbf{x}_j - \mathbf{x}_i)^\perp}{2A_{ijk}}.$$

Using the property that $\mathbf{d} \cdot \mathbf{d}^{\perp} = 0$ and $\mathbf{d}_1 \cdot \mathbf{d}_2^{\perp} = \mathbf{d}_1^{\perp} \cdot (\mathbf{d}_2^{\perp})^{\perp} = -\mathbf{d}_1^{\perp} \cdot \mathbf{d}_2$, the inner product of these vectors is

$$\nabla u_{\tau_{ijk}}^{\perp} \cdot \nabla v_{\tau_{ijk}}$$

$$= \frac{\left\{-(u_j - u_i)(\mathbf{x}_i - \mathbf{x}_k) - (u_k - u_i)(\mathbf{x}_j - \mathbf{x}_i)\right\} \cdot \left\{(v_j - v_i)(\mathbf{x}_i - \mathbf{x}_k)^{\perp} + (v_k - v_i)(\mathbf{x}_j - \mathbf{x}_i)^{\perp}\right\}}{4 A_{ijk}^2}$$

$$= \frac{\left\{-(u_j - u_i)(v_k - v_i) + (u_k - u_i)(v_j - v_i)\right\}\left\{(\mathbf{x}_i - \mathbf{x}_k) \cdot (\mathbf{x}_j - \mathbf{x}_i)^{\perp}\right\}}{4 A_{ijk}^2}.$$

Focusing on the left half of the numerator, we have

$$- (u_j - u_i)(v_k - v_i) + (u_k - u_i)(v_j - v_i)$$

$$= -u_j v_k + u_j v_i + u_i v_k \cancel{- u_i v_i} + u_k v_j - u_k v_i - u_i v_j \cancel{+ u_i v_i}$$

$$= - \det \begin{pmatrix} u_i & u_j \\ v_i & v_j \end{pmatrix} - \det \begin{pmatrix} u_j & u_k \\ v_j & v_k \end{pmatrix} - \det \begin{pmatrix} u_k & u_i \\ v_k & v_i \end{pmatrix}. \qquad (1.60)$$

Here, $\det \begin{pmatrix} u_i & u_j \\ v_i & v_j \end{pmatrix}$ represents twice the signed area of the triangle formed by the origin and the directed edge ij in the UV space, so the sum of the three determinants is equal to twice the signed area $\tilde{A}_{ijk}$ of the triangle τ_{ijk} in the UV space. The right half of the numerator is

$$(\mathbf{x}_i - \mathbf{x}_k) \cdot (\mathbf{x}_j - \mathbf{x}_i)^{\perp} = -(\mathbf{x}_k - \mathbf{x}_i) \cdot (\mathbf{x}_j - \mathbf{x}_i)^{\perp}$$

$$= -2 A_{ijk}$$

where we used the fact that $(\mathbf{x}_k - \mathbf{x}_i) \cdot (\mathbf{x}_j - \mathbf{x}_i)^{\perp} / \|\mathbf{x}_j - \mathbf{x}_i\|$ represents the height of the vertex k with respect to the edge (i, j) as the base.

In summary, we have

$$\nabla u_{\tau_{ijk}}^{\perp} \cdot \nabla v_{\tau_{ijk}} = \frac{(-2\tilde{A}_{ijk})(-2A_{ijk})}{4 A_{ijk}^2}$$

$$= \frac{\tilde{A}_{ijk}}{A_{ijk}},$$

and the energy function of LSCM can be written as

$$E_{\text{LSCM}}(u, v) = \frac{1}{2} \sum_{\tau \in \mathcal{F}} \|\nabla u\|^2 A_\tau + \frac{1}{2} \sum_{\tau \in \mathcal{F}} \|\nabla v\|^2 A_\tau - \frac{1}{2} \sum_{\tau \in \mathcal{F}} 2 \frac{\tilde{A}_\tau}{A_\tau} A_\tau$$

$$= E_{\text{Dirichlet}}(u) + E_{\text{Dirichlet}}(v) - \tilde{A}(u, v)$$

where $\tilde{A}$ is the total area of the triangular mesh in the UV space.

By introducing the vector $\mathbf{w} := (\mathbf{u}^\top, \mathbf{v}^\top)^\top$ that combines the U and V coordinates, the above energy can be written simply using matrices and vectors as

$$E_{\text{LSCM}}(\mathbf{w}) = \frac{1}{2}\mathbf{w}^\top \underbrace{\left(\begin{pmatrix} -\mathbf{L} & \mathbf{O} \\ \mathbf{O} & -\mathbf{L} \end{pmatrix} - 2\mathbf{A}\right)}_{\mathbf{Q}} \mathbf{w} \tag{1.61}$$

Here, $\mathbf{L}$ is the cotangent Laplacian matrix, and $\mathbf{A}$ is a matrix that calculates the area of the triangular mesh in the UV space. Considering the summation of areas of two triangles in the UV space that share an edge, it is evident from Eq. (1.60) that the matrix determinants for the two oppositely directed edges ij and ji cancel each other out. Therefore, the sum of all the triangle areas in the UV space can be calculated using only the boundary edges. Specifically, for each edge (i, j) on the boundary, we set

$$\mathbf{A}_{i,|\mathcal{V}|+j} = \frac{1}{2}$$

$$\mathbf{A}_{|\mathcal{V}|+i,j} = -\frac{1}{2}$$

and now the total area can be calculated as $\mathbf{w}^\top \mathbf{A}\mathbf{w}$. The matrix $\mathbf{A}$ is not symmetric in this form, however, which is inconvenient for the subsequent numerical solving, so we replace it by $\mathbf{A} \leftarrow \frac{\mathbf{A}+\mathbf{A}^\top}{2}$ to make it symmetric.

1.3.2.5 Boundary Conditions for LSCM

Similar to the harmonic parameterization, the U and V coordinates that minimize E_{LSCM} are the solutions to the equation

$$\frac{\partial E_{\text{LSCM}}}{\partial \mathbf{w}} = \mathbf{Q}\,\mathbf{w} = 0. \tag{1.62}$$

To avoid the trivial solution $\mathbf{w} = \mathbf{0}$, we need to impose some boundary conditions. Unlike the harmonic parameterization, however, we need not fix all the boundary vertices, and a unique solution can be determined by fixing as few as two vertices. A simple method of choosing the two vertices to be fixed is to find a pair of vertices that are relatively far apart on the original 3D mesh [18, 19]. An example of executing the LSCM method is shown in Fig. 1.18.

1.3.2.6 Conformal Mapping Without Explicit Boundary Conditions

The LSCM method is quite practical and is actually incorporated into many 3D modeling software. However, because of the imposed boundary conditions that fix the

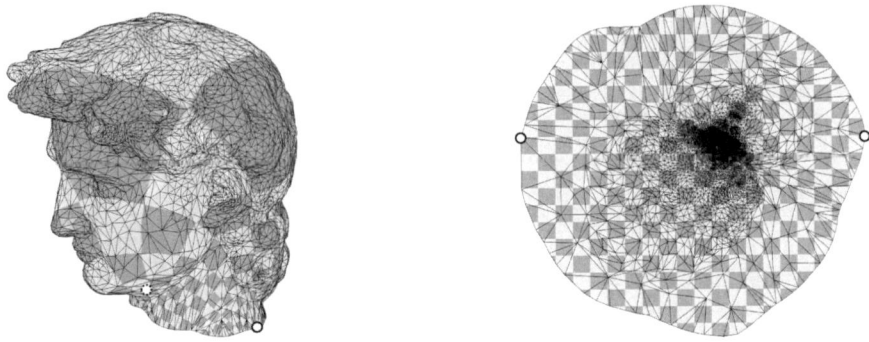

Fig. 1.18 An example of the LSCM method. The two white points represent the vertices where the UV coordinates were fixed as boundary conditions (in the 3D representation, one is hidden, so it is represented by a dashed contour line)

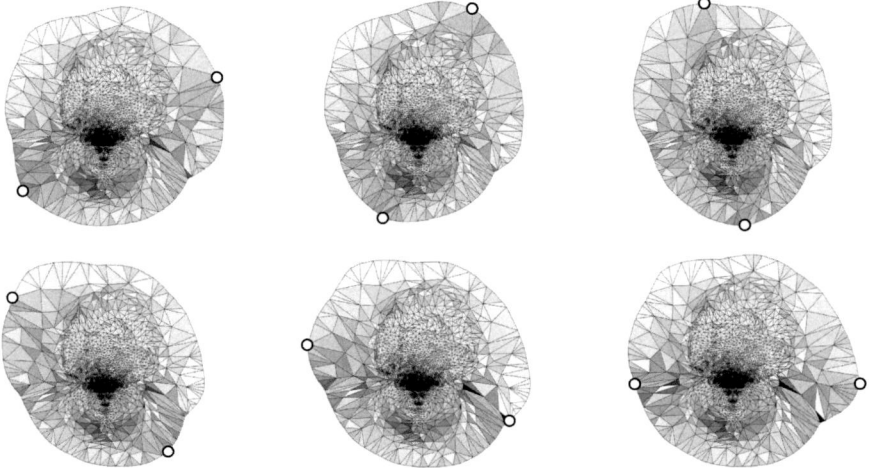

Fig. 1.19 Bias that occurs by fixing two vertices in the LSCM method. The color intensity of the triangle represents the magnitude of the angle distortion

UV coordinates of two vertices, the result contains some bias, and in particular the angle distortion becomes somewhat larger near the fixed vertices (Fig. 1.19). Mullen et al. pointed out these problems and proposed *Spectral Conformal Parameterization* (SCP), a method that can obtain solutions without explicitly giving boundary conditions by solving a generalized eigenvalue problem [20]. The basic idea is instead of fixing the UV coordinates of several vertices as in the LSCM method, impose a constraint that the norm of the vector **w** is 1 while minimizing the energy so as to avoid the trivial solutions.

The condition that the norm of the vector $\mathbf{w}$ is 1 can be written as

$$\mathbf{w}^\top \mathbf{B}\,\mathbf{w} = 1 \tag{1.63}$$

Here, instead of the ordinary $\mathcal{L}^2$ norm, a generalized norm is used, and a symmetric positive definite matrix $\mathbf{B}$ is introduced (described in detail later). The problem of minimizing a quadratic objective function under a quadratic constraint is generally difficult to solve, but if the constraint takes this specific form of Eq. (1.63), it can be solved as a generalized eigenvalue problem using the method of Lagrange multipliers.

By introducing the Lagrange multiplier λ, the objective function is defined as

$$E_{\text{SCP}}(\mathbf{w}, \lambda) := \frac{1}{2}\mathbf{w}^\top \mathbf{Q}\,\mathbf{w} + \frac{\lambda}{2}(1 - \mathbf{w}^\top \mathbf{B}\,\mathbf{w}) \tag{1.64}$$

At the stationary points of this function, the following conditions are satisfied:

$$\frac{\partial E_{\text{SCP}}}{\partial \mathbf{w}} = \mathbf{Q}\,\mathbf{w} - \lambda \mathbf{B}\,\mathbf{w} = \mathbf{0} \tag{1.65}$$

$$\frac{\partial E_{\text{SCP}}}{\partial \lambda} = \frac{1}{2}(1 - \mathbf{w}^\top \mathbf{B}\,\mathbf{w}) = 0 \tag{1.66}$$

In other words, it suffices to find the solutions $\mathbf{w}, \lambda$ to the following generalized eigenvalue problem:

$$\mathbf{Q}\,\mathbf{w} = \lambda \mathbf{B}\,\mathbf{w} \tag{1.67}$$

If we denote the eigenvalue and eigenvector that satisfy equations (1.63) and (1.67) as λ^*, $\mathbf{w}^*$, then the energy of the LSCM method is

$$\begin{aligned}
E_{\text{LSCM}}(\mathbf{w}^*) &= \frac{1}{2}\mathbf{w}^{*\top}\mathbf{Q}\,\mathbf{w}^* \\
&= \frac{1}{2}\mathbf{w}^{*\top}\left(\lambda^* \mathbf{B}\,\mathbf{w}^*\right) \\
&= \frac{\lambda^*}{2}
\end{aligned}$$

which is proportional to the eigenvalue λ^*. That is, all we need to do is find the eigenvector corresponding to the smallest eigenvalue of the generalized eigenvalue problem (1.67).

Another perspective on eigenvalues and eigenvectors is the Rayleigh quotient

$$R_{\mathbf{Q},\mathbf{B}}(\mathbf{w}) := \frac{\mathbf{w}^\top \mathbf{Q}\,\mathbf{w}}{\mathbf{w}^\top \mathbf{B}\,\mathbf{w}} \tag{1.68}$$

The minimum and maximum values of the Rayleigh quotient coincide with the smallest and largest eigenvalues of the generalized eigenvalue problem (1.67), respectively, and are obtained when the corresponding eigenvectors are substituted. In the SCP method, finding the smallest eigenvector is equivalent to minimizing the Rayleigh quotient, which means finding $\mathbf{w}$ that makes the LSCM energy $\mathbf{w}^\top \mathbf{Q}\, \mathbf{w}$ in the numerator smaller while making the norm $\mathbf{w}^\top \mathbf{B}\, \mathbf{w}$ in the denominator larger. By balancing the energy and the norm this way, we can avoid the trivial solution of $\mathbf{w} = \mathbf{0}$.

One notable property of the matrix $\mathbf{Q}$ is that it is positive semi-definite, i.e., it has a zero eigenvalue and there exists $\mathbf{w} \neq \mathbf{0}$ satisfying $\mathbf{w}^\top \mathbf{Q}\, \mathbf{w} = 0$. This occurs when all the UV coordinates of the vertices are concentrated at one point, i.e., when $(u_i, v_i) = (c, d) \quad \forall i \in \mathcal{V}$ for constants $c, d \in \mathbb{R}$, because in this configuration the Dirichlet energy is zero (as the function is constant) and the total area is also zero (as all the vertices coincide). The number of dimensions of the null space of $\mathbf{Q}$ is 2, and its two basis vectors $\mathbf{w}_1^*$, $\mathbf{w}_2^*$ can be expressed as $\mathbf{w}_1^* = (\mathbf{1}_{|\mathcal{V}|}^\top, \mathbf{0}_{|\mathcal{V}|}^\top)^\top$, $\mathbf{w}_2^* = (\mathbf{0}_{|\mathcal{V}|}^\top, \mathbf{1}_{|\mathcal{V}|}^\top)^\top$ using the constant vectors $\mathbf{0}_{|\mathcal{V}|} := (0, \ldots, 0)^\top$, $\mathbf{1}_{|\mathcal{V}|} := (1, \ldots, 1)^\top \in \mathbb{R}^{|\mathcal{V}|}$. In the SCP method, these trivial solutions are avoided by seeking the smallest non-zero eigenvalue of the generalized eigenvalue problem (1.67). If we denote the eigenvector corresponding to the smallest non-zero eigenvalue as $\mathbf{w}^*$, from the orthogonality of the eigenvectors, we have

$$\mathbf{w}^{*\top} \mathbf{B}\, \mathbf{w}_1^* = \mathbf{w}^{*\top} \mathbf{B}\, \mathbf{w}_2^* = 0.$$

This means that the average of the U and V coordinates are both zero, i.e., the centroid of the triangular mesh in the UV space is at the origin.

The simplest way to define the norm using the symmetric positive definite matrix $\mathbf{B}$ is to use the mass matrix $\mathbf{M}$ introduced in Eq. (1.46) and define

$$\mathbf{B} := \begin{pmatrix} \mathbf{M} & \mathbf{O} \\ \mathbf{O} & \mathbf{M} \end{pmatrix}.$$

This approach, however, unnecessarily interferes with the minimization of the LSCM energy $\mathbf{w}^\top \mathbf{Q}\, \mathbf{w}$ in the Rayleigh quotient (1.68), because all the vertices are used in the calculation of the norm $\mathbf{w}^\top \mathbf{B}\, \mathbf{w}$. When the 3D surface is far from developable, inversion and extreme shrinkage of triangles in the UV space can easily occur especially for those triangles that are far from the boundary. The essence of the SCP method is to constrain the resulting map to have a certain size in the UV space to avoid the trivial solution $\mathbf{w} = \mathbf{0}$, and there is no reason to use all the vertices in the calculation of this "size". The method proposed by Mullen et al. is to zero out all the entries in the diagonal matrix $\mathbf{B}$ that correspond to the interior vertices. This method can greatly reduce the possibility of triangle flipping (although it does not guarantee that flipping will not occur).

Finally, let's talk about the specific numerical calculation method to solve the generalized eigenvalue problem (1.67). Since our problem is to find small eigenvalues and corresponding eigenvectors for the large sparse matrix $\mathbf{Q}$, the power method can

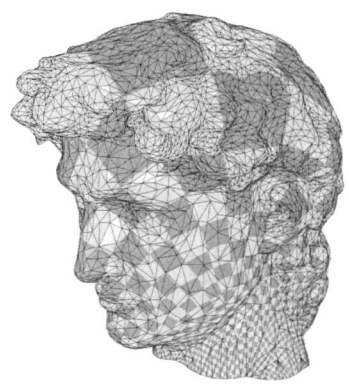
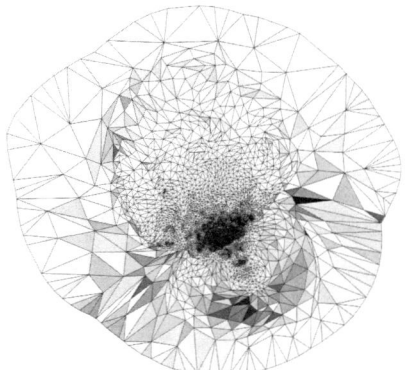

Fig. 1.20 An example of the SCP method. Note that unlike the LSCM method (Fig. 1.19), there are no vertices fixed as boundary conditions

be used. However, because the smallest eigenvalue is zero, the calculation will diverge as it is, so it is necessary to shift the diagonal elements slightly.

An example is shown in Fig. 1.20.

1.4 Deformation

Deformation can be described as a problem where each vertex $i \in \mathcal{V}$ of the mesh $\mathcal{M} = (\mathcal{V}, \mathcal{E}, \mathcal{F})$, which has a 3D coordinate $\mathbf{x}_i \in \mathbb{R}^3$, is assigned a new 3D coordinate $\mathbf{x}'_i \in \mathbb{R}^3$. There are various ways to generate deformations, but here we will explain a simple handle-based deformation method that does not require any auxiliary data such as skeletons or skinning weights. In this handle-based deformation method, the user gives a position constraint to a part of the mesh vertices $i \in C \subset \mathcal{V}$ (referred to as handles) as

$$\mathbf{x}'_i = \mathbf{c}_i \qquad (1.69)$$

where the right-hand side is a 3D coordinate specified by the user, and the positions of the other vertices are automatically calculated by some optimization.

1.4.1 Harmonic Deformation

The simplest method is to use the harmonic functions explained in Sect. 1.3.1. In this method, we first consider the *displacement* between the vertex coordinates before and after deformation:

$$\mathbf{d}_i := \mathbf{x}'_i - \mathbf{x}_i. \qquad (1.70)$$

Fig. 1.21 Triangular mesh
used in the deformation
experiment

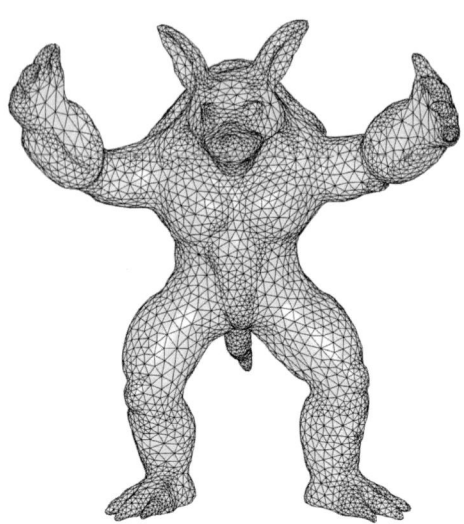

We consider a harmonic function of the displacement

$$\Delta \mathbf{d} = \mathbf{0} \tag{1.71}$$

under the boundary condition $\mathbf{d}_i = \mathbf{c}_i - \mathbf{x}_i, i \in C$. The obtained displacement is
added to the original vertex coordinates, yielding the vertex coordinates after
deformation:

$$\mathbf{x}'_i = \mathbf{x}_i + \mathbf{d}_i. \tag{1.72}$$

The result of applying this algorithm to the triangular mesh shown in Fig. 1.21 is
shown in Fig. 1.22a.

1.4.2   Biharmonic Deformation

As seen in Sect. 1.3.1, when the scalar field $f : \mathcal{M} \to \mathbb{R}$ is harmonic, f minimizes
the Dirichlet energy

$$E_{\text{Dirichlet}}(f) = \frac{1}{2} \iint_{\mathcal{M}} \|\nabla f\|^2 \, dA. \tag{1.73}$$

Here, as a substitute for the Dirichlet energy that takes the sum of the squares of the
magnitudes of the gradient vectors, we consider the *Laplacian energy*, which takes
the sum of the squares of the Laplacians,

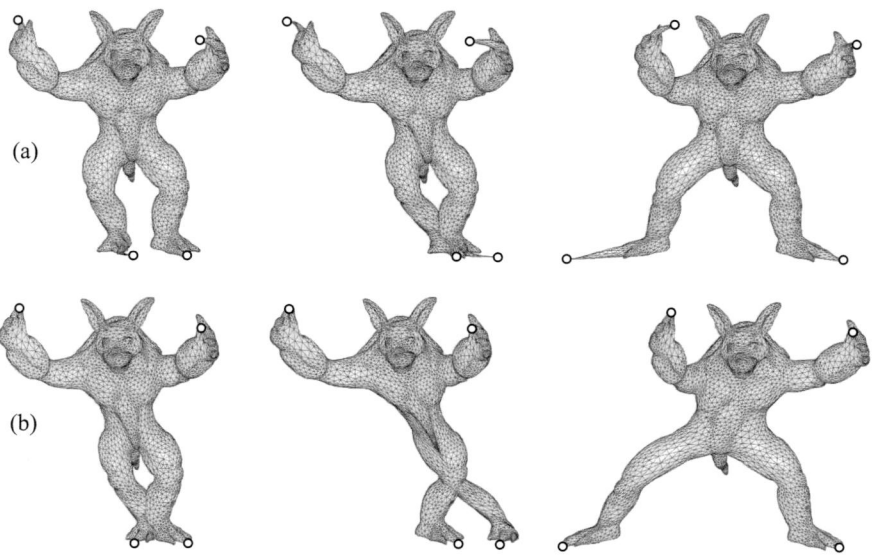

(a)

(b)

Fig. 1.22 **a** Deformation based on the harmonic function, **b** Deformation based on the biharmonic function

$$E_{\text{Laplacian}}(f) := \frac{1}{2} \iint_{\mathcal{M}} (\Delta f)^2 \, dA. \tag{1.74}$$

As described in Sect. 1.2.5, the Laplacian at each vertex, per unit area, can be written as $\mathbf{M}^{-1}\mathbf{L}\mathbf{f}$ using the mass matrix $\mathbf{M}$ and the cotangent Laplacian matrix $\mathbf{L}$. The Laplacian energy that sums the squares of the Laplacians at each vertex multiplied by the local area of each vertex (i.e., the mass matrix $\mathbf{M}$) can be succinctly written using vectors and matrices as

$$E_{\text{Laplacian}}(\mathbf{f}) = \frac{1}{2} \left(\mathbf{M}^{-1}\mathbf{L}\mathbf{f}\right)^{\top} \mathbf{M} \left(\mathbf{M}^{-1}\mathbf{L}\mathbf{f}\right) \tag{1.75}$$

$$= \frac{1}{2}\mathbf{f}^{\top} \underbrace{\left(\mathbf{L}\mathbf{M}^{-1}\mathbf{L}\right)}_{\mathbf{L}_2} \mathbf{f} \tag{1.76}$$

Its minimizer can be obtained by solving

$$\frac{\partial E_{\text{Laplacian}}}{\partial \mathbf{f}} = \mathbf{L}_2\mathbf{f} = \mathbf{0} \tag{1.77}$$

under the boundary conditions. The function f that minimizes the Laplacian energy in this way is called a *biharmonic* function, and it is obtained as a solution to the *bi-Laplace equation*

$$\Delta^2 f = 0. \tag{1.78}$$

The differential operator Δ^2 is called the *bi-Laplacian*, and it is represented by the sparse symmetric matrix $\mathbf{L}_2$ when implemented on a triangular mesh.

Harmonic functions minimize the sum of the gradient magnitudes squared, in other words, they penalize the change in the function at each point. Intuitively, among the functions that satisfy the boundary conditions, the harmonic function is the one that is closest to a constant function. Therefore, it has the property that the value of the function approaches the overall average value rapidly from the boundary of the domain toward the interior. In deformation, this property appears as a phenomenon where the displacement is concentrated near the handle.

Biharmonic functions, on the other hand, minimize the sum of the Laplacians squared, in other words, they penalize the extent to which the function deviates from linear at each point (since the Laplacian of a linear function is zero). Intuitively, among the functions that satisfy the boundary conditions, the biharmonic function is the one that bends the least. As a result of this property, the displacement in the deformation does not excessively concentrate near the handle, resulting in a smoother deformation result (Fig. 1.22b).

1.4.3   As-Rigid-As-Possible Deformation

As we saw in Sect. 1.3.1, the Dirichlet energy can be written as the weighted sum of the squares of the differences in values at both ends of an edge:

$$E_{\text{Dirichlet}}(\mathbf{d}) = \frac{1}{2} \sum_{ij \in \mathcal{E}} w_{ij} \left\| \mathbf{d}_i - \mathbf{d}_j \right\|^2 \tag{1.79}$$

Here, the weight w_{ij} is the off-diagonal component of the cotangent Laplacian. If we rewrite this using the vertex coordinates $\mathbf{x}'$ after deformation instead of the displacement $\mathbf{d}$, we get

$$E_{\text{Dirichlet}}(\mathbf{x}') = \frac{1}{2} \sum_{ij \in \mathcal{E}} w_{ij} \left\| (\mathbf{x}'_i - \mathbf{x}_i) - (\mathbf{x}'_j - \mathbf{x}_j) \right\|^2 \tag{1.80}$$

$$= \frac{1}{2} \sum_{ij \in \mathcal{E}} w_{ij} \| \underbrace{(\mathbf{x}'_i - \mathbf{x}'_j)}_{\mathbf{e}'_{ij}} - \underbrace{(\mathbf{x}_i - \mathbf{x}_j)}_{\mathbf{e}_{ij}} \|^2 . \tag{1.81}$$

Intuitively, the harmonic deformation can be interpreted as determining the vertex coordinates after deformation in such a way that the edge vectors after deformation $\mathbf{e}'_{ij}$ become as close as possible to the edge vectors before deformation $\mathbf{e}_{ij}$ (we call them *target edge vectors* hereafter).

There is a major problem with this method, however, which is that it cannot consider the local surface rotation that should occur with the deformation. For example, suppose we apply a certain rotation matrix $\mathbf{R} \in \mathbb{R}^{3 \times 3}$ to the handles

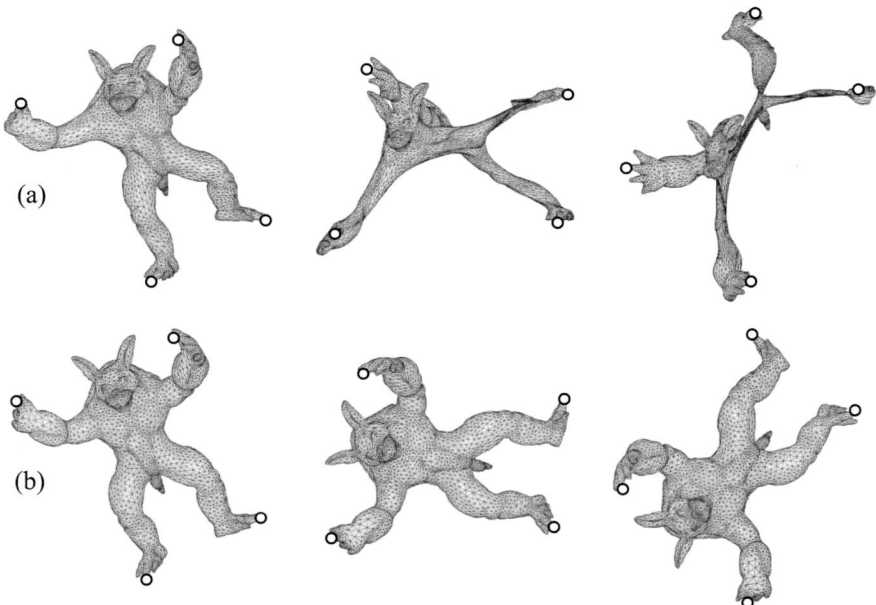

Fig. 1.23 Using the harmonic or biharmonic deformation method, rotations accompanying deformations cannot be handled well (**a**). By appropriately rotating the target edge vectors, the expected result can be obtained (**b**)

($\mathbf{x}'_i = \mathbf{R}\mathbf{x}_i$, $i \in C$). In this case, it is expected that the result of the deformation will be the same as rotating the entire shape by the same $\mathbf{R}$, but with the harmonic or biharmonic deformation method described above, such a result cannot be obtained (Fig. 1.23a). By modifying the Dirichlet energy with the target edge vectors pre-rotated by $\mathbf{R}$, $\frac{1}{2} \sum_{ij \in \mathcal{E}} w_{ij} \left\| \mathbf{e}'_{ij} - \mathbf{R}\mathbf{e}_{ij} \right\|^2$, we get the expected result (Fig. 1.23b).

In general, complex deformations induce different rotations for each part of the shape. In the *As-Rigid-As-Possible* (ARAP) deformation method [21] explained below, this locally varying rotation is represented by assigning a rotation matrix $\mathbf{R}_i \in \mathbb{R}^{3 \times 3}$ to each vertex $i \in \mathcal{V}$. $\mathbf{R}_i$ is an unknown variable, and it is sought as the best *rigid transformation* against spatial changes in the local 1-ring neighborhood of the vertex i.

In order to derive the energy of the ARAP deformation, first, the base Dirichlet energy is rewritten as the total sum for each vertex:

$$E_{\text{Dirichlet}}(\mathbf{x}') = \frac{1}{4} \sum_{i \in \mathcal{V}} \sum_{j \in \mathcal{N}_*(i)} w_{ij} \left\| \mathbf{e}'_{ij} - \mathbf{e}_{ij} \right\|^2. \tag{1.82}$$

Note that the first coefficient is halved because each edge is counted twice by the vertices at both ends.

By applying the rotation $\mathbf{R}_i$ for each vertex to the target edge vector, the ARAP deformation energy is defined:

$$E_{\text{ARAP}}(\mathbf{x}', \mathbf{R}) := \frac{1}{4} \sum_{i \in \mathcal{V}} \sum_{j \in \mathcal{N}_*(i)} w_{ij} \left\| \mathbf{e}'_{ij} - \mathbf{R}_i \mathbf{e}_{ij} \right\|^2 \tag{1.83}$$

As mentioned earlier, note that the rotation for each vertex $\mathbf{R} = (\mathbf{R}_1, \ldots, \mathbf{R}_{|\mathcal{V}|})$ is also a variable of optimization. Due to the constraint that $\mathbf{R}$ must be a rotation matrix, this optimization problem becomes nonlinear, making it impossible to find a global optimum at once. Therefore, it is necessary to start from an appropriate initial solution and converge to a local optimum through iterations. The ARAP deformation algorithm employs a characteristic method of dividing this iterative computation into two steps. In the first step, the vertex coordinates $\mathbf{x}'$ are fixed and the rotation $\mathbf{R}$ is optimized, while the second step performs the reverse. These are respectively called the local step and the global step, and this method of alternately repeating them is thus referred to as *local-global optimization*.

1.4.3.1 Local Step

Here, with the transformed vertex coordinates $\mathbf{x}'$ known, we seek the rotation $\mathbf{R}$ that minimizes E_{ARAP}. As can be seen from Eq. (1.83), it is clear that the rotations $\mathbf{R}_i$, $\mathbf{R}_j$ held by different vertices $i, j \in \mathcal{V}$ contribute independently to the energy. In other words, for each vertex i, we only need to solve the following separate optimization problem:

$$\underset{\mathbf{R}_i}{\arg\min} \sum_{j \in \mathcal{N}_*(i)} w_{ij} \left\| \mathbf{e}'_{ij} - \mathbf{R}_i \mathbf{e}_{ij} \right\|^2 . \tag{1.84}$$

If we expand the equation, we get

$$\underset{\mathbf{R}_i}{\arg\min} \sum_{j \in \mathcal{N}_*(i)} w_{ij} (\mathbf{e}'_{ij} - \mathbf{R}_i \mathbf{e}_{ij})^\top (\mathbf{e}'_{ij} - \mathbf{R}_i \mathbf{e}_{ij})$$

$$= \underset{\mathbf{R}_i}{\arg\min} \sum_{j \in \mathcal{N}_*(i)} w_{ij} (\mathbf{e}'^{\top}_{ij} \mathbf{e}'_{ij} - 2\mathbf{e}'^{\top}_{ij} \mathbf{R}_i \mathbf{e}_{ij} + \mathbf{e}^{\top}_{ij} \mathbf{e}_{ij})$$

$$= \underset{\mathbf{R}_i}{\arg\max} \sum_{j \in \mathcal{N}_*(i)} w_{ij} \mathbf{e}'^{\top}_{ij} \mathbf{R}_i \mathbf{e}_{ij} .$$

By noting the fact that for any n-dimensional vectors $\mathbf{a}, \mathbf{b}$ we have $\mathbf{a}^\top \mathbf{b} = \text{Tr}(\mathbf{b}\mathbf{a}^\top)$ (where $\text{Tr}(\cdot)$ is the trace of a matrix, i.e., the sum of its diagonals), we further transform the equation as

$$\underset{\mathbf{R}_i}{\arg\max} \sum_{j \in \mathcal{N}_*(i)} w_{ij} \, \text{Tr}(\mathbf{R}_i \mathbf{e}_{ij} \mathbf{e}'^{\top}_{ij})$$

$$= \arg\max_{\mathbf{R}_i} \text{Tr} \left(\mathbf{R}_i \underbrace{\sum_{j \in \mathcal{N}_*(i)} w_{ij} \mathbf{e}_{ij} \mathbf{e}_{ij}'^{\top}}_{\mathbf{S}_i} \right).$$

The matrix $\mathbf{S}_i \in \mathbb{R}^{3\times3}$, defined this way is called a *covariance* matrix. To find the rotation matrix $\mathbf{R}_i \in \mathbb{R}^{3\times3}$ that maximizes $\text{Tr}(\mathbf{R}_i \mathbf{S}_i)$, we use the singular value decomposition (SVD) of the covariance matrix

$$\mathbf{S}_i = \mathbf{U}_i \underbrace{\begin{pmatrix} \sigma_{i,1} & 0 & 0 \\ 0 & \sigma_{i,2} & 0 \\ 0 & 0 & \sigma_{i,3} \end{pmatrix}}_{\Sigma_i} \mathbf{V}_i^{\top} \tag{1.85}$$

as proposed by Sorkine-Hornung in 2017 [22]. Here, $\mathbf{U}_i, \mathbf{V}_i \in \mathbb{R}^{3\times3}$ are orthogonal matrices, and $\sigma_{i,1} \geq \sigma_{i,2} \geq \sigma_{i,3} \geq 0$ are singular values. Using the property that for any square matrices $\mathbf{A}$ and $\mathbf{B}$, $\text{Tr}(\mathbf{AB}) = \text{Tr}(\mathbf{BA})$, we can transform

$$\begin{aligned} \text{Tr}(\mathbf{R}_i \mathbf{S}_i) &= \text{Tr}(\mathbf{R}_i \mathbf{U}_i \Sigma_i \mathbf{V}_i^{\top}) \\ &= \text{Tr}(\underbrace{\mathbf{V}_i^{\top} \mathbf{R}_i \mathbf{U}_i}_{\mathbf{T}_i} \Sigma_i) \\ &= \sum_{j=1}^{3} (\mathbf{T}_i)_{jj} \sigma_{i,j}. \end{aligned}$$

Since all singular values are non-negative, $\text{Tr}(\mathbf{R}_i \mathbf{S}_i)$ is maximized when the coefficients $(\mathbf{T}_i)_{jj}$ (the diagonals of $\mathbf{T}_i$) multiplied to the singular values are maximized. Since we are assuming that $\mathbf{R}_i$ is a rotation matrix, $\mathbf{T}_i = \mathbf{V}_i^{\top} \mathbf{R}_i \mathbf{U}_i$, which is a product of orthogonal matrices, is also an orthogonal matrix, and the length of its column vectors is all 1. The diagonals of $\mathbf{T}_i$ are maximized when $\mathbf{T}_i$ coincides with the identity matrix $\mathbf{I}$. Hence,

$$\mathbf{V}_i^{\top} \mathbf{R}_i \mathbf{U}_i = \mathbf{I} \quad \Leftrightarrow \quad \mathbf{R}_i = \mathbf{V}_i \mathbf{U}_i^{\top} \tag{1.86}$$

gives us the optimal rotation $\mathbf{R}_i$.

One thing to be careful is that in the case where $\det(\mathbf{S}_i) < 0$, the $\mathbf{R}_i$ obtained above becomes an orthogonal matrix that includes a mirror inversion which is not a correct rotation. A simple remedy for this case is to negate the last row of $\mathbf{V}_i$.

In the local step, we generate the covariance matrix and perform its SVD for each vertex independently, so parallel processing for all vertices is naturally possible. Also, by using the algorithm specialized for 3×3 matrices developed by McAdams et al. [23], the SVD can be performed quickly.

1.4.3.2 Global Step

Here, we assume the rotation $\mathbf{R}$ is known and seek the vertex positions after deformation $\mathbf{x}'$ that minimize E_{ARAP}. When calculating E_{ARAP}, $\mathbf{x}'_i$ is referenced in two cases: (1) each time an adjacent vertex j is visited for the summation of the edge vector differences centered at the vertex i (using the rotation $\mathbf{R}_i$), and (2) each time the vertex i is visited for the summation of the edge vector differences centered at each adjacent vertex j (using the rotation $\mathbf{R}_j$). Therefore, the derivative of E_{ARAP} with respect to $\mathbf{x}'_i$ is

$$\frac{\partial E_{\text{ARAP}}}{\partial \mathbf{x}'_i} = \frac{1}{4} \frac{\partial}{\partial \mathbf{x}'_i} \left(\sum_{j \in \mathcal{N}_*(i)} w_{ij} \left\| \mathbf{e}'_{ij} - \mathbf{R}_i \mathbf{e}_{ij} \right\|^2 + \sum_{j \in \mathcal{N}_*(i)} w_{ji} \left\| \mathbf{e}'_{ji} - \mathbf{R}_j \mathbf{e}_{ji} \right\|^2 \right)$$

Noting that $w_{ji} = w_{ij}$ and $\mathbf{e}_{ji} = -\mathbf{e}_{ij}$, expanding the above gives

$$\frac{1}{4} \frac{\partial}{\partial \mathbf{x}'_i} \left(\sum_{j \in \mathcal{N}_*(i)} w_{ij} \left(\mathbf{e}'^{\top}_{ij} \mathbf{e}'_{ij} - 2 \mathbf{e}'^{\top}_{ij} \mathbf{R}_i \mathbf{e}_{ij} + \mathbf{e}^{\top}_{ij} \mathbf{e}_{ij} \right) + \right.$$

$$\left. \sum_{j \in \mathcal{N}_*(i)} w_{ji} \left(\mathbf{e}'^{\top}_{ji} \mathbf{e}'_{ji} - 2 \mathbf{e}'^{\top}_{ji} \mathbf{R}_j \mathbf{e}_{ji} + \mathbf{e}^{\top}_{ji} \mathbf{e}_{ji} \right) \right)$$

$$= \frac{1}{2} \frac{\partial}{\partial \mathbf{x}'_i} \left(\sum_{j \in \mathcal{N}_*(i)} w_{ij} \left(\mathbf{e}'^{\top}_{ij} \mathbf{e}'_{ij} - 2 \mathbf{e}'^{\top}_{ij} \frac{\mathbf{R}_i + \mathbf{R}_j}{2} \mathbf{e}_{ij} + \mathbf{e}^{\top}_{ij} \mathbf{e}_{ij} \right) \right)$$

$$= \sum_{j \in \mathcal{N}_*(i)} w_{ij} \left(\mathbf{e}'_{ij} - \frac{\mathbf{R}_i + \mathbf{R}_j}{2} \mathbf{e}_{ij} \right).$$

We want to find $\mathbf{x}'$ such that this becomes zero, so for vertex i, the following holds:

$$\sum_{j \in \mathcal{N}_*(i)} w_{ij} \mathbf{e}'_{ij} = \sum_{j \in \mathcal{N}_*(i)} w_{ij} \frac{\mathbf{R}_i + \mathbf{R}_j}{2} \mathbf{e}_{ij}. \tag{1.87}$$

If we denote the Laplacian as $\mathbf{L}$, the left-hand side is precisely the i-th row of $\mathbf{L}\mathbf{x}'$. If we stack the above equation for all the vertices, we get

$$\mathbf{L}\,\mathbf{x}' = \mathbf{b}. \tag{1.88}$$

This generalized form of the Laplace equation where the right-hand side is a non-zero function is called the *Poisson equation*. By solving this Poisson equation under the boundary condition $\mathbf{x}'_i = \mathbf{c}_i$, $i \in C$, we can obtain the vertex coordinates $\mathbf{x}'$ that minimize E_{ARAP}.

1.4.3.3 Local-Global Optimization

When updating $\mathbf{x}'$ by the global step, the optimal rotation $\mathbf{R}$ also changes accordingly, so we perform the local step again to update $\mathbf{R}$. The optimal $\mathbf{x}'$ then changes accordingly, so we repeat the global step. This is the so-called local-global optimization. What's important here is that the energy is always reduced in both steps, ensuring that it will always converge to some appropriate state.

1.4.3.4 Interactive Deformation

As mentioned earlier, initial values are required to solve the nonlinear optimization iteratively. When there is no additional information, it is appropriate to initialize the vertex coordinates and rotations with the original vertex coordinates $\mathbf{x}'_i = \mathbf{x}_i$ and the unit matrix $\mathbf{R}_i = \mathbf{I}$, respectively. On the other hand, in applications where deformations are performed interactively, an effective method is to use the vertex coordinates and rotations calculated in the previous frame as the initial values, under the assumption that the changes in these quantities are continuous over time.

In addition, repeating the optimization until convergence can yield higher quality results, but this can increase computation time and potentially interfere with the interactive experience. In cases where speed is prioritized over quality, it can be effective to not wait for complete convergence but to cut off the iterations at a predefined number.

An example of the ARAP deformation method is shown in Fig. 1.24.

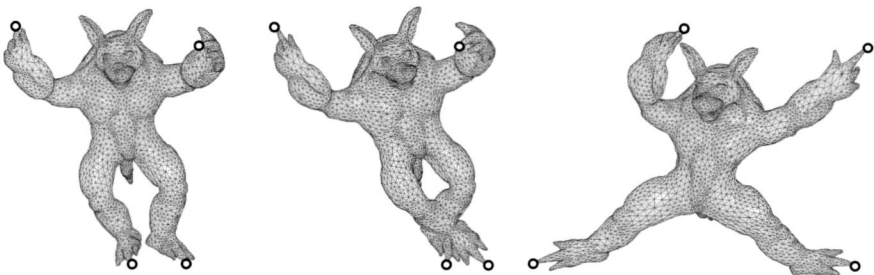

Fig. 1.24 An example of the ARAP deformation method. Note that more natural deformations are obtained compared to the harmonic deformation method (Fig. 1.22b)

1.4.4 Modification of E_{ARAP}

In a follow-up research, Chao et al. pointed out that there are problems with the original definition of E_{ARAP} by Sorkine et al., and proposed a modification [24]. Before explaining that, first note that the off-diagonal component of the Laplacian w_{ij} can be written as the sum of the weights $\tilde{w}_{ij}$, $\tilde{w}_{ji}$ corresponding to the half-edges ij and ji, using the angles θ_{ij}^k and θ_{ji}^l of the corners opposite the edges in the triangles τ_{ijk} and τ_{jil}:

$$w_{ij} = \underbrace{\frac{1}{2}\cot\theta_{ij}^k}_{\tilde{w}_{ij}} + \underbrace{\frac{1}{2}\cot\theta_{ji}^l}_{\tilde{w}_{ji}} \tag{1.89}$$

Using this, the Dirichlet energy can be rewritten as the total sum for each half-edge:

$$E_{\text{Dirichlet}}(\mathbf{x}') = \frac{1}{2}\sum_{\tau\in\mathcal{F}}\sum_{ij\in\mathcal{H}(\tau)}\tilde{w}_{ij}\left\|\mathbf{e}_{ij}' - \mathbf{e}_{ij}\right\|^2 \tag{1.90}$$

where $\mathcal{H}(\tau)$ denotes the set of three half-edges composing the triangle τ. Rewriting this into a vertex-wise summation, we get

$$E_{\text{Dirichlet}}(\mathbf{x}') = \frac{1}{6}\sum_{i\in\mathcal{V}}\sum_{\tau\in\mathcal{N}_\blacktriangle(i)}\sum_{jk\in\mathcal{H}(\tau)}\tilde{w}_{jk}\left\|\mathbf{e}_{jk}' - \mathbf{e}_{jk}\right\|^2 \tag{1.91}$$

where the initial coefficient $1/6$ is due to the fact that a single triangle is counted three times from its three vertices. By rotating the target edge vector $\mathbf{e}_{jk}$ by the vertex's rotation $\mathbf{R}_i$, the modified ARAP deformation energy is defined:

$$E_{\text{ARAP}}(\mathbf{x}', \mathbf{R}) := \frac{1}{6}\sum_{i\in\mathcal{V}}\sum_{\tau\in\mathcal{N}_\blacktriangle(i)}\sum_{jk\in\mathcal{H}(\tau)}\tilde{w}_{jk}\left\|\mathbf{e}_{jk}' - \mathbf{R}_i\mathbf{e}_{jk}\right\|^2. \tag{1.92}$$

By performing the same derivation as in the previous section, the covariance matrix used in the local step is

$$\mathbf{S}_i = \sum_{\tau\in\mathcal{N}_\blacktriangle(i)}\sum_{jk\in\mathcal{H}(\tau)}\tilde{w}_{jk}\mathbf{e}_{jk}\mathbf{e}_{jk}'^{\top} \tag{1.93}$$

and the optimal rotation $\mathbf{R}_i$ is obtained by performing the SVD of this matrix.

For the global step, we derive the derivative of the modified ARAP deformation energy with respect to $\mathbf{x}_i'$. For a single triangle τ_{ijk}, each of its three vertices i, j, k contributes once to the energy (using $\mathbf{R}_i, \mathbf{R}_j, \mathbf{R}_k$ respectively). Also, among the half-edges of τ_{ijk}, those that involve vertex i are ij and ki, so we have

$$
\frac{\partial E_{\text{ARAP}}}{\partial \mathbf{x}'_i} = \frac{1}{6} \frac{\partial}{\partial \mathbf{x}'_i} \sum_{\tau_{ijk} \in \mathcal{N}_\blacktriangle(i)} \left(\tilde{w}_{ij} \left\| \mathbf{e}'_{ij} - \mathbf{R}_i \mathbf{e}_{ij} \right\|^2 + \tilde{w}_{ki} \left\| \mathbf{e}'_{ki} - \mathbf{R}_i \mathbf{e}_{ki} \right\|^2 \right.
$$

$$
+ \tilde{w}_{ij} \left\| \mathbf{e}'_{ij} - \mathbf{R}_j \mathbf{e}_{ij} \right\|^2 + \tilde{w}_{ki} \left\| \mathbf{e}'_{ki} - \mathbf{R}_j \mathbf{e}_{ki} \right\|^2
$$

$$
\left. + \tilde{w}_{ij} \left\| \mathbf{e}'_{ij} - \mathbf{R}_k \mathbf{e}_{ij} \right\|^2 + \tilde{w}_{ki} \left\| \mathbf{e}'_{ki} - \mathbf{R}_k \mathbf{e}_{ki} \right\|^2 \right).
$$

Expanding this, we get

$$
\frac{1}{2} \frac{\partial}{\partial \mathbf{x}'_i} \sum_{\tau_{ijk} \in \mathcal{N}_\blacktriangle(i)} \left(\tilde{w}_{ij} \left(\mathbf{e}'^{\mathsf{T}}_{ij} \mathbf{e}'_{ij} - 2 \mathbf{e}'^{\mathsf{T}}_{ij} \frac{\mathbf{R}_i + \mathbf{R}_j + \mathbf{R}_k}{3} \mathbf{e}_{ij} + \mathbf{e}^{\mathsf{T}}_{ij} \mathbf{e}_{ij} \right) \right.
$$

$$
\left. + \tilde{w}_{ki} \left(\mathbf{e}'^{\mathsf{T}}_{ki} \mathbf{e}'_{ki} - 2 \mathbf{e}'^{\mathsf{T}}_{ki} \frac{\mathbf{R}_i + \mathbf{R}_j + \mathbf{R}_k}{3} \mathbf{e}_{ki} + \mathbf{e}^{\mathsf{T}}_{ki} \mathbf{e}_{ki} \right) \right)
$$

$$
= \underbrace{\sum_{\tau_{ijk} \in \mathcal{N}_\blacktriangle(i)} \left(\tilde{w}_{ij} \mathbf{e}'_{ij} + \tilde{w}_{ki} \mathbf{e}'_{ik} \right)}_{= \sum_{j \in \mathcal{N}_\bullet(i)} w_{ij} \mathbf{e}'_{ij}} - \sum_{\tau_{ijk} \in \mathcal{N}_\blacktriangle(i)} \frac{\mathbf{R}_i + \mathbf{R}_j + \mathbf{R}_k}{3} \left(\tilde{w}_{ij} \mathbf{e}_{ij} + \tilde{w}_{ki} \mathbf{e}_{ik} \right).
$$

In other words, the optimality condition for the vertex i is

$$
\sum_{j \in \mathcal{N}_\bullet(i)} w_{ij} \mathbf{e}'_{ij} = \sum_{\tau_{ijk} \in \mathcal{N}_\blacktriangle(i)} \frac{\mathbf{R}_i + \mathbf{R}_j + \mathbf{R}_k}{3} \left(\tilde{w}_{ij} \mathbf{e}_{ij} + \tilde{w}_{ki} \mathbf{e}_{ik} \right). \qquad (1.94)
$$

By using the above instead of Eq. (1.87) for the right-hand side of the Poisson equation, we can find the deformed vertex positions $\mathbf{x}'$ for the modified ARAP energy. We will omit the explanation of why this modification is advantageous over the original scheme as it would require complex theories. However, the practical difference appears when many of the triangles in the mesh become obtuse. In the example of the original method shown earlier in Fig. 1.24, the results were natural because most of the triangles of the input mesh shown in Fig. 1.21 were close to equilateral. If a mesh containing many obtuse triangles like the one shown in Fig. 1.25 is given as input, the result of the original method becomes highly jagged and far from the original shape (Fig. 1.26a). For such an input, the modified method produces much more natural deformations (Fig. 1.26b).

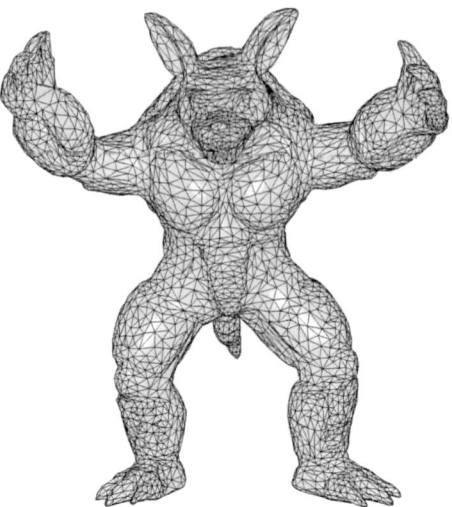

Fig. 1.25 A mesh that includes many obtuse triangles. Compare this to the one shown in Fig. 1.21

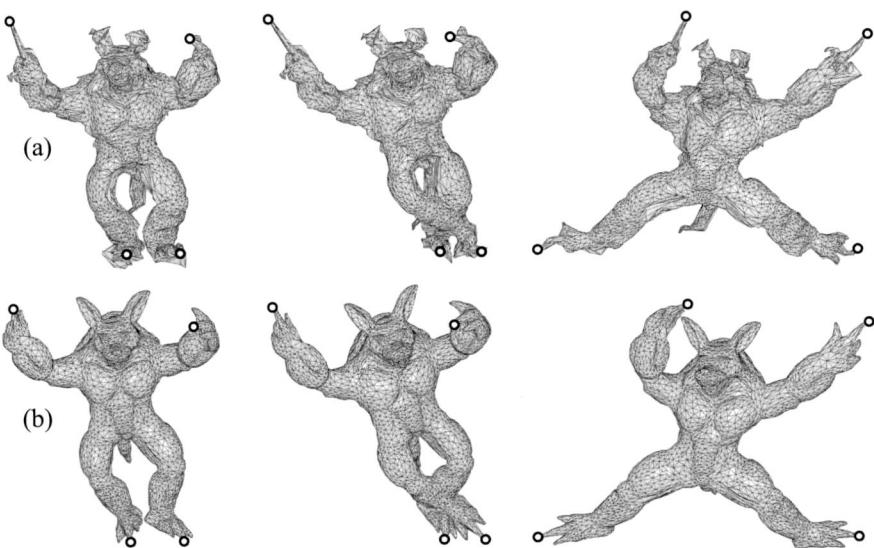

Fig. 1.26 The deformation results of the triangular mesh shown in Fig. 1.25 when used as input: the original method by Sorkine et al. (**a**), and the modified method by Chao et al. (**b**)

1.5 Conclusion

In this chapter, as an introduction to the field of surface geometry processing in 3DCG, we discussed three topics: smoothing, parameterization, and deformation, along with some of the basic concepts and important algorithms for each. In particular, we demonstrated that some fundamental tools like the cotangent Laplacian and the Dirichlet energy are commonly used across different topics. The data structures and algorithms discussed in this article have already been implemented and made public in various libraries, so there may be no actual need to implement them yourself in practice. However, understanding these basics is important when embarking on new research.

So far, we have assumed that a relatively clean triangular mesh is given as input, but in reality, there is a great challenge in extracting a clean triangular mesh from raw data obtained by scanning real 3D objects, a task called *3D shape reconstruction*, which is a central theme in the field of computer vision rather than computer graphics. Furthermore, the meshes output by 3D shape reconstruction algorithms, or those exported by CAD software, often contain artifacts (e.g., noise, holes, extremely long triangles) that hinder the application of geometry processing algorithms, and methods to fix or circumvent them are also being studied. In recent years, there has been significant progress in the study of robust geometry processing algorithms that can maintain consistency even when the quality of the input mesh is poor. Particularly in parameterization, various algorithms have been proposed to prevent or repair the flipping of triangles in the mapped space.

Although not mentioned in this chapter, generating volumetric meshes such as tetrahedral meshes or hexahedral meshes inside 3D shapes is also an important topic. Volumetric meshes are data structures necessary for performing physical simulations considering the internal structure of 3D shapes, and the goal is to reduce the number of elements while ensuring the high quality of the mesh elements (tetrahedron or hexahedron). There are many cases where the 2D concept of surface mesh processing can be naturally extended to 3D volumetric settings, but generally, the amount of data increases, and various problems unique to 3D occur. Therefore, the problem becomes significantly harder, and the room for development remains large today.

Finally, the technology of deep learning, which has been developing significantly in recent years, is also beginning to be applied in the field of geometry processing. 2D images are easy to handle due to the regularity of the pixel grids, but triangular meshes have vertices that are irregularly connected, making it non-trivial to incorporate them into deep learning. However, efforts to overcome this problem have been increasing in recent years, and future developments are expected.

References

1. Lorensen, W. & Cline, H. Marching cubes: A high resolution 3D surface construction algorithm. *Proceedings Of The 14th Annual Conference On Computer Graphics And Interactive Techniques*. pp. 163-169 (1987), https://doi.org/10.1145/37401.37422
2. Jacobson, A., Panozzo, D. & Others libigl: A simple C++ geometry processing library. (2018), https://libigl.github.io/
3. Project, T. CGAL User and Reference Manual. (CGAL Editorial Board,2024), https://doc.cgal.org/6.0/Manual/packages.html
4. Möbius, J. & Others OpenMesh: A generic and efficient polygon mesh data structure. (2024), https://www.graphics.rwth-aachen.de/software/openmesh/
5. Sharp, N., Crane, K. & Others GeometryCentral: A modern C++ library of data structures and algorithms for geometry processing. (2019), https://geometry-central.net/
6. Sieger, D. & Botsch, M. The Polygon Mesh Processing Library. (2023), https://github.com/pmp-library/pmp-library
7. Botsch, M., Kobbelt, L., Pauly, M., Alliez, P. & Levy, B. Polygon Mesh Processing. (A K Peters/CRC Press,2010)
8. Taubin, G. A signal processing approach to fair surface design. *Proceedings Of The 22nd Annual Conference On Computer Graphics And Interactive Techniques*. pp. 351-358 (1995), https://doi.org/10.1145/218380.218473
9. Desbrun, M., Meyer, M., Schröder, P. & Barr, A. Implicit fairing of irregular meshes using diffusion and curvature flow. *Proceedings Of The 26th Annual Conference On Computer Graphics And Interactive Techniques*. pp. 317-324 (1999), https://doi.org/10.1145/311535.311576
10. Meyer, M., Desbrun, M., Schröder, P. & Barr, A. Discrete Differential-Geometry Operators for Triangulated 2-Manifolds. *Visualization And Mathematics III*. pp. 35-57 (2003)
11. Kazhdan, M., Solomon, J. & Ben-Chen, M. Can Mean-Curvature Flow be Modified to be Non-singular?. *Comput. Graph. Forum*. **31**, 1745-1754 (2012,8), https://doi.org/10.1111/j.1467-8659.2012.03179.x
12. Tutte, W. How to Draw a Graph. *Proceedings Of The London Mathematical Society*. **s3-13**, 743-767 (1963), https://londmathsoc.onlinelibrary.wiley.com/doi/abs/10.1112/plms/s3-13.1.743
13. Floater, M. Parametrization and smooth approximation of surface triangulations. *Comput. Aided Geom. Des.*. **14**, 231-250 (1997,4), https://doi.org/10.1016/S0167-8396(96)00031-3
14. Floater, M. Mean value coordinates. *Computer Aided Geometric Design*. **20**, 19-27 (2003), https://www.sciencedirect.com/science/article/pii/S0167839603000025
15. Bobenko, A. & Springborn, B. A Discrete Laplace-Beltrami Operator for Simplicial Surfaces. *Discrete & Computational Geometry*. **38**, 740-756 (2007), https://doi.org/10.1007/s00454-007-9006-1
16. Sharp, N., Soliman, Y. & Crane, K. Navigating intrinsic triangulations. *ACM Trans. Graph.*. **38** (2019,7), https://doi.org/10.1145/3306346.3322979
17. Sharp, N. & Crane, K. A Laplacian for Nonmanifold Triangle Meshes. *Comput. Graph. Forum*. **39**, 69-80 (2020), https://onlinelibrary.wiley.com/doi/abs/10.1111/cgf.14069
18. Lévy, B., Petitjean, S., Ray, N. & Maillot, J. Least squares conformal maps for automatic texture atlas generation. *ACM Trans. Graph.*. **21**, 362-371 (2002,7), https://doi.org/10.1145/566654.566590
19. Desbrun, M., Meyer, M. & Alliez, P. Intrinsic Parameterizations of Surface Meshes. *Comput. Graph. Forum*. **21**, 209-218 (2002), https://onlinelibrary.wiley.com/doi/abs/10.1111/1467-8659.00580
20. Mullen, P., Tong, Y., Alliez, P. & Desbrun, M. Spectral Conformal Parameterization. *Comput. Graph. Forum*. **27**, 1487-1494 (2008), https://onlinelibrary.wiley.com/doi/abs/10.1111/j.1467-8659.2008.01289.x
21. Sorkine, O. & Alexa, M. As-rigid-as-possible surface modeling. *Proceedings Of The Fifth Eurographics Symposium On Geometry Processing*. pp. 109-116 (2007)

22. Sorkine-Hornung, O. & Rabinovich, M. Least-squares rigid motion using SVD. (ETH Zurich,2017)
23. McAdams, A., Selle, A., Tamstorf, R., Teran, J. & Sifakis, E. Computing the Singular Value Decomposition of 3×3 matrices with minimal branching and elementary floating point operations. (University of Wisconsin-Madison,2011)
24. Chao, I., Pinkall, U., Sanan, P. & Schröder, P. A simple geometric model for elastic deformations. *ACM Trans. Graph.*. **29** (2010,7), https://doi.org/10.1145/1778765.1778775

Chapter 2
Rendering

Yoshinori Dobashi⊙

Abstract Rendering has meanings such as "to give," "to make into a state," and "to express," and it is not a term limited to the field of computer graphics. It is also used in various contexts, such as sound rendering, video rendering, and web page rendering. Rendering can be thought of as expressing or transforming original data into a different state or format. In this chapter, we will explain the rendering process of generating 2D images from 3D information that describes synthetic scenes. In particular, we will focus on the intensity calculation of synthetic objects, beginning with the input information required for the calculation. We will cover global illumination techniques used to generate photorealistic images and precomputation-based methods for fast rendering. Furthermore, we will explain the rendering of light scattering effects to enhance realism. Finally, we will briefly introduce advanced rendering techniques.

2.1 Introduction

Rendering in computer graphics is the process of synthesizing digital images from numerical data that describes synthetic scenes. The process simulates capturing a synthetic scene composed of virtual objects with a virtual camera, resulting in a digital image of the virtual world. Rendering is a central and crucial field in computer graphics, and it is not an overstatement to say that many computer graphics techniques have evolved alongside the development of rendering techniques.

Various techniques are required to realize the rendering process. Firstly, we need to define a computational model for the virtual camera to capture synthetic scenes. In computer graphics, a simplified model known as the pinhole camera model is often used. This model does not produce lens blur, meaning all points in the scene are in focus. Next, we need to calculate the intensity (or color) of each pixel in the digital image. This chapter explains how to perform this calculation. The contents of each section of this chapter are summarized in the following (Fig. 2.1). While each section is related to others, they are generally independent, allowing readers to focus on the sections of most interest to them.

© The Editor(s) (if applicable) and The Author(s), under exclusive license to Springer Nature Singapore Pte Ltd. 2025
J. Mitani et al., *Mathematics and Applications of Computer Graphics*, https://doi.org/10.1007/978-981-96-2933-6_2

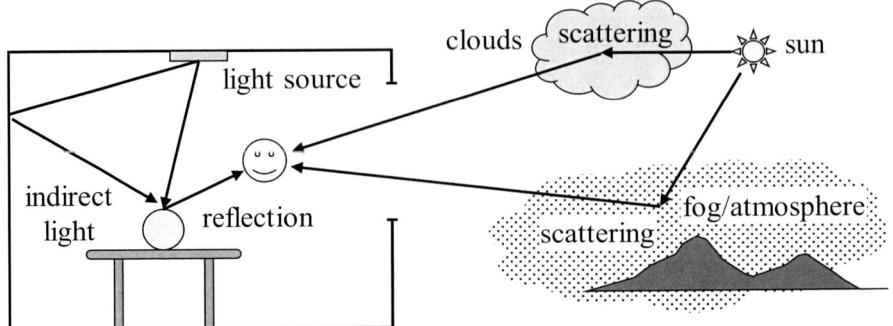

Fig. 2.1 Contents of this chapter

Section 2.2 explains the basic *shading models*. When we see an object in the real
world, we perceive the reflected light that has reached the object from a light source.
This means that the appearance of an object depends on its material properties and its
lighting environment. To reproduce a realistic appearance, we need computational
models for both the material of the object and the light source. This section explains
these models.

Section 2.3 explains the *global illumination model*. To generate synthetic images
of higher quality, it is essential to accurately simulate the behavior of light in the real
world. Early computer graphics used a *local illumination model* that only considered
direct light from the light source, which was limited in its realism. For more realistic
images, it is necessary to account for both direct and indirect light, including the
interreflections of light between objects. This advanced approach is known as the
global illumination model. By incorporating global illumination, one can produce
highly realistic images that are difficult to distinguish from real photographs. This
section covers the fundamental equations representing this model and its numerical
solution methods.

Section 2.4 explains methods to accelerate intensity calculations. The global illumination model often requires significant computation time. Depending on the complexity of the scene, generating a single image can take more than several minutes.
Additionally, the entire computation must be repeated whenever the scene description changes. This presents a serious challenge for interactive applications like video
games. Precomputation-based methods have been developed to address this issue by
calculating intermediate information in advance for use in real-time rendering. This
section provides an overview of these methods.

Section 2.5 discusses the rendering of participating media and translucent objects.
Participating media refers to a substance or medium in which tiny particles, such as
dust, smoke, or water droplets, interact with light as it passes through. These particles
scatter, absorb, and sometimes emit light, affecting how we perceive objects within

or behind the medium. Examples of participating media include fog, smoke, clouds, and water. The behavior of light in participating media is more complex than in clear air or vacuum, as it involves particle interactions that influence the overall appearance of a scene, such as softening shadows or creating atmospheric effects like haze or glow. This section covers methods for rendering these *light scattering* effects.

Finally, in Sect. 2.6, we briefly introduce recent rendering techniques, including *machine learning* and *differentiable rendering*. Both are expected to make significant contributions to the future development of rendering technology.

2.2 Shading and Lighting

There are two factors that determine the intensity of each point on the surface of an object: *shading* and *shadowing* (see Fig. 2.2). Shading refers to how light interacts with the surface of the object based on its material properties and the direction of the light source. Shadowing, on the other hand, occurs when an object blocks light from reaching certain areas, creating regions of darkness or reduced intensity. Both factors work together to define the overall appearance of an object's surface in a rendered scene. Various calculation models have been proposed regarding the material properties of objects and the types of light sources.

Let us consider the case shown in Fig. 2.2, where a point on a sphere is illuminated by light coming from the direction ω_i. The intensity of the incident light is denoted by L_i. The intensity of the reflected light, denoted by I, can be expressed by the following equation:

$$I = f_r(\omega_o, \omega_i)V(\omega_i)L_i(\omega_i)\cos\theta, \tag{2.1}$$

where f_r is the *Bidirectional Reflectance Distribution Function* (*BRDF*), which describes the reflectance based on the directions of the incident and reflected light. V is a visibility function that returns 0 if the light from the source is occluded by other objects, and 1 otherwise. θ is the angle between the normal direction at the point and

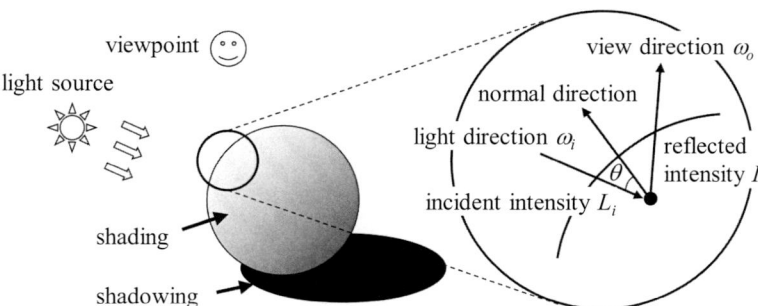

Fig. 2.2 Shading and shadowing

the direction of the light source. The term $\cos\theta$ accounts for the light energy received by the fractional surface area at that point. When light strikes the surface at a steep angle, the effective area over which the light is distributed is larger, resulting in less light being reflected compared to when it is illuminated directly from the normal direction. This makes the surface appear darker.

Various computational models have been developed to account for different reflectance properties and types of light sources when computing f_r and L_i, resulting in diverse appearances. In the following, we will first explain the reflectance properties, and then discuss different intensity calculation methods based on various types of light sources.

2.2.1 Reflectance Property

The appearance of an object is dominated by its reflectance property, that is, by the Bidirectional Reflectance Distribution Function (BRDF). The BRDF represents the fraction of incident light that is reflected in a specific direction, given the direction of the incoming light and the direction of the outgoing light. Thus, the BRDF is a function of the incident and the reflection directions. Since both the incident and the reflection directions are represented by two variables, the azimuth angle and the zenith angle, the BRDF becomes a four-dimensional function. The BRDF must satisfy the following properties.

- Energy Conservation: For a fixed incident direction, the integral of the BRDF over all possible reflection directions is less than or equal to 1. This property ensures that the total energy of the reflected light does not exceed the energy of the incident light.
- Reciprocity: The BRDF is symmetric with respect to the exchange of incoming and outgoing light directions. The BRDF value remains the same when the incident direction and the reflection direction are swapped.

To create realistic images that accurately reflect physical phenomena, it is important to use a BRDF that adheres to these properties. The reflectance of an object can be categorized into two types: *diffuse reflection* and *specular reflection*. Figure 2.3 shows typical examples of both types of reflections. At the top, the distribution of reflected light for light incident from a certain direction is illustrated.

For diffuse reflection, light incident on a certain point is reflected uniformly in all directions (Fig. 2.3a). Diffuse reflection typically corresponds to the color of an object. A key characteristic of a surface with diffuse reflection is that it appears to have consistent brightness from any viewing angle. Typical examples of objects with diffuse reflection include paper and concrete. For diffuse reflection, the BRDF is constant and is given by $f_r = \rho_d/\pi$, where ρ_d is the diffuse reflectance, a constant between 0 and 1 specified by the user. $1/\pi$ is a normalization constant that ensures energy conservation.

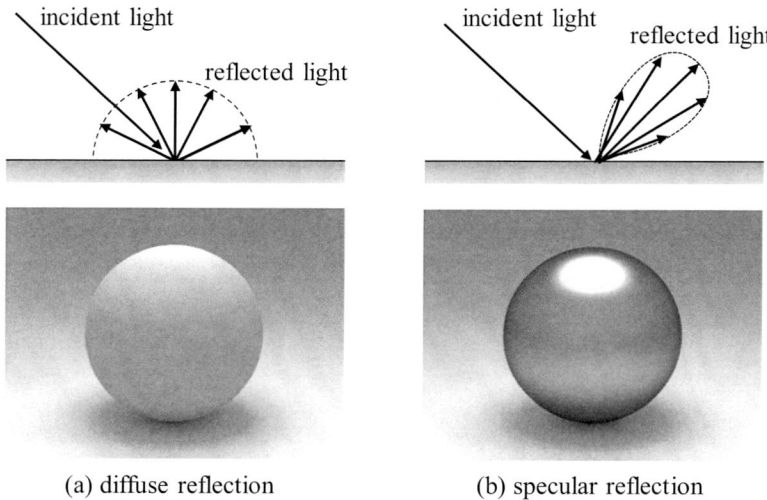

(a) diffuse reflection   (b) specular reflection

Fig. 2.3 Comparison of diffuse and specular reflections

Specular reflection is used to represent glossy materials such as plastic and metal (Fig. 2.3b). The incident light is primarily reflected in the direction opposite to the incident direction, creating a bright area known as a *highlight* on the object's surface. Various calculation models for specular reflection have been proposed, which are described in the following sections.

2.2.1.1 Ideal Specular Reflection

This is a special case of specular reflection where the incident light is reflected perfectly in the ideal reflection direction. As a result, on a surface with this reflection model, the observer sees a clear reflected image of the surrounding objects (Fig. 2.4). The BRDF for ideal specular reflection is represented by a Dirac delta function with respect to the reflection direction. It has a non-zero value only for the ideal specular reflection direction and is zero otherwise. The specular reflection direction can be determined by a simple geometric calculation from the incident direction and the normal vector at the calculation point. In the case of Fig. 2.4, the normal vector aligns with the direction of the vector obtained by subtracting the incident vector ω_i from the reflection vector ω_o. Its magnitude is twice $\cos\theta$, where θ is the angle between the incident vector and the normal vector. Therefore, the specular reflection direction is given by: $\omega_o = \omega_i + 2\omega_n \cos\theta$, where ω_n represents the normal vector.

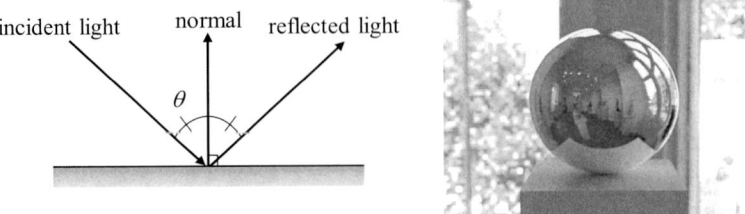

Fig. 2.4 Ideal specular reflection

2.2.1.2 Phong Model

This is the first computational model for glossy reflection, known as the Phong model, named after its inventor, Bui Tuong Phong [1]. As shown in Fig. 2.5, the intensity of the reflected light is calculated to be proportional to the power of the cosine of the deviation angle γ from the ideal reflection direction, expressed as $\cos^n \gamma$. The degree of glossiness can be adjusted using the power n. This is a heuristic model designed for the simplified rendering of glossy materials and does not account for the physical reflection process. Therefore, it does not satisfy the aforementioned energy conservation. Therefore, an improved model was later proposed that introduces a normalization factor to ensure that the total reflected light does not exceed 1, thereby generating physically accurate images. The Phong model, developed in 1975, remains widely used due to its simplicity in calculations.

2.2.1.3 Microfacet Model

This is a physically based reflection model that accounts for the microgeometry of the object's surface [2]. When magnified, the object's surface is not flat but consists of numerous tiny bumps, which can be considered as a collection of microfacets (Fig. 2.6). From a macroscopic view, the reflected light can be considered as the sum of the reflections from each tiny microfacet. In this model, each microfacet is

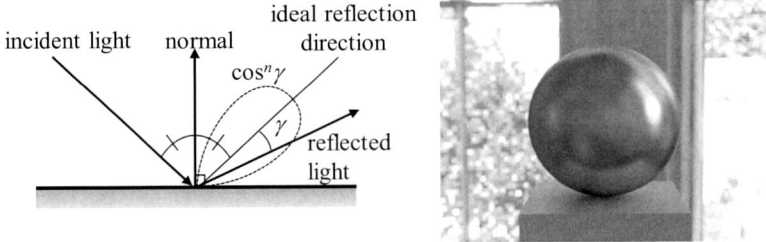

Fig. 2.5 Phong reflection model

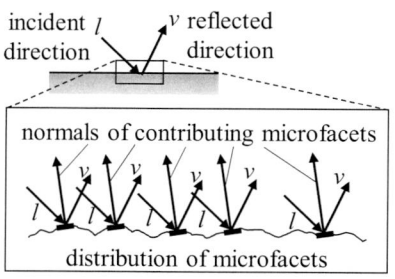 

Fig. 2.6 Microfacet model

assumed to be a perfect mirror. In this case, as shown in Fig. 2.6, the intensity of the reflected light is the sum of the contributions from the microfacets whose normals align with the half-vector direction between the incident light l and the viewing direction v. The microfacet model is based on this concept. Instead of calculating the reflection from each microfacet individually, the model considers the distribution of microfacets and derives a formula that statistically represents the macroscopic BRDF. The distribution of the microfacets is described using the *normal distribution function*, also known as the *NDF*. Commonly used NDFs include the Beckmann distribution function [2] and the GGX distribution function [3]. The model accounts for how microfacets can occlude both the incident and reflected light, as well as changes in reflectance due to differences in the refractive index, known as *Fresnel reflection*. This model, based on the distribution of microfacets, is well suited for rendering the reflections of metals such as aluminum and copper.

The microfacet model, developed in 1981, has been widely used as a physically based BRDF that satisfies the key properties mentioned above, namely energy conservation and reciprocity, and continues to be refined by many researchers. Comparing Figs. 2.5 and 2.6, a noticeable difference can be observed, particularly at the edges of the sphere. In the Phong model, the edges appear unnaturally dark, while the microfacet model addresses this issue, producing a more natural appearance.

2.2.1.4 Anisotropic Reflection

The reflection models described so far are categorized as *isotropic reflection* models, where the reflected intensity at a point remains unchanged even if the object is rotated around the normal vector at that point. For example, if you place a disc-shaped metal piece on a desk, fix the light source and viewpoint, and rotate the metal piece, its intensity does not change. However, the intensity changes in the case of *anisotropic reflection* [4], as described in this section (Fig. 2.7). Anisotropic reflection is observed on metal surfaces that have been polished in a specific direction. This is because the normal direction of the microsurface becomes biased based on the polishing direction.

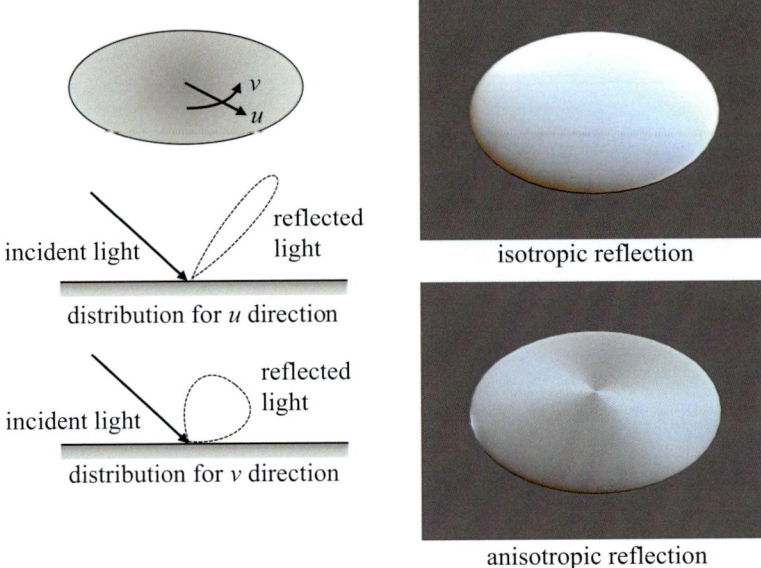

Fig. 2.7 Anisotropic reflection model

Figure 2.7 illustrates the difference between isotropic and anisotropic reflection. Let us assume a uv coordinate system on the surface of the disk, as shown in the figure. When the disk is polished along the u direction, the reflection distribution becomes sharper along the u direction compared to the v direction. As a result, the reflection appears more diffuse along the v direction, and the intensity changes when the disk is rotated about its normal. For anisotropic reflection, the highlight appears elongated in the direction of the surface's polishing. Anisotropic reflection is used not only to represent polished metals but also to depict the texture of hair [5, 6].

2.2.2 Light Sources

Common light sources in computer graphics include point lights, directional lights, linear lights, and area lights. A special type of light source, known as an environment light, represents light coming from all directions and is also commonly used. This will be discussed in detail in Sect. 2.4.1. Once we specify the reflection model and the type of light source, we can calculate the intensity at a point on the object's surface. This section explains the four types of light sources, as well as the intensity calculation.

2.2.2.1 Point Light

A *point light source* is the most basic light source. It represents an infinitesimally small point that emits light uniformly in all directions (Fig. 2.8). In the real world, it is analogous to a light bulb. A key characteristic of a point light source is that its light intensity decreases proportionally to the square of the distance from the source. The intensity of light at a point illuminated by a point light source is given by the following equation.

$$I = f_r(\omega_o, \omega_i) V(\omega_l) \frac{I_l}{r^2} \cos\theta, \tag{2.2}$$

where ω_i and ω_o represent the directions of the incoming light and the viewpoint, respectively, as observed from the point. V represents the visibility function, I_l denotes the intensity of the light source, and r is the distance between the point and the light source. V is determined by testing for intersections between the line segment connecting the point to the light source and any other objects.

Shadows cast by point light sources have well-defined boundaries between shadowed and non-shadowed regions. Additionally, the size of the shadows depends on the distance between the object and the light source; shadows of objects closer to the light source are larger, while those of objects farther away are smaller. By constraining the direction and angle of light emission, effects such as those from car headlights and spotlights can be simulated.

2.2.2.2 Directional Light

A *directional light source* represents light arriving in parallel from a single direction, effectively serving as a point light source located at infinity. It is often used to represent sunlight. Unlike a point light, directional light does not account for attenuation with distance. Therefore, the intensity calculation for a directional light source is formulated by omitting the $1/r^2$ term from the point light Eq. 2.2. Shadows created

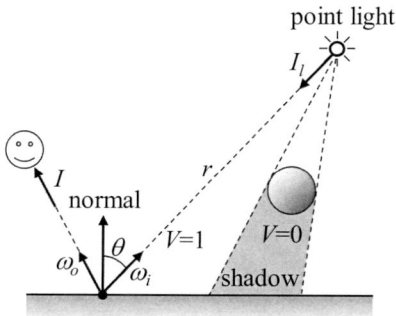

Fig. 2.8 Point light

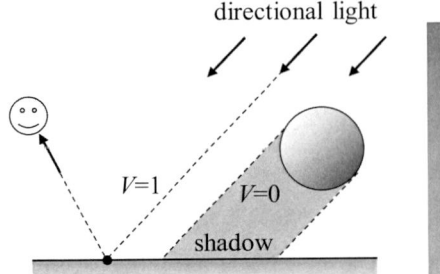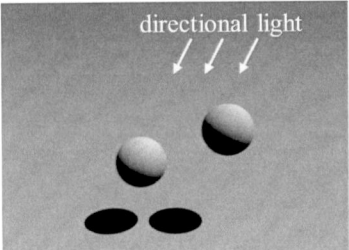

Fig. 2.9 Directional light

by a directional light source, like those from a point light, have well-defined boundaries, but the size of the shadows remains the same regardless of the distance from
the light source (see Fig. 2.9).

The intensity calculation using point or directional light sources is relatively simple, and shadows can be computed efficiently, making them suitable for real-time
applications such as video games and virtual reality. However, the boundaries of the
shadows are sharp, and soft shadows commonly seen in the real world cannot be
represented. Therefore, the realism of synthetic images generated using point light
sources and directional light sources is limited.

2.2.2.3   Linear Light/Area Light

A *linear light source* represents a line segment that emits light, similar to fluorescent
lights, while an *area light source* represents a plane that emits light, analogous to
panel-shaped light sources (Fig. 2.10). An area light source is often represented by
a polygon such as a rectangle. All the light arriving from every point on the line
segment or polygon must be taken into account to calculate the intensity at a point on
the surface of an object. The intensity is thus determined by accumulating the light
from those points on the source. As a result, the intensity calculation is formulated
using an integral, as expressed by the following equation.

$$I(\omega_o) = \int_A f_r(\omega_o, \omega_i) V(\omega_i) \frac{I_l}{r^2} \cos\alpha \cos\theta dA, \qquad (2.3)$$

where ω_i represents the direction from a point on the object to a point on the light
source, and r represents the distance between these two points. α represents the angle
between the vector connecting these points and the normal vector of the area light
source (see Fig. 2.10). The term $\cos\alpha$ determines the amount of light energy per unit
area from the point on the light source to the point on the object. A represents the set
of all points on the area light source, while dA represents an infinitesimal surface

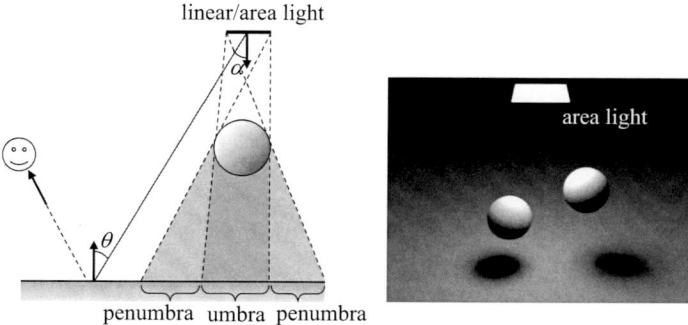

Fig. 2.10 Linear light/area light

element on the area light source. The equation for a linear light source is similar but involves a line integral along the line segment, instead of an area integral.

The linear and area light sources can represent *penumbra*. Unlike point light sources and directional light sources, linear and area light sources create regions illuminated by a part of a line segment or polygon. When observing the light source from a point on the object, there are three cases: the light source can be completely occluded by other objects, partially occluded, or completely visible. The partially occluded area is referred to as the penumbra, which allows for the expression of soft shadows with unclear boundaries. The completely occluded area is called the *umbra*. These light sources can produce more realistic images, though they require higher computational costs.

2.3 Global Illumination

The previous section explained methods for calculating intensity by considering only the light that arrives directly from the light source (direct lighting). Such a calculation model is called a *local illumination model* because the intensity is determined using only local information, such as the reflection property at a point and the light source. However, in the real world, we also need to consider indirect light that arrives at a point after being reflected from other points (see Fig. 2.11). In this case, global calculations are required because the intensity is influenced by light interactions with all surrounding objects. Therefore, a calculation model that accounts for indirect light is referred to as a *global illumination model*. The global illumination model can be mathematically formulated as an integral equation known as the rendering equation, for which various solutions have been proposed. In this section, we derive three forms of the rendering equation and introduce their typical solutions.

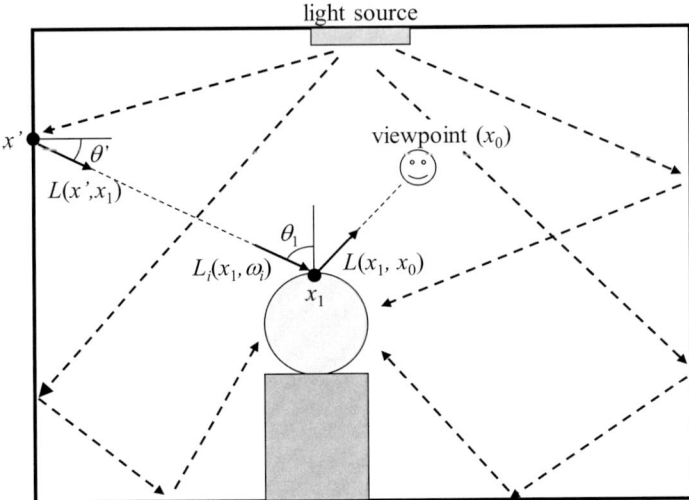

Fig. 2.11 Global illumination

2.3.1 Rendering Equation

The *rendering equation*, proposed by James T. Kajiya, is the fundamental equation for global illumination calculation [7]. The rendering equation describes the relationship between the input and output of light at a certain point on an object.

Let us consider the intensity at point x when observed from direction ω_o. The intensity at x consists of two components: the light emitted directly by x (which is non-zero if x is on the light source) and the reflected light at x, which includes contributions from the light source as well as light reflected from other points. As a result, the intensity is given by the following equation:

$$L(x, \omega_o) = L_e(x, \omega_o) + \int_\Omega L_i(x, \omega_i) f_r(\omega_o, \omega_i) \cos \theta d\omega_i. \qquad (2.4)$$

Equation 2.4 is called the rendering equation. The left side of the equation represents the intensity L observed from direction ω_o at point x. The first term on the right side denotes the intensity of light emitted by point x itself in direction ω_o, while the second term represents the total reflected light in direction ω_o due to the incident light L_i at point x. f_r represents the BRDF, Ω denotes the set of all directions within the hemisphere centered around the normal direction at point x, and θ is the angle between the normal direction at point x and the incident light direction ω_i. This rendering equation must be valid at all points within the scene.

The rendering equation is an *integral equation* for which no analytical solution has been found. To determine the intensity $L(x, \omega_o)$ at point x, we have to evaluate the two terms on the right side. The first term can be easily evaluated, as it corresponds to the intensity of the light source, which is typically provided as part of the scene description. The second term, however, is not easy to evaluate due to the recursive nature of the equation. The second term, an angular integral, represents the sum of contributions from the reflected light coming from all directions of light incident on point x. Among the integrands of this second term, f_r and $\cos \theta$ are easily evaluated from information on the materials and shapes of objects, but evaluating the incident light L_i is challenging. The incident light L_i includes light that arrives from reflections off other object surfaces, and to evaluate this reflected light, the rendering equation at that point must be solved again. This recursive relationship means that the intensity $L(x, \omega_o)$ must be determined such that the rendering equation holds at every point within the scene, making it challenging to solve the rendering equation.

To clarify the above discussion mathematically, let us derive an alternative form of the rendering equation. Equation 2.4 describes the relationship between incident and outgoing light at point x as an integral with respect to the direction. Let us derive the equation in the form of an area integral with respect to the object surface. As shown in Fig. 2.11, let us assume that the viewpoint is at x_0, the point directly visible from the viewpoint is x_1, and the intensity of light arriving at x_0 from x_1 is denoted as $L(x_1, x_0)$. When considering light arriving at x_1 from direction ω_i, we see that this light is actually the light reflected at point x' and coming to x_1, which can be denoted as $L(x', x_1)$. Considering the above discussion, the rendering equation can be expressed as follows.

$$L(x_1, x_0) = L_e(x_1, x_0) + \int_A L(x', x) f_r(x', x_1, x_0) G(x_1, x') dx', \qquad (2.5)$$

where A represents the set of all points on the surfaces of objects in the scene. $f_r(x', x_1, x_0)$ denotes the reflectance when light reflects toward the direction of x_0 via point x_1 from point x', which corresponds to the BRDF. $G(x_1, x')$ is called the *geometric term*, which represents the fraction of light reflected at point x' that reaches point x_1. It is calculated using the following equation.

$$G(x_1, x') = V(x_1, x') \frac{\cos \theta' \cos \theta_1}{|x_1 - x'|^2}. \qquad (2.6)$$

$V(x_1, x')$ is the *visibility function*, which returns 1 if there are no other objects between x_1 and x', and 0 otherwise. θ' is the angle between the normal vector at point x' and the vector connecting x_1 and x', and θ_1 is the angle between the normal vector at x_1 and the vector connecting x_1 and x' (see Fig. 2.11).

Let's analyze Eq. 2.5. The first term on the right side represents self-emission, as mentioned earlier, and is 0 except at the light source. The second term represents the reflected light reaching point x_1 from all points other than x_1. This is written as an area integral, derived from Eq. 2.4, where the geometric term G is introduced to convert the directional integral into an area integral. Comparing with the directional integral form, we can see that the unknown function L appears explicitly on both sides of the equation, which provides a clearer intuition of the integral equation. If this equation can be solved, it allows us to determine the intensity of the object while accounting for global illumination effects. Mathematically, the integral Eq. 2.5 is known as a Fredholm equation of the second kind. It has been shown that its solution can be expressed as an infinite series.

Finally, let us intuitively derive the third form of the solution to the rendering equation, which is the infinite series representation. We replace x' in Eq. 2.5 with x_2 and the product of f_r and G with K. The rendering equation for the intensity at point x_2, that is, $L(x_2, x_1)$ representing the intensity of light from x_2 to x_1, is then expressed by the following equation.

$$L(x_2, x_1) = L_e(x_2, x_1) + \int_A L(x_3, x_2)K(x_3, x_2, x_1)dx_3. \tag{2.7}$$

By substituting the above equation into Eq. 2.5, the following equation is obtained.

$$L(x_1, x_0) = L_e(x_1, x_0) + \int_A L_e(x_2, x_1)K(x_2, x_1, x_0)dx_2$$
$$+ \int_A \int_A L(x_3, x_2)K(x_2, x_1, x_0)K(x_3, x_2, x_1)dx_2dx_3. \tag{2.8}$$

The first term on the right represents the self-emission at point x_1. The second term corresponds to the self-emission at point x_2, which reaches the viewpoint x_0 after reflecting at point x_1. The third term represents the light from point x_3 that arrives at the viewpoint x_0 after bouncing at points x_2 and x_1. The third term is a double integral over points x_2 and x_3, representing the light that reaches the viewpoint after at least two reflections. If we consider the rendering equation for point x_3 and substitute it into the equation above, we obtain a similar equation with an additional triple integral term. By repeating this process, $L(x_1, x_0)$ is eventually expressed as an infinite series as follows.

$$L(x_1, x_0) = L_e(x_1, x_0) + \sum_{k=1}^{\infty} L_k(x_1, x_0), \tag{2.9}$$

where L_k represents the light that reaches x_0 after being reflected k times, given by the following equation.

$$L_k(x_1, x_0) = \int_A \cdots \int_A K(x_2, x_1, x_0)K(x_3, x_2, x_1)$$
$$\cdots K(x_{k+1}, x_k, x_{k-1})L_e(x_{k+1}, x_k)dx_2 \cdots dx_{k+1}, \tag{2.10}$$

and,

$$K(x_{i+1}, x_i, x_{i-1}) = f_r(x_{i+1}, x_i, x_{i-1})G(x_i, x_{i+1}). \tag{2.11}$$

The first term on the right side of Eq. 2.9 represents the self-emission at point x_1, and the second term represents the sum of light reflected k times ($k = 1, 2, \cdots \infty$).

In the following sections, numerical solutions to the rendering equation will be explained. The radiosity method and path tracing, discussed in the next section, are based on the second (Eq. 2.5) and third (Eq. 2.9) forms of the rendering equations described above. The method presented in Sect. 2.4 is based on the first form (Eq. 2.4) and achieves fast rendering by expanding the integrand into a series of some basis functions.

2.3.2 Radiosity Method

The *radiosity method* is one of the earliest numerical techniques developed for simulating global illumination. This method is named after the physical quantity known as radiant flux, which represents the light energy leaving a surface through emission, reflection, or transmission. In computer graphics, however, it is used as a general term for a set of methods used to calculate global illumination. The method was originally invented for interior lighting design in architectural fields but has been significantly extended and adapted for use in computer graphics. In the context of the radiosity method, B and E are often used for intensity and emission instead of L and L_e, respectively. We will follow this convention in this section.

The basic idea of the radiosity method is as follows. The method subdivides surfaces of objects in a scene, like walls and floors, into small surface elements, such as triangles and quadrilaterals, as shown in Fig. 2.12a. These surface elements are called *patches*, and they are used to discretize the rendering equation. We can mathematically define the relationship in terms of light energy exchange between any

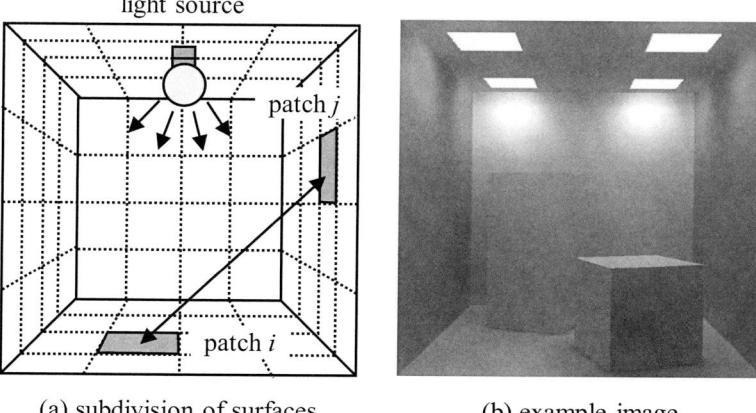

(a) subdivision of surfaces   (b) example image

Fig. 2.12 Radiosity method

pair of patches in the scene. This results in a linear system of equations that can be solved using common numerical methods, such as Jacobi method and Gauss-Seidel method.

The radiosity method can synthesize realistic images that account for indirect light, as shown in Fig. 2.12b. In the following sections, the formulation and several numerical solutions are explained.

2.3.2.1 Formulation

This section derives the formulation of the original radiosity method for diffuse reflection only. Extensions to account for specular reflection will be described later. In the case of diffuse reflection, the BRDF is constant, meaning that light incident on a surface is reflected uniformly in all directions. That is, the intensity depends only on position x on object surfaces. The rendering Eq. 2.5 is then simplified as follows.

$$B(x) = E(x) + \int_A B(x')\frac{\rho(x')}{\pi}G(x, x')dx', \qquad (2.12)$$

where $\frac{\rho(x')}{\pi}$ is the diffuse BRDF and ρ is the diffuse reflectance. B is the intensity at point x, also known as radiosity, and E represents self-emission.

Let us now assume that the surface of the object in the scene is subdivided into N patches. The integral term in the equation above can be expressed as the sum of integrals over each patch, resulting in the following equation.

$$B(x) = E(x) + \sum_{j=1}^{N} \int_{A_j} B(x')\frac{\rho(x')}{\pi}G(x, x')dx', \qquad (2.13)$$

where A_j represents the set of points within patch j. Next, when we assume that point x lies within patch i, the total radiosity emitted from patch i can be obtained by integrating $B(x)$ over patch i. Applying the integral operator to both sides of the above equation yields the following equation.

$$\int_{A_i} B(x)dx = \int_{A_i} E(x)dx + \sum_{\substack{j=1 \\ i \neq j}}^{N} \int_{A_i}\int_{A_j} B(x')\frac{\rho(x')}{\pi}G(x, x')dx'dx. \qquad (2.14)$$

Furthermore, when the surfaces are subdivided into fine patches, we can assume that the radiosity, self-emission, and reflectance within each patch are constant, resulting in the following equation.

$$B_i = E_i + \rho_i \sum_{\substack{j=1 \\ i \neq j}}^{N} F_{ij} B_j \quad (i = 1, \cdots, N), \tag{2.15}$$

where B_i and ρ_i are the radiosity and diffuse reflectance of patch i, respectively. F_{ij}, called the *form factor*, represents the fraction of energy emitted from patch i that reaches patch j and is given by the following equation.

$$F_{ij} = \frac{1}{A_i} \int_{A_i} \int_{A_j} \frac{\cos \theta_i \cos \theta_j}{\pi r_{ij}^2} V(x', x) dx' dx. \tag{2.16}$$

It is important to note that Eq. 2.16 does not contain terms related to the unknown variable B_i. This implies that the form factor F_{ij} can be computed using numerical integration methods, given the geometric shape of the object and the patch subdivision.

By solving the linear system of Eqs. 2.15 for B_i, we can determine the radiosity of each patch. A straightforward method is to compute the inverse of the coefficient matrix, but this approach is impractical for realistic problems due to the large number of patches. The computational and memory costs for such a matrix become prohibitive. For example, consider a rectangular room of 10 m × 10 m × 5 m. To assume constant radiosity over each patch, the patch size should be a few to several tens of centimeters. Using a patch size of 10 cm × 10 cm results in 70,000 patches. Thus, a 70,000 × 70,000 matrix must be stored, which requires 20 to 30 GB of storage. Since few patch combinations have a form factor value of 0, the coefficient matrix becomes dense with numerous non-zero elements. Consequently, computing the inverse matrix directly is impractical, so an iterative method that updates the solution sequentially is used instead.

2.3.2.2 Numerical Solution

The representative numerical solutions to the radiosity equation are the *gathering method* [8] and the *shooting method* [9] (see Fig. 2.13). As the names suggest, the gathering method collects light from other patches, while the shooting method emits light to other patches.

Gathering Method

The idea of this method is straightforward and is based on Eq. 2.15. Initially, the radiosity of each patch, except for those corresponding to light sources, is set to zero. The patches representing light sources are assigned the energy of the light source. Subsequently, the radiosity of each patch is updated iteratively using the following equation.

$$B_i^k = B_i^{k-1} + \rho_i \sum_{\substack{j=1 \\ i \neq j}}^{N} F_{ij} B_j^{k-1} \quad (i = 1, \cdots, N). \tag{2.17}$$

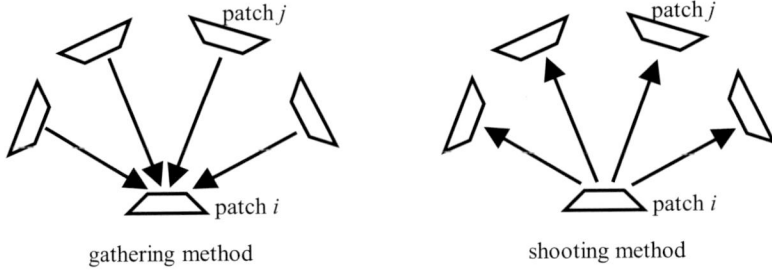

gathering method   shooting method

Fig. 2.13 Numerical solutions to radiosity equation

While the gathering method is conceptually straightforward, it can be time-consuming for convergence. Each iteration involves computing the summation in the second term on the right, which requires calculating form factors N times. The calculation of a form factor involves evaluating the visibility function V, which requires checking for occlusions between patches, resulting in high computational cost. Additionally, using Eq. 2.17, only one patch is updated per iteration, despite the high-cost form factor calculations being performed N times. To update the radiosities of all patches, N^2 form factor calculations are necessary. This iterative process continues until convergence is achieved, leading to extensive computation time. The shooting method, described below, addresses this issue.

Shooting Method

In this method, each patch is considered a secondary light source that emits reflected light, and the radiosities of the patches are updated by iteratively illuminating the scene from each patch. First, the patch representing the light source illuminates the scene, and the energy received by each patch is computed. Next, one of the patches is selected as a new light source to illuminate the scene again. This process is repeated until convergence. Conceptually, this method can be considered to simulate the propagation of light.

To realize this concept, new variable U_i is introduced for each patch in addition to the radiosity B_i. U_i records unshot energy of light or unshot radiosity. B_i and U_i are respectively updated according to the following equations.

$$B_j^k = B_j^{k-1} + \rho_j F_{ij} U_i^{k-1} \quad (j = 1, \cdots, N; j \neq i), \tag{2.18}$$

$$U_j^k = U_j^{k-1} + \rho_j F_{ij} U_i^{k-1} \quad (j = 1, \cdots, N; j \neq i). \tag{2.19}$$

In the initial state ($k = 0$), only the patch corresponding to the light source has the unshot radiosity that is equivalent to the energy of light source. Both the radiosities and the unshot radiosities of all other patches are set to 0. After patch i has emitted radiosity to other patches, the unshot radiosity for patch i is reset to zero, that is, $U_i = 0$.

In this method, it is sufficient to evaluate Eq. 2.19 only once to update the radiosity of one patch using Eq. 2.18. This indicates that N patches are updated by N evaluations of the form factors. In contrast, the gathering method requires N^2 evaluations of the form factors to update N patches. The shooting method achieves a significant speedup. However, to accelerate convergence, it is crucial to select an appropriate patch to emit the unshot radiosity. A common strategy is to choose the patch with the largest unshot radiosity.

2.3.2.3 Extension to Specular Reflection

Although the radiosity method was originally developed for diffuse reflection only, numerous approaches have since been developed to handle specular reflections as well. While a detailed discussion of these methods is beyond the scope of this book, a brief summary of some representative techniques is provided below.

When considering specular reflections, the radiosity of each patch becomes a function of the outgoing directions. The first method to account for specular reflections extended the original radiosity method by recording the directional distribution of radiosity for each patch [10], using discrete directional samples. However, to achieve accurate calculations, a large number of directional samples must be used. This increases the number of unknowns and, consequently, leads to significant computational costs.

A method using *spherical harmonics* was subsequently proposed to reduce storage costs [11]. Spherical harmonics are well suited for representing functions defined on the unit sphere. This method utilizes spherical harmonics to represent the BRDF. Consequently, the directional distribution at each point is also expressed using spherical harmonics, and the calculation of radiosity is reduced to determining the coefficients of the spherical harmonic functions, allowing for more efficient computation.

The method proposed in 2007 achieves a significant acceleration in computation by eliminating the need for visibility function calculations [12]. Instead of explicitly calculating the visibility function, the method introduces an implicit approach by using negative radiosity, or anti-radiosity, to cancel out light that should not reach certain areas due to occlusions. To implement this approach, the method records the directional distribution of radiosity using discrete samples, similar to the method described above [10], but also allows negative light to be stored for each direction. Therefore, this method can naturally handle specular reflections. Although the number of unknowns increases as mentioned above, the computation converges significantly faster because visibility calculations are no longer required. Furthermore, with advancements in computer performance, the memory capacity needed to record the radiosity for each direction is no longer an issue. Using this method, it is possible to generate images that account for global illumination in real time, even when the light source or objects move, or when the material properties of the objects change.

2.3.3 Path Tracing Method

The *path tracing* method is a technique that applies the *Monte Carlo method*, a numerical approach using random numbers, to solve the rendering equation [7]. Unlike the radiosity method, which requires subdividing surfaces into patches, path tracing does not need such processing. As a result, it can be applied to complex objects that are difficult to subdivide into patches, such as trees. The method does not explicitly discretize the rendering equation to find its numerical solution, making it versatile enough to handle various surface types, including diffuse, specular, and even transparent surfaces. Path tracing can synthesize highly realistic images and is used in various applications, including movies, video games, cosmetic and product designs. The following sections explain the concept of integral calculation using the Monte Carlo method and describe the principles of path tracing.

2.3.3.1   Monte Carlo Integration

Monte Carlo integration is often used for integrating high-dimensional functions, such as those that appear in the rendering Eq. 2.9 in Sect. 2.3.1. The basic idea behind Monte Carlo integration is as follows.

Let us consider the integral I of the function $f(x)$. In the Monte Carlo method, x is treated as a *random variable* that follows a *probability density function* $p(x)$. We generate N samples X_i $(i = 1, \ldots, N)$ of x using $p(x)$, and the integral is approximately estimated by its average, $\bar{I}_N$, computed from these samples. That is,

$$I = \int f(x)dx = \int \frac{f(x)}{p(x)}p(x)dx \approx \bar{I}_N = \frac{1}{N}\sum_{i=1}^{N}\frac{f(X_i)}{p(X_i)}. \tag{2.20}$$

An important property of this method is that the *expected value* of $\bar{I}_N$ equals I, which can be mathematically proven. In other words, as N increases, $\bar{I}_N$ converges to the exact value of I.

The role of the probability density function $p(x)$ is important for efficient computation. The optimal probability density function is one that is proportional to the integrand $f(x)$. If we can use $cf(x)$ as $p(x)$, then $f(X_i)/p(X_i)$ is equal to c, a constant, regardless of the random sample X_i, allowing the integral to be calculated instantly. In contrast, if $p(x)$ is very different from $f(x)$, the variance of $f(X_i)/p(X_i)$ becomes large, leading to significant errors in the estimate. The variance of the estimate is often used as a measure to evaluate the quality of Monte Carlo integration, with smaller variance indicating better performance.

For complex problems where the Monte Carlo integration is required, however, the form of $f(x)$ is unknown, so we cannot choose a probability density function like $p(x) = cf(x)$. Therefore, we need to analyze the problem and the integrand carefully to design a good probability density function to minimize the variance.

2.3.3.2 Concept of Path Tracing

Let us apply the Monte Carlo integration to the rendering Eq. 2.9. In the case of k-th order reflected light, the random variable is a k-dimensional vector $(x_1, \ldots, x_k)$. $(x_1, \cdots, x_k)$ represents the path of light from the light source to the viewpoint, which is called a *light path*. In path tracing, this light path is treated as a random variable and sampled by random numbers to evaluate the integral value. The ray tracing technique is typically used for sampling the light path. The basic procedure for generating a light path is as follows (see Fig. 2.14).

First, a *ray* of light passing through each pixel from the viewpoint is generated to compute the first intersection point, which is determined deterministically without using random numbers.[1] Next, random numbers are employed to decide whether a reflection occurs at this intersection point. If a reflection occurs, the reflection direction is determined using random numbers, and a new ray is generated in that direction to compute the next intersection point. These steps are repeated until the ray reaches a light source or it is determined that no reflection occurs.

The above process is repeated to generate multiple light paths, and the energy of light reaching the viewpoint is calculated for each path. The intensity of each pixel is then estimated as the average energy of these paths. This is the basic idea of path tracing, which is simple enough to implement easily. However, the resulting images often contain significant noise unless an appropriate probability density function is chosen for generating random numbers. A good probability density function should be proportional to the contribution of each light path to the pixel intensity, and it should minimize generation of light paths with small contributions. The probability density function needs to be designed with these considerations in mind. In the following, some strategies for designing an effective probability density function are discussed.

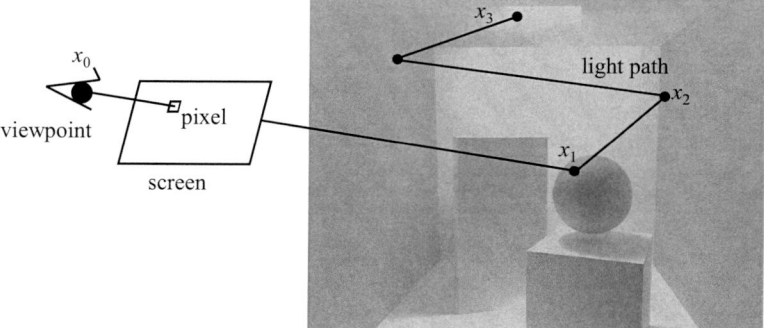

Fig. 2.14 Path tracing

---

[1] The direction of the ray could be perturbed using random numbers for anti-aliasing, but it is omitted here for simplicity.

First, let us consider the probability of a specific light path generated using the procedure described. This probability is determined by the product of the probabilities associated with the random numbers used to generate the light path. For each intersection point along the light path, two random numbers are generated: one to decide whether reflection occurs and another to determine the direction of the reflected ray. Therefore, the probability density function for each intersection point is the product of the density functions used for these two random numbers. Consequently, the probability density function for the entire light path is the product of the probability density functions for each intersection point. This is given as the value of the integrand function in Eq. 2.9. It is the product of the reflectance, geometric term, and intensity of the light source at all intersection points.

Considering the above discussion, a straightforward choice for the probability density function is one proportional to the product of the reflection function (BRDF) and the geometric term for each intersection point. This function helps to reduce the generation of paths with small contributions, as light paths including points with low reflectance or geometric term values are likely to contribute less. Since the BRDF and geometric terms can be calculated from the scene information, designing a probability density function proportional to these terms is feasible.

Unfortunately, considering only the BRDF and geometric terms does not always yield the expected improvement in accuracy. Even if a light path consists of points with high BRDF or geometric term values, its contribution could still be small if it does not reach the light source. The probability of finding a light path that reaches the light source is very low, as the path is determined stochastically from the viewpoint using random numbers. Consequently, light paths that do not reach the light source contribute nothing, making the effort of generating such paths wasted. A relatively simple improvement is to explicitly generate a special ray toward the light source from each intersection point. This approach increases the likelihood of finding light paths that reach the light source, thereby improving the calculation accuracy.

The above idea has been further developed into a method called *bidirectional path tracing* [13], where light paths are constructed not only from the viewpoint but also from the light source, as shown in Fig. 2.15. First, two light paths are generated: one from the viewpoint and one from the light source, using the path generation procedure described earlier. Next, a set of new light paths is formed by connecting all possible combinations of vertices between the two paths. Figure 2.15 illustrates this process, where the two paths consist of N_e and N_l vertices, respectively, excluding the viewpoint and the light source. By considering all combinations of these vertices, $N_e \times N_l$ light paths can be generated. These newly created paths connect the light source and the viewpoint as long as there are no obstacles between the connecting vertices, and their contributions are expected to be significant. This method can find paths with non-zero contributions by computing just two paths from the viewpoint and the light source, greatly improving computational efficiency.

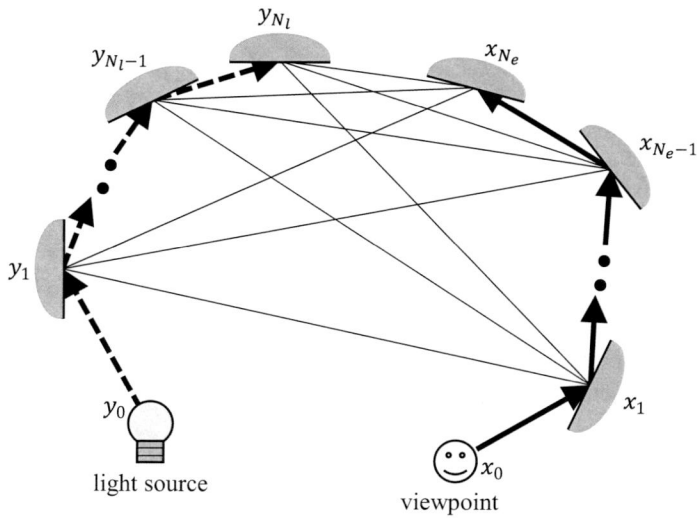

Fig. 2.15 Bidirectional path tracing

2.3.3.3 Metropolis Light Transport

The calculation accuracy of the path tracing method depends on its ability to efficiently find light paths with high contributions. The *Metropolis Light Transport* [14] described in this section is a method that has successfully made significant improvements in this regard.

As mentioned in the previous section, designing an appropriate probability density function is important for efficiently discovering paths with high contributions. While it is reasonable to design the probability density function based on the BRDF and geometric terms, this approach relies solely on local information at each intersection point. Bidirectional path tracing takes a more global approach by connecting the two light paths starting from the viewpoint and the light source. However, the paths it finds do not always yield high contributions. These methods do not consider the contribution of the path itself when generating new paths; instead, they rely on heuristic approaches to generate contributing paths. The Metropolis Light Transport addresses this.

In the path tracing method, the random variable is the light path. Considering all possible light paths in a given three-dimensional scene (known as the light path space), previous methods search for paths with high contributions based on local information and heuristic approaches. For more efficient computation, it is desirable to adaptively explore the light path space according to the contribution of the light path. The Metropolis Light Transport method achieves this by generating light paths proportional to their contributions.

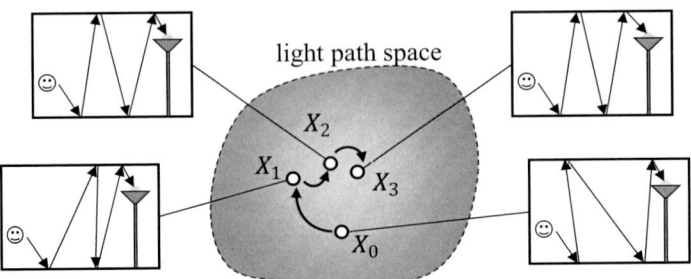

Fig. 2.16 Concept of metropolis light transport

The concept of Metropolis Light Transport is illustrated in Fig. 2.16. In this figure, the light path space is illustrated as a two-dimensional space where each point corresponds to a specific light path. The shading indicates the contribution of each light path, with brighter areas representing higher contributions. Starting from an initial light path X_0 in this space, new light paths $X_1, X_2, \cdots$ are generated sequentially.[2] Initial light paths X_0 are typically generated using path tracing or bidirectional path tracing. The contribution of the initial path X_0 is evaluated, and the algorithm then searches the neighborhood to move to a new sample point X_1 in a region with higher contribution. This process, known as state transition, is probabilistic. By repeating these transitions, sample points become denser in regions of high contribution. In the following, we provide a brief explanation of how light paths are generated in the Metropolis Light Transport method.

To generate a new light path X_{i+1} from the current path X_i, a tentative light path X_i' is first created by mutating X_i. *Mutation* involves making partial changes to the light path, such as moving some of its vertices to nearby positions. This mutation process is probabilistic and uses random numbers, with the probability density function for the mutation being arbitrarily chosen. This probability distribution is referred to as the proposal distribution, and the likelihood of transitioning from X_i to X_i' is called the mutation probability.

Next, the contribution of the tentative light path X_i' is evaluated by computing the integrand. Based on this contribution and the mutation probability, the algorithm probabilistically decides whether to accept X_i' as the new light path X_{i+1}. The acceptance probability increases if the contribution of X_i' is higher than that of X_i. If accepted, the transition from X_i to $X_{i+1}(= X_i')$ is made. This process is repeated until the desired number of light paths is generated.

The advantage of Metropolis Light Transport is that there is no need to explicitly design a probability density function proportional to the contribution of the light path. It is sufficient to be able to evaluate the integrand for any given light path. While the

---

[2] Updating from one state to another based only on the current state is known as a Markov chain. When used for statistical sampling, this process is called the Markov Chain Monte Carlo (MCMC) method.

proposal distribution must be designed by the user, it can be a simple distribution such as uniform or Gaussian. Unlike previous methods, Metropolis Light Transport adaptively explores the light path space based on the contributions of light paths. When a high-contribution light path is found, the method focuses on exploring its surroundings, significantly enhancing both accuracy and efficiency.

2.3.4 Photon Mapping

Photon mapping [15] is widely used as well as the radiosity method and path tracing method. It combines the advantages of both methods. The method consists of two steps: the first step generates the photon map described later, and the second step renders an image. The photon map does not need to be regenerated when the viewpoint changes, and explicit discretization by patch division is not necessary. Photon mapping can produce high-quality images at relatively low cost. The concept of photon mapping is illustrated in Fig. 2.17.

In the first step, a large number of virtual particles called *photons* are emitted from the light source. Each photon is assigned the energy of the emitted light, and its emission direction is determined using random numbers. The intersection point between each photon and an object is then computed using the ray tracing method. At each intersection, the coordinates, incoming direction, and energy of the photon are recorded. Next, the method statistically determines, using random numbers, whether the photon is absorbed or reflected. If it is reflected, the reflection direction is calculated using random numbers, and a new intersection point is computed. This process continues until the photon is absorbed. As a result, numerous sample

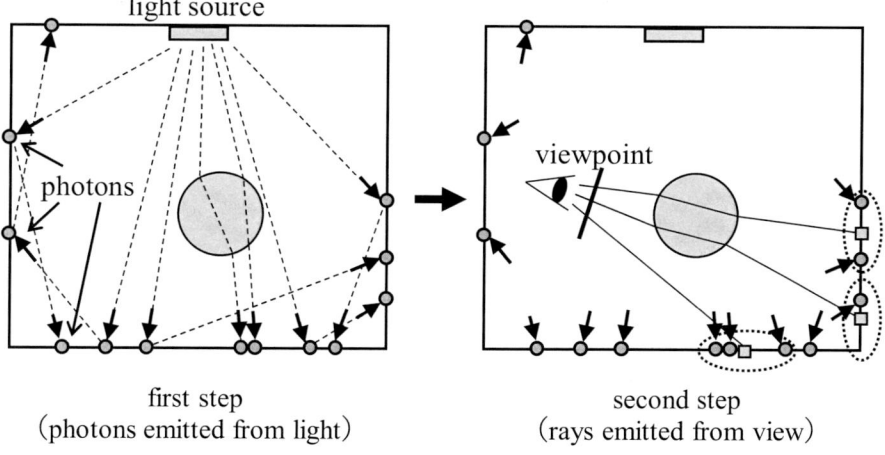

first step   second step
(photons emitted from light)   (rays emitted from view)

Fig. 2.17 Photon mapping

points recording the positions, incoming directions, and light energies are stored on the object surfaces. This information forms the *photon map*, representing the energy (illumination) distribution on the object surfaces through a set of sample points.

In the second step, an image is generated using the photon map. The intersection point between the viewing ray passing through each pixel and the object is calculated, and the intensity at this point is determined through interpolation based on the photon map. First, information about the photons in the vicinity of this point is extracted from the photon map, with the neighborhood range specified by the user in advance. Then, the intensity of the reflected light is calculated based on the incoming direction and light energy recorded for each photon. The average intensity of the reflected light is used as the intensity for this point. This process is repeated for every pixel.

Since the photon map records the incident direction and energy of photons, rather than the reflected light, it can be reused to render images from different viewpoints by repeating only the second step. The photon map only needs to be updated if the light source or object information changes. The number of photons emitted from the light source typically ranges from thousands to millions, so a fast search method is required to locate photons near a query point. Many approaches use a data structure called a kd-tree for this purpose [16], which accelerates the search process by adaptively and hierarchically subdividing the search space based on the distribution of photons.

Although photon mapping is similar to path tracing, a key difference is that photon mapping does not guarantee convergence to the true solution. This limitation stems from the use of a finite number of photons and the interpolation process in the second step. Even if the number of photons is increased, the intensity calculated through interpolation does not converge to the exact value. To address this issue, a method called progressive photon mapping was developed [17]. This method reverses the processing order. First, rays are emitted from the viewpoint through each pixel to identify the points where intensity needs to be computed for rendering the image. Then, photons are emitted from the light source toward these points to calculate the intensity, and this second step is repeated, sequentially updating the intensity. This approach eliminates the need to specify the number of photons to be emitted in advance, and theoretically, an infinite number of photons can be used, ensuring convergence to the correct solution.

2.4   Fast Rendering with Precomputation

When using computer graphics, images are often generated under varying conditions such as viewpoint, lighting, and object materials. In applications like video games, images must be rendered quickly to provide real-time feedback to the user. However, rendering realistic images that account for global illumination can be computation-ally expensive, and recalculating everything is necessary whenever any condition changes. This section introduces precomputation-based methods that enable fast rendering even when some of these conditions are altered.

2.4.1 Image-Based Lighting

Image-based lighting is a technique used to simulate complex real-world lighting environments by representing the lighting as an image, enabling highly realistic image synthesis [18]. It is commonly applied in movie production to integrate live-action and CG footage. The intensity calculation with the image-based lighting can be considered as an approximate form of the rendering equation.

When the size of an object is sufficiently small such that its influence on the surrounding environment can be neglected in terms of optical interactions, the rendering Eq. 2.4 for this small object can be approximated as follows.

$$L(x, \omega_o) = \int_\Omega f_r(\omega_o, \omega_i) V(\omega_i) L_e(\omega_i) \cos\theta d\omega_i. \tag{2.21}$$

$L_e(\omega_i)$ represents the intensity of light incident on the object from the direction ω_i, and Ω denotes the set of all possible incident directions. $L_e(\omega_i)$ describes the surrounding light environment and acts as a light source when viewed from the object, hence it is referred to as an *environmental light source* (Fig. 2.18). Environmental light sources are commonly used to recreate real-world lighting conditions. Conceptually, it can be thought of as a spherical light source with an infinite radius, where the intensity of light incident from each direction is recorded on the surface of a sphere.

In practice, a cube, or a *cube map*, is often used instead of a sphere. As shown in Fig. 2.18, six images are captured around the location where the light environment is to be represented and are mapped onto each face of the cube. Each pixel on the cube corresponds to a direction in the light environment, with the pixel value representing the intensity of light from that direction. This setup effectively simulates a directional light source for each pixel direction, without considering distance-based attenuation of the light.

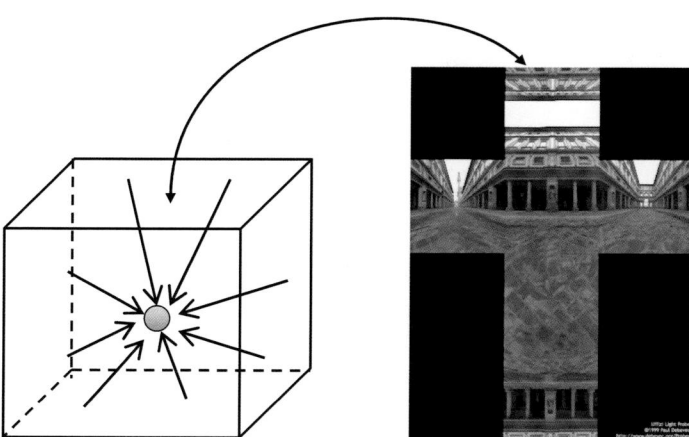

Fig. 2.18 Image-based lighting. Image courtesy of Paul Debevec

Image-based lighting can accurately simulate real-world lighting environments and produce highly realistic images. However, the integral calculation over all directions, as represented by Eq. 2.21, is computationally intensive. Specifically, evaluating the visibility function V involves time-consuming intersection calculations between the ray toward each pixel and the object.

2.4.2 Fast Calculation with Precomputation

Many methods have been developed that incorporate precomputation to achieve real-time rendering based on Eq. 2.21. These methods are suitable for applications that require real-time performance, such as video games and virtual reality, because they can generate high-quality images quickly. In the following, the basic idea and applications of these methods are explained.

2.4.2.1 Basic Idea

The intensity distribution of an environmental light source and/or a BRDF is expanded into a set of *basis functions*, and the integral is precomputed to achieve fast rendering [19, 20]. Figure 2.19 illustrates the basic idea.

In this method, the environmental light source is represented as a weighted sum of basis functions: $L_e(\omega_i) = \sum_k a_k \phi_k(\omega_i)$, where a_k denotes the coefficient. Substituting this into Eq. 2.21 yields the following equation.

$$L(x, \omega_o) = \sum_k a_k B_k(x, \omega_o), \qquad (2.22)$$

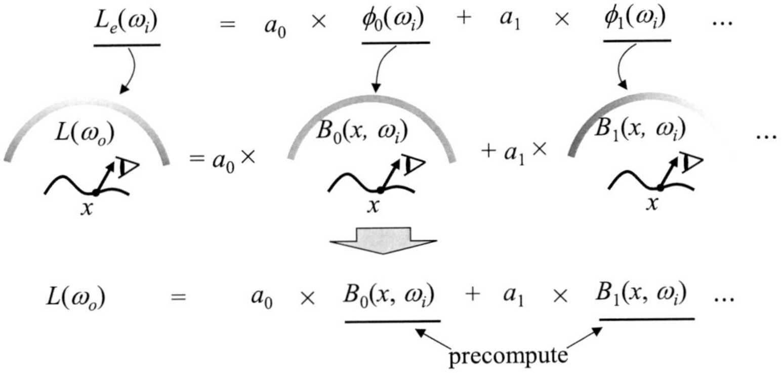

Fig. 2.19 Precomputed radiance transfer

where,

$$B_k(x, \omega_o) = \int_\Omega f_r(\omega_o, \omega_i) V(\omega_i) \phi_k(\omega_i) \cos \theta d\omega_i. \qquad (2.23)$$

$B_k(x, \omega_o)$ represents the intensity at point x illuminated by the environmental light source with distribution $\phi_k(\omega_i)$. Since $\phi_k(\omega_i)$ is predetermined, $B_k(x, \omega_o)$ can be precomputed and stored in advance.

The intensity $L(x, \omega_o)$ can then be quickly computed through the following procedure. First, $B_k(x, \omega_o)$ is precomputed at sample points on the object's surface. If the object is represented by polygons or triangular meshes, these vertices could serve as the sample points. Next, the environmental light source $L_e(\omega_i)$ is expanded into a series of basis functions, and the coefficient a_k for each basis function is computed. The intensity at each sample point is then determined by a weighted sum of the precomputed values $B_k(x, \omega_o)$, as described by Eq. 2.22. Since the computation of Eq. 2.22 only involves simple multiplication and addition, it can be executed very quickly. A key advantage of this method is the fast intensity computation, provided that the environmental light source is represented with basis functions. Although the coefficients a_k must be updated to reflect changes in the distribution of the light source $L_e(\omega_i)$, this calculation is relatively inexpensive, enabling real-time image updates. The visibility function V, which is typically the most computationally intensive factor, is precomputed. Additionally, since $L_e(\omega_i)$ is independent of x, the coefficients need to be calculated only once, rather than for each point.

The method described above is known as *Precomputed Radiance Transfer (PRT)*. In this explanation, the light source distribution L_e is expanded into basis functions, but there are several variations of the method. For instance, one variation allows for changes in the material properties of the object by expanding the reflection distribution function f_r into basis functions. The choice of basis functions ϕ_k is a crucial factor in the PRT method. In the following sections, we explore some commonly used basis functions and discuss their respective advantages and disadvantages.

2.4.2.2 Spherical Harmonic Functions

The environmental light can be considered a spherical light source with an infinite radius, and its intensity distribution can be regarded as a function defined on a unit sphere. *Spherical harmonics* are frequently used to express such functions. Each basis function of spherical harmonics is indexed by two parameters, l and m, and is commonly written as $Y_{lm}(\omega)$. The parameter l indicates the degree of the function, while m ($-l \leq m \leq l$) represents its directionality. Some of these basis functions are illustrated in Fig. 2.20. The top functions in the figure correspond to lower degrees, while those on the left and right have the same degree but different m values. As the degree increases, the distribution becomes more intricate.

Spherical harmonic functions form an *orthonormal basis* on the sphere, essentially functioning as a Fourier basis on the sphere. An orthonormal basis is a series of functions that satisfy the following properties:

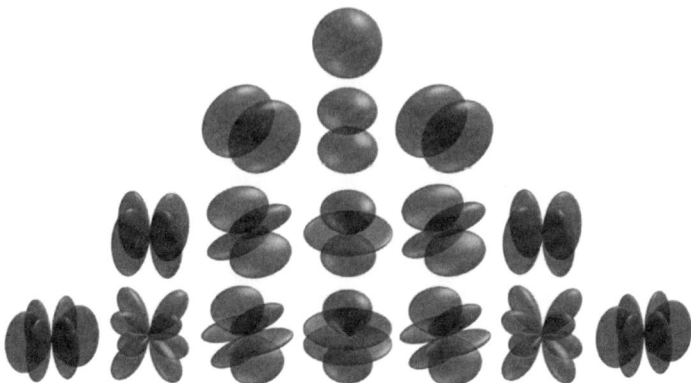

Fig. 2.20 Examples of spherical harmonics functions

$$\int_\Omega Y_{lm}(\omega)Y_{l'm'}(\omega)d\omega = \begin{cases} 1 & (l,m) = (l',m') \\ 0 & (l,m) \neq (l',m') \end{cases}. \tag{2.24}$$

This equation shows that the integral of the product of two spherical harmonic functions is 1 only when $l = l'$ and $m = m'$, and 0 otherwise. Using this property, the expansion coefficient a_k can be computed by the following equation:

$$a_{lm} = \int_\Omega L_e(\omega_i)Y_{lm}(\omega_i)d\omega_i. \tag{2.25}$$

That is, the coefficient a_{lm} is calculated as the integral of the product of the spherical harmonic function and the environmental light source.

The advantage of spherical harmonic functions is their rotation invariance. Once a function is represented using spherical harmonics, the rotated version of the function can also be expressed in spherical harmonics. The coefficients for the rotated function can be obtained through simple arithmetic, without requiring any integral calculations [20]. As a result, when rotating the environmental light source, the coefficients a_{lm} after the rotation are computed quickly, allowing for fast image updates.

Figure 2.21 shows an example of an image generated using spherical harmonic functions. In Fig. 2.21a, the environmental light source is expanded using spherical harmonic functions, resulting in realistic shading on the object [20]. In Fig. (b), the light distribution curve of a point light source is expanded with spherical harmonic functions. This allows for quick updates when the light distribution curve of the point light source is changed. The interreflection of light between walls is also considered [21].

The disadvantage of spherical harmonic functions is their difficulty in representing complex distributions. Since the basis functions are smooth across the entire domain (the sphere), functions with discontinuous changes cannot be accurately captured, even with high-order basis functions. As a result, spherical harmonic functions are

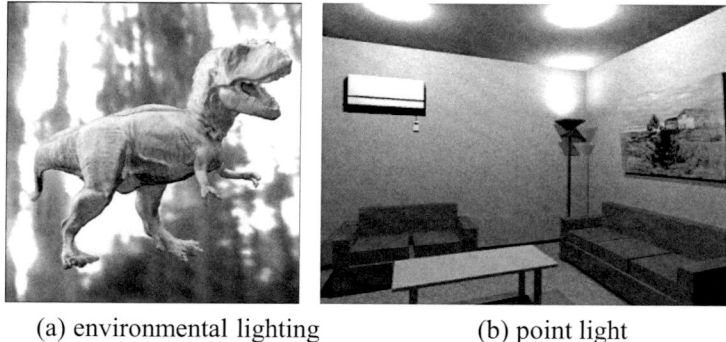

(a) environmental lighting   (b) point light

Fig. 2.21 Examples using spherical harmonics. Image **a** courtesy of Peter-Pike Sloan

often used to approximate relatively smooth distributions that can be represented by low-order basis functions, i.e., low-frequency components. For instance, they are suitable for approximating the intensity distribution of the sky and light reflected from diffuse surfaces but are not effective for light sources with sharp intensity changes.

2.4.2.3 Wavelet Function

The *wavelet function* can accurately approximate complex functions containing high-frequency components, addressing the limitation of spherical harmonic functions. In spherical harmonics, the support (the interval where the value is not zero) of the basis function spans the entire domain (the entire sphere), which prevents accurate representation of complex functions. Wavelet functions, however, resolve this issue. Furthermore, the wavelet basis has a hierarchical structure, with support size varying by level in the hierarchy, allowing efficient representation of both local and global features of a given function.

There are various types of wavelet functions, but in the field of computer graphics, the *Haar wavelet* is commonly used. Similar to spherical harmonic functions, Haar wavelets possess orthogonality, and their expansion coefficients can be easily computed. The Haar wavelet is particularly well suited for representing discrete signals, such as images, due to the shape of its basis functions. The basis functions consist of two functions, as shown in Fig. 2.22a. Their amplitude and support are variable, changing with the hierarchical level. For discrete signals, the expansion coefficients can be obtained through a simple process, described below.

An example of the expansion process using the Haar wavelet is shown in Fig. 2.22b. In this example, the wavelet transform is applied to a discrete signal [9, 7, 3, 5]. The basic principle is to recursively compute the local average and the deviation from the average for each pair of values in the signal. First, two pairs are considered: [9, 7] and [3, 5]. The average of the first pair is 8, with deviations of 1 and −1, so only 1 is recorded. For the second pair, the average is 4 and the deviation

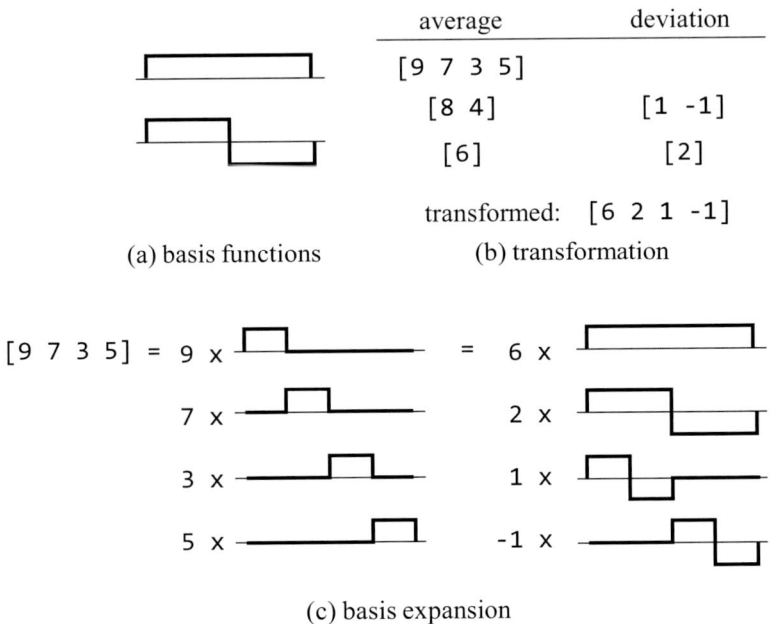

(a) basis functions   (b) transformation

(c) basis expansion

Fig. 2.22 Haar wavelets

is −1. From the initial sequence [9, 7, 3, 5], the resulting averages are [8, 4], and the deviations are [1, −1]. By repeating the process on [8, 4], the average is 6 with a deviation of 2. Thus, the final transformed sequence becomes [6, 2, 1, −1].

The above process corresponds to expanding the original function using wavelet bases, as illustrated in Fig. 2.22c. The input sequence, [9, 7, 3, 5], can be viewed as a multiplication of these values by four horizontally shifted unit box functions, shown in the middle of Fig. 2.22c. After applying the wavelet transform, the sequence is converted into a different function representation depicted on the right. The first term represents the overall average, while the second to fourth terms recursively express the deviations from that average. The third and fourth terms represent local and high-frequency components, and the absolute values of their expansion coefficients are relatively small. If we remove these small coefficients by setting them to 0, we can approximate the function effectively.

Furthermore, the third and fourth terms represent information specific to the left and right halves of the original function, respectively. These terms capture frequency information in their corresponding local segments. In segments where the variation is small (i.e., low frequency), the coefficient values become small. This demonstrates that wavelet functions can detect segments with significant changes. In other words, wavelet functions reveal both spatial and frequency information. In contrast, when using spherical harmonic functions, spatial information is entirely lost after transformation, making it impossible to identify high-frequency segments. Therefore, even when only part of the function exhibits significant variation, the wavelet function can accurately approximate the function with a relatively small number of terms.

For image-based lighting, the wavelet transform is applied to the images mapped onto each face of the cube map. A two-dimensional wavelet transform is required, which can be achieved by applying a one-dimensional wavelet transform to the x and y dimensions successively. There are two possible approaches: one is to apply a one-dimensional wavelet transform for the y component after doing so for the x component, while the other alternates between the x and y wavelet transforms. Although the former method is easier to implement, the latter offers better performance for function approximation.

Figure 2.23 compares images generated using the Haar wavelet and spherical harmonic functions [22]. In Fig. 2.23a, the environment map is approximated, and in Fig. 2.23b, rendered images based on the approximated maps are shown. These examples illustrate that wavelet functions offer greater approximation accuracy compared to spherical harmonics. The spherical harmonics struggle to capture complex

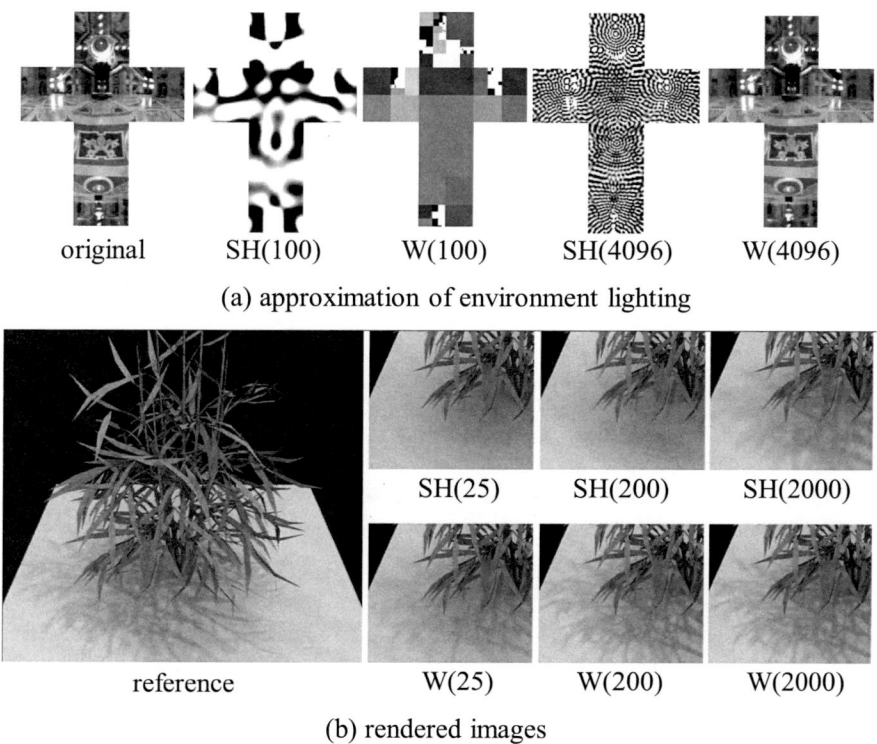

original   SH(100)   W(100)   SH(4096)   W(4096)

(a) approximation of environment lighting

SH(25)   SH(200)   SH(2000)

reference   W(25)   W(200)   W(2000)

(b) rendered images

Fig. 2.23 Comparison between spherical harmonics (SH) and Haar Wavelet (W). Numbers in the brackets indicate the numbers of the basis functions. Images courtesy of Ravi Ramamoorthi

variations in the environment light, leading to blurry and poorly defined shadows on the floor. In contrast, the wavelet function effectively resolves this issue, producing sharper, more accurately rendered shadows.

A drawback of the wavelet function is that when the light source rotates, the wavelet transform must be recalculated. In contrast, spherical harmonics allow for quick computation of the expansion coefficients for a rotated function using simple operations, making them more efficient in such scenarios. As a result, if the light source undergoes frequent rotation, the wavelet function incurs a higher computational cost compared to spherical harmonics.

2.4.2.4 Spherical Gaussian Function

The *spherical Gaussian function*, as its name implies, is a Gaussian function defined on the surface of a sphere, possessing several highly useful properties. It is characterized by two parameters: ξ, which defines the axial direction, and λ, which controls the sharpness of the distribution. These correspond to the mean and the inverse of the variance in a standard Gaussian function (see Fig. 2.24). The spherical Gaussian function is straightforward in its formulation and is expressed by the following equation.

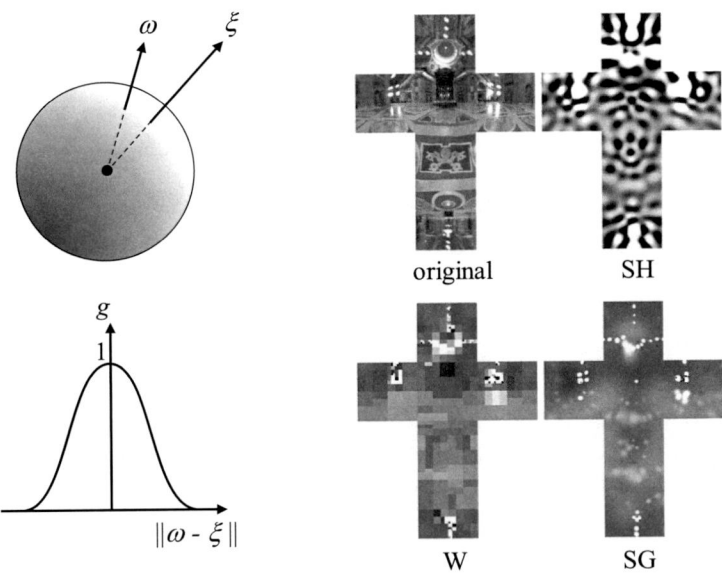

(a) spherical Gaussian   (b) approximation of environment lighting

Fig. 2.24 Approximation of environment lighting using spherical Gaussian functions. SH, W, and SG denote spherical harmonics, Haar wavelets, and spherical Gaussian functions, respectively. In each case, 972 basis functions are used. Images courtesy of Yu-Ting Tsai

$$G(\omega, \xi, \lambda) = g(||\omega - \xi||, 1/\lambda) = \exp\left(-\frac{||\omega - \xi||}{2(1/\lambda)^2}\right), \qquad (2.26)$$

g denotes the Gaussian function. The parameter ξ specifies the axial direction of the spherical Gaussian function, where the function reaches its maximum value of 1 when $\omega = \xi$. The parameter λ controls the spread of the Gaussian distribution, with smaller values resulting in a sharper, more concentrated peak.

A key advantage of the spherical Gaussian function is its ability to provide an analytical solution for the integral of the product of spherical Gaussian functions over the sphere. This property enables the integral component of Eq. 2.21 in the intensity calculation to be evaluated analytically. To illustrate, we rewrite the integrand of Eq. 2.21 as follows:

$$L(x, \omega_o) = \int_S L_e(\omega_i) H(\omega_o, \omega_i) d\omega_i, \qquad (2.27)$$

where S denotes the entire spherical domain, and H is defined as

$$H(\omega_o, \omega_i) = f_r(\omega_o, \omega_i) V(\omega_i) \max(0, \cos\theta). \qquad (2.28)$$

The term $\max(0, \cos\theta)$ ensures that light from the negative direction, relative to the surface normal at point x, is excluded. Next, both $L_e(\omega_i)$ and $H(\omega_o, \omega_i)$ are approximated as linear sums of spherical Gaussian functions:

$$L_e(\omega_i) = \sum_k a_k G_k(\omega_i, \xi_k, \lambda_k), \qquad (2.29)$$

$$H(\omega_o, \omega_i) = \sum_l b_l(\omega_o) G_j(\omega_i, \xi_l, \lambda_l). \qquad (2.30)$$

Thus, the intensity $L(x, \omega_o)$ at point x is expressed as

$$L(x, \omega_o) = \sum_k \sum_l a_k b_l(\omega_o) \int_S G_k(\omega_i, \xi_k, \lambda_k) G_j(\omega_i, \xi_l, \lambda_l) d\omega_i. \qquad (2.31)$$

The integral of the product of the spherical Gaussian functions on the right-hand side can be computed analytically, allowing for rapid evaluation. In addition, spherical Gaussian functions offer analytical solutions for their own integrals, and the rotation of distributions represented by these functions can be handled easily.

A drawback of spherical Gaussian functions is the high computational cost for approximating a function. In the above example, determining the coefficients a_i and b_j, along with the optimal axis directions ξ_k, ξ_l and the sharpness parameters λ_k, λ_l, is necessary to approximate L_e or H using spherical Gaussian functions. Unlike spherical harmonic functions or Haar wavelets, spherical Gaussian functions are not orthogonal, making this determination more complex. Solving this requires tackling a *nonlinear optimization problem* [23]. However, this optimization is performed only once in advance, enabling fast intensity calculations during image generation.

2.5 Light Scattering Phenomenon

We have so far discussed on intensity calculations based on light reflection from object surfaces. In this section, we focus on the optical effects that arise when light interacts with particles suspended in media, such as air or water. For example, the atmosphere contains various particles, including dust, dirt, tiny water droplets, and air molecules, all of which scatter light in different directions when illuminated. In fact, many materials like water, milk, skin, marble, and cheese can be modeled as containing small particles that also cause *light scattering*. These scattering materials are referred to as *participating media*. Accurately simulating light scattering in participating media is crucial for achieving highly realistic images. This section will explore the fundamental principles and techniques for rendering the visual effects produced by light scattering.

2.5.1 Light Scattering

In light scattering, two key physical processes—*scattering* and *attenuation*—play a crucial role (Fig. 2.25). Scattering occurs when light interacts with particles, causing it to be deflected in multiple directions. The *phase function*, which describes this behavior, depends on the angle between the incident and scattered light (Fig. 2.25a). Attenuation, on the other hand, refers to the reduction in light intensity as it travels through a medium. This reduction is due to both scattering and absorption by particles. The extent of attenuation is described by an exponential function, known as the *attenuation function* (Fig. 2.25b). A common measure of attenuation is the *mean free path*, which represents the average distance light travels before scattering again. In denser media, like clouds or thick smoke, the mean free path is shorter, leading to a higher attenuation rate.

The simplest scattering model assumes a constant phase function, meaning that light scatters uniformly in all directions when it interacts with a particle. This is known as *isotropic scattering*. Although isotropic scattering is rare in real-world scenarios, it is frequently used in computer graphics due to its computational simplicity and ability to still produce visually realistic images. By assuming isotropic scattering and further assuming that the intensity of scattered light is uniform everywhere, the resulting light intensity reaching the viewer can be computed analytically.

For realistic simulation of scattering phenomena, it is essential to consider more complex properties of the scattering process, where the intensity depends on the direction of the scattered light. This is known as *anisotropic scattering*. There are two types of anisotropic scattering based on particle size: *Rayleigh* and *Mie scattering*.

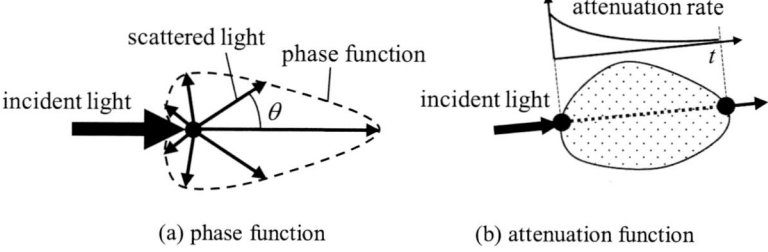

(a) phase function   (b) attenuation function

Fig. 2.25 Scattering and attenuation of light

Rayleigh scattering occurs with particles smaller than the wavelength of light, such as air and water molecules. The intensity of scattered light from Rayleigh scattering is inversely proportional to the fourth power of the wavelength, meaning shorter wavelengths are scattered more strongly. This wavelength dependence accounts for the color variations of the sky-blue during the day and red in the evening. The blue appearance of clear water is also a result of Rayleigh scattering. Conversely, scattering by larger particles, such as dust, corresponds to Mie scattering. Mie scattering exhibits strong directionality, with light scattering predominantly in the direction of propagation and low wavelength dependence. Media such as clouds and smoke are characterized by Mie scattering, resulting in a strong reflection of the light source's color.

In the following sections, we will explain three types of scattering models: the simplest model, the *single scattering model*, and the *multiple scattering model*, each designed to simulate different visual effects caused by scattering. The single scattering model considers only the light that is scattered once along each viewing ray, allowing for relatively fast computations. This model is effective for participating media with a long mean free path, such as the atmosphere, water, and thin smoke. In contrast, for participating media with a short mean free path, the multiple scattering model must be employed. In this case, light from a source reaches the viewpoint after undergoing multiple scattering events. Similar to global illumination calculations, multiple scattering calculations involve solving complex integral equations, resulting in a high computational cost. The unknown function in these equations represents the intensity distribution at every location within the participating media, and the equations take on a form akin to the rendering equation. While the rendering equation is limited to object surfaces, scattering phenomena require consideration of all points within the participating media, significantly increasing the problem's complexity. Methods that extend radiosity and path tracing have been developed to address these challenges.

2.5.2 The Simplest Model

Consider a highly simplified scattering model. Here, the particle density is uniform throughout, and the intensity of the light incident on the particles, L_s, remains constant everywhere. Additionally, we assume the phase function is isotropic, meaning light scatters uniformly in all directions. In this scenario, the light reaching the viewpoint, L_v, consists of two components: the intensity of an object, L_p, and the accumulated scattered light along the viewing ray. This relationship can be expressed as follows (see Fig. 2.26).

$$L_v = L_p \exp(-\kappa T) + \int_0^T \rho L_s \exp(-\kappa t)dt. \qquad (2.32)$$

where T is the distance between the viewpoint and the object, ρ is the *scattering albedo*, and κ represents the *extinction coefficient*. The scattering albedo, a constant between 0 and 1, indicates the fraction of incident light that is scattered by particles. For isotropic scattering, the albedo itself works as the phase function, with ρL_s corresponding to the intensity of the scattered light. Given that the incident light intensity L_s is constant, the scattered light intensity remains uniform everywhere. The extinction coefficient, κ, defines the rate at which light diminishes per unit length. In a uniform participating medium (i.e., with constant particle density), the extinction coefficient remains constant, causing the attenuation function to take the form of an exponential decay with respect to the light's travel distance. The first term on the right-hand side of the equation describes the object's intensity, L_p, reaching the viewpoint after being attenuated by particles. The second term accounts for the accumulated scattered light along the viewing ray, where the scattered light at each point also decays exponentially before reaching the viewpoint.

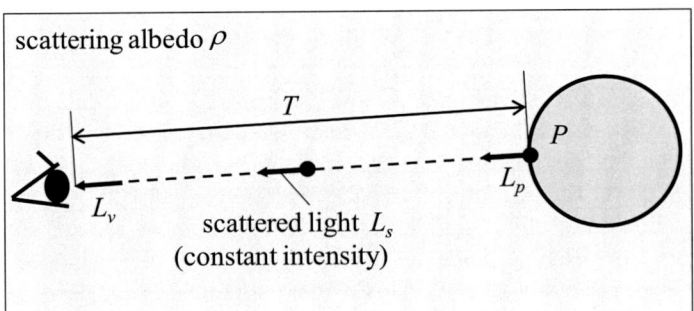

Fig. 2.26 The simplest model

Using this simplified model, Eq. 2.32 can be solved analytically, yielding the following expression:

$$L_v = L_p \exp(-\kappa T) + \frac{\rho L_s}{\kappa}(1 - \exp(-\kappa T)). \tag{2.33}$$

By substituting $\alpha = \exp(-\kappa T)$ and $L_\infty = \frac{\rho L_s}{\kappa}$ into the equation, we obtain a more compact form:

$$L_v = \alpha L_p + (1 - \alpha)L_\infty. \tag{2.34}$$

As $T \to \infty, \alpha \to 0$, and therefore $L_v \to L_\infty$. Here, L_∞ represents the light intensity reaching the viewpoint in the absence of an object. Since $0 \le \alpha \le 1$, this simple model blends L_p and L_∞ according to the ratio α, which is based on the distance T. This makes the calculation straightforward. Additionally, the user can control the color of the participating medium by specifying L_∞.

2.5.3 Single Scattering Model

The single scattering model accounts for light that reaches the viewpoint after being scattered only once along the viewing ray. Unlike the simplified model from the previous section, where both the scattered light intensity and particle density are uniform, the single scattering model allows these properties to vary with location, providing a more accurate representation of real-world physical phenomena. The phase function is no longer isotropic, and the attenuation of light is calculated through integration, reflecting the spatially dependent nature of the scattering process (Fig. 2.27).

Consider point Q at a distance t from the viewpoint, where the intensity of light reaching Q from the light source is $L_i(t)$. The scattered light in the viewing direction

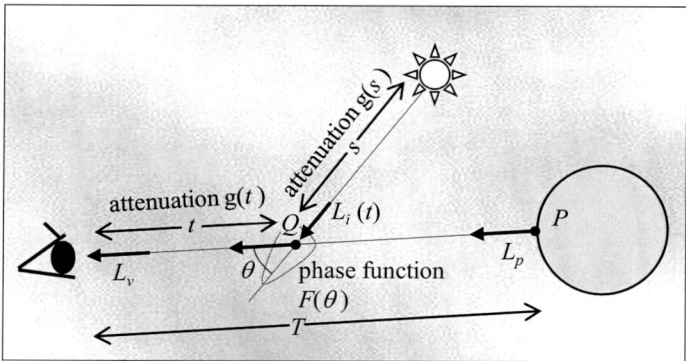

Fig. 2.27 Single scattering model

is $\rho F(\theta) L_i(t)$, where ρ is the scattering albedo and F is the phase function. Here, θ represents the angle between the incident light direction and the viewing direction at Q. The scattered light accumulates along the viewing ray. However, light attenuates both as it travels from the light source to Q and from Q to the viewpoint after scattering. Denoting the attenuation function as g, the intensity at the viewpoint is expressed as

$$L_v = L_p g(T) + \int_0^T \rho F(\theta) L_i(t) g(s) g(t) dt. \tag{2.35}$$

As in the previous section, the first term represents the object's intensity after attenuation, while the second term represents the scattered light intensity. $g(T)$ refers to the object's attenuation, while $g(s)$ and $g(t)$ represent the light attenuation to and from Q, respectively.

Let us now examine the attenuation function g in more detail. In the case of a uniform participating medium, as discussed earlier, g is modeled as an exponential function of the light's travel distance. However, for non-uniform participating media, the attenuation occurs exponentially relative to the *optical distance* τ. The optical distance represents the integrated extinction coefficient along the light path and is defined as follows:

$$\tau(t) = \int_0^t \kappa(t^*) dt^*. \tag{2.36}$$

Using this definition, the attenuation function is given by $g(t) = \exp(-\tau(t))$. It is important to note that the extinction coefficient at any point is proportional to the local density of the participating medium.

As described above, the single scattering model involves double integrals: one for accumulating the scattered light along the viewing ray (Eq. 2.35) and the other for computing the optical distance (Eq. 2.36). Unlike the simplified model discussed earlier, the single scattering model lacks an analytical solution, requiring numerical integration to compute the intensity, which can be computationally expensive. A common approach is to generate sample points along the viewing ray and numerically integrate Eq. 2.35. At each sample point, additional sample points are generated along the line between the sample point and the light source, and the optical distance, defined by Eq. 2.36, is computed via numerical integration.

Acceleration by GPU: The intensity from the single scattering model can be efficiently evaluated using polygon rendering, taking advantage of *GPU* (Graphics Processing Unit) parallel processing to achieve real-time image generation [24]. As illustrated in Fig. 2.28, multiple virtual planes parallel to the screen are created, and the scattered light intensity at each point on these planes is computed. By rendering these virtual planes and accumulating their intensities in the frame buffer, the integral calculation is effectively replaced by the rendering process. Since the per-pixel operations for calculating and accumulating scattered light intensity are performed in parallel by the GPU, images can be generated at high speed.

Fig. 2.28 Single scattering
model by GPU

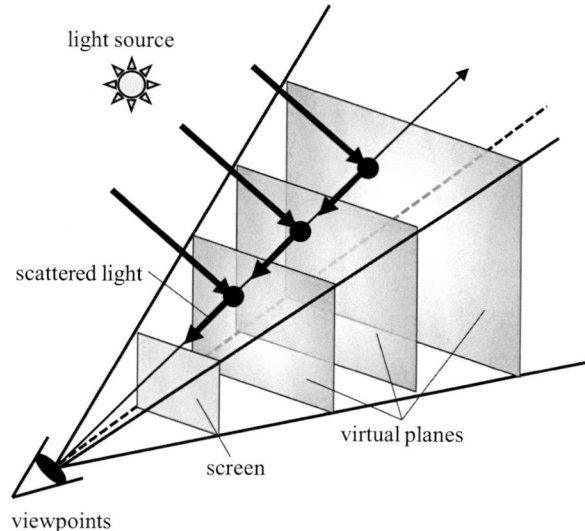

2.5.4 Multiple Scattering Model

For participating media with a short mean free path, such as clouds or dense smoke, multiple scattering must be considered, where light from the source reaches the viewpoint after undergoing multiple scattering events. In Sect. 2.3, we discussed the global illumination model and the rendering equation, which represents the energy balance of reflected light between objects. A similar equation, known as the *volume rendering equation* [25], can be defined for multiple scattering. This equation governs the energy balance of scattered light among all points within the participating medium.

The concept of the volume rendering equation can be illustrated using Fig. 2.29. The intensity of light scattered in the direction ω_o from a point x within the participating medium is denoted as $L(x, \omega_o)$, while the light incident from the direction ω_i

Fig. 2.29 Derivation of
volume rendering equation

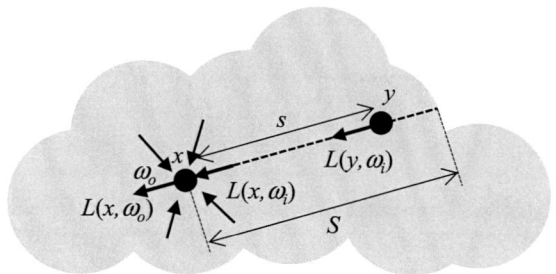

to the point x is denoted as $L_i(x, \omega_i)$. Since light arrives at point x from all directions, $L(x, \omega_o)$ is obtained by accumulating light contributions from all directions:

$$L(x, \omega_o) = \int_\Omega \rho F(\omega_o, \omega_i) L_i(x, \omega_i) d\omega_i, \qquad (2.37)$$

where Ω represents the set of all possible incident directions, ρ is the scattering albedo, and F is the phase function. Next, the incident light $L_i(x, \omega_i)$ is obtained by integrating the scattered light along the ray from x toward $-\omega_i$. Consider a point y located at distance s along this ray, as shown in Fig. 2.29. If the intensity of light scattered in the direction ω_i at point y is represented by $L(y, \omega_i)$, then $L_i(x, \omega_i)$ can be expressed as

$$L_i(x, \omega_i) = \int_0^S L(y, \omega_i) g(s) ds, \qquad (2.38)$$

where S represents the distance to the boundary of the participating medium, and $g(s)$ is the attenuation function.

The combination of the two equations above forms the rendering equation for participating media. To determine the scattered light intensity $L(x, \omega_o)$ at point x, we must first compute the incident light L_i. However, calculating L_i requires knowing the scattered light intensity $L(y, \omega_i)$ at point y, and the same applies recursively for $L(y, \omega_i)$. This creates an integral equation where the scattered light intensity at each point in the participating medium is an unknown variable. For participating media that involve combustion, such as flames or explosions, self-emission must also be considered. Additionally, when there are solid objects within or near the participating medium, the interaction between light and these objects must be accounted for. As a result, solving the volume rendering equation is highly complex.

Methods that extend both radiosity and path tracing have been developed to handle multiple scattering as well. In the radiosity-based approach, the simulation space is subdivided into a grid, and energy transfer between every pair of grid points is formulated, resulting in a large system of linear equations. However, solving these equations comes with high computational and storage costs, which limits the complexity of participating media that can be handled by this method. As a result, recent research has increasingly focused on path-tracing-based approaches, which are more scalable for complex media.

In path tracing-based methods, multiple light paths from the viewpoint to the light source are generated probabilistically, and the average contribution of each path is calculated. The key difference from global illumination is the way the light paths are determined, which involves two main processes (see Fig. 2.30): free path sampling and scattering direction sampling. Free path sampling determines the distance to the next scattering point after scattering occurs at the current location, while scattering direction sampling determines the direction in which light scatters at each point. The attenuation function is often used as the probability density function for free path sampling, whereas the phase function is typically used for scattering direction sampling.

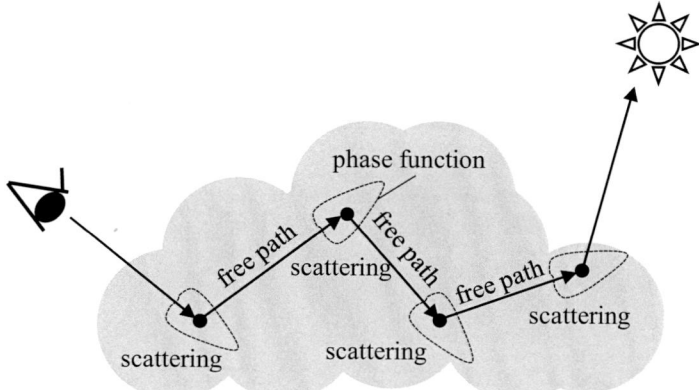

Fig. 2.30 Path tracing for participating media

Path tracing for participating media is generally time-consuming, particularly for non-uniform media like smoke or clouds. This is because free path sampling becomes computationally expensive; the probability density function for free path sampling is difficult to define explicitly, often requiring inefficient techniques like rejection sampling. To address this issue, methods have been developed to improve efficiency by adaptively subdividing the space based on the density distribution of the medium, allowing for more efficient sampling and faster computations [27].

2.5.5 Examples of Various Scattering Phenomena

In this section, we show examples of the scattering effects using the methods described above.

2.5.5.1 Fog

For outdoor scenes with fog, the simplified model from Sect. 2.5.2 is effective in creating realistic images. This is because sunlight provides uniform illumination, and the fog density is nearly constant. Figure 2.31 illustrates this effect: without fog, the terrain remains clearly visible regardless of distance from the viewpoint, whereas simulating fog causes the terrain's appearance to vary with distance, creating a more realistic effect. This simple model is commonly implemented as a core function in standard graphics APIs like *OpenGL* and is widely used.

(a) without fog   (b) with fog

Fig. 2.31   Effect of fog

2.5.5.2   Atmosphere

The atmosphere contains two types of particles: air molecules and *aerosols*, which are responsible for determining the color of the sky. The densities of these particles are not uniform; they decrease exponentially with altitude from the Earth's surface. Since the mean free path in the atmosphere is long, realistic images can be produced using the single scattering model. To simulate atmospheric scattering, we must account for light scattered on a global scale. The atmosphere is approximately 30 km thick, so a large virtual sphere is modeled by adding this thickness to the Earth's radius of about 6,400 km. For numerical integration of the scattered light, sample points are generated along the viewing ray and its intersection with the virtual sphere [28, 29].

Figure 2.32 illustrates an example of the sky, where the atmospheric color transitions beautifully from blue to red based on the sun's altitude. This color shift is strongly influenced by the scattering behavior of air molecules. Since these molecules

(a) sky dome   (b) outdoor scene

Fig. 2.32   Example of the sky.

are much smaller than the wavelength of light, their scattering follows Rayleigh scattering theory, where the intensity of scattered light is inversely proportional to the fourth power of the wavelength. During the day, when the sun is high, sunlight travels a shorter distance through the atmosphere, allowing the shorter wavelength blue light to scatter and reach the viewpoint, making the sky appear blue. In contrast, at sunset, when the sun is near the horizon, the sunlight travels a much longer path through the atmosphere. The scattered blue light is significantly attenuated before reaching the viewpoint, allowing the longer wavelength red light to dominate, giving the evening sky its reddish hue.

On the other hand, scattering by aerosols is most noticeable around the sun. Since the particle size of aerosols is larger than the wavelength of light, their scattering follows Mie scattering theory, which results in strong forward scattering. Consequently, a bright region is observed around the sun. This effect is also visible in Fig. 2.32, where the bright area near the top corresponds to the direction of the sun.

2.5.5.3 Light Beams

Figure 2.33 illustrates examples of *light beams* resulting from the scattering caused by dust particles in the air [30, 32]. These scattering effects are commonly utilized in live stage performances with spotlights. Similar phenomena can also be observed in outdoor environments, where sunlight passes through gaps in the clouds, creating what are often referred to as god rays.

To render such effects, it is necessary to identify the segments along each viewing ray that are illuminated by the light source. This is achieved by generating shadow rays from each sample point on the viewing ray toward the light source to check visibility. If obstacles block the light, the point lies in shadow. By incorporating semi-transparent objects, such as windows, beautiful light beams can be simulated, as seen when light passes through stained glass [32] (Fig. 2.33).

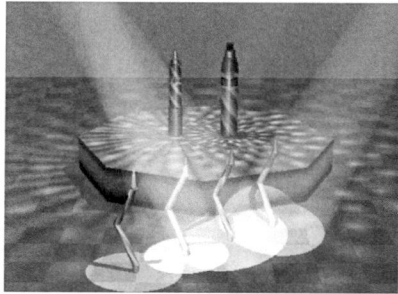

Fig. 2.33 Light beams. Image courtesy of Tomoyuki Nishita

The technique for rendering such effects was initially developed in the 1980s, and at that time, generating images required several minutes to tens of minutes. However, with the advancements in GPU technology, these effects can now be rendered in real time, making the method widely adopted in video games to enhance realism.

2.5.5.4 Water

The color of water is influenced by the scattering properties of water molecules. These molecules are much smaller than the wavelength of light, and similar to the atmosphere, they follow Rayleigh scattering theory, which explains the blue hue of water. However, unlike the atmosphere, water also has a surface that causes unique visual effects. The phenomenon known as *caustics*, caused by the refraction of light through the water surface, produces impressive and beautiful patterns on object surfaces.

Caustics refer to the distinctive patterns formed by the refraction of light at the water surface. This refraction focuses light, creating brighter spots on object surfaces. When this focusing effect is combined with light scattering by particles, multiple light beams appear underwater, resulting in a visually stunning scene (see Fig. 2.34a). However, accurately computing the focal ratio is challenging due to the complexities of refraction, as light paths must be traced from the source. To address this, volume photon mapping, an extension of photon mapping, was developed [26], enabling efficient representation of caustics by storing photons in the volume as well as on object surfaces. A GPU-accelerated method was later introduced for real-time rendering of caustics [33]. In this approach, transparent triangular prisms are used to simulate caustics, as shown in Fig. 2.34b. These prisms are generated by subdividing the water surface into a triangular mesh, and refracted rays are calculated at each vertex. The light focusing rate is determined by the ratio of the areas between the top

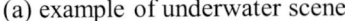
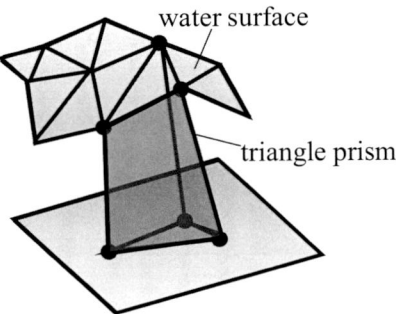

(a) example of underwater scene   (b) Computation with GPU

Fig. 2.34 Scattering by water

and bottom surfaces of each prism. The intensity of the scattered light within each prism is computed based on this ratio, allowing for real-time rendering by using the GPU to process the transparent prisms and accumulate the resulting intensities.

2.5.5.5 Smoke and Clouds

Cloud and smoke particles are larger than the wavelength of light, causing them to follow Mie scattering theory. As a result, the mean free path is short, and multiple scattering effects must be taken into account to achieve realistic shading.

Figure 2.35 shows a comparison between images rendered with and without multiple scattering. Figure 2.35a, b are generated using single scattering and multiple scattering, respectively. With multiple scattering, the smoke appears brighter and more diffuse, resulting in a whiter appearance. Figure 2.36 illustrates an image of clouds rendered with multiple scattering [27], using path tracing to account for the overall light interactions in the scene, including scattering from the clouds, the atmosphere, and reflections from the ground. A highly realistic image is generated.

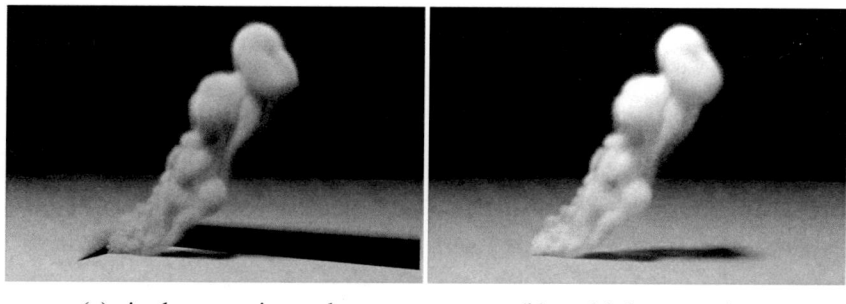

(a) single scattering only   (b) multiple scattering

Fig. 2.35 Single scattering versus multiple scattering

Fig. 2.36 Clouds

2.5.5.6   Subsurface Scattering

Finally, let us discuss *subsurface scattering*, a phenomenon observed in *translucent materials* like marble and human skin. In such objects, scattering occurs beneath the surface. Light enters the object, scatters within, and exits at a different point. By simulating this subsurface scattering, the appearance of translucent objects can be realistically rendered. This phenomenon gained widespread attention following the work by Jensen et al. [34], leading to its popular use in rendering translucent materials.

In the model proposed by Jensen et al., they introduce the *BSSRDF* (Bidirectional Scattering Surface Reflectance Distribution Function) to describe the relationship between incident and scattered light, assuming a locally flat surface. Unlike the BRDF, the BSSRDF depends on both the incident and exit locations of light. It models the fraction of light that enters at one point, scatters within the material, and exits at another point. While the BSSRDF is an approximation of subsurface scattering, it is widely used for its simplicity and effectiveness in producing realistic appearances.

Figure 2.37 illustrates the effect of subsurface scattering. In Fig. 2.37a, the image is rendered without subsurface scattering, while Fig. 2.37b includes the effect. The material used in this example is marble, showcasing the soft and unique appearance resulting from its translucent properties.

(a) without subsurface scattering   (b) with subsurface scattering

Fig. 2.37 Effects of subsurface scattering. Images courtesy of Henrik Wann Jensen

2.6 Advanced Rendering Techniques

So far, we have discussed global illumination and scattering phenomena in the context of rendering realistic images—areas that have been well-established and extensively studied in computer graphics over the years. However, recent advances in emerging technologies, namely *deep learning* and *differentiable rendering*, have driven significant innovations in the field. These technologies offer a broad range of applications and present new approaches to solving various challenges. In this section, we provide an overview of how deep learning and differentiable rendering are being applied to rendering techniques.

2.6.1 Deep Learning for Rendering

Deep learning is a form of *machine learning*, developed as an extended version of *neural networks*. Neural networks, initially developed in the 1960s, are composed of multiple layers of interconnected units. Recent advances in computing power have enabled the expansion of these networks, allowing for a significant increase in the number of layers and units, which is the core of what is referred to as deep learning today.

Deep learning demonstrates remarkable capabilities when provided with large datasets, enabling it to implicitly model complex rules or nonlinear functions derived from the data. It has been successfully applied across various fields, often surpassing traditional mathematical approaches. Particularly, deep learning excels in tasks involving images as both input and output, making it highly compatible with computer graphics, a field focused on image generation. With deep learning, real-time global illumination simulation becomes feasible. Although the training process can be time-consuming, the computational cost for predicting outputs from inputs is minimal once training is complete. This allows for significant acceleration of the rendering process by incorporating deep learning into some or all of the calculations. The following sections highlight several applications of deep learning to rendering problems.

For the path tracing method discussed in Sect. 2.3, a noise reduction technique utilizing deep learning has been introduced [35]. Since light paths are sampled randomly, rendering with a small number of samples often results in noisy images. To address this, deep learning can be applied by preparing large datasets of noisy and noiseless image pairs from various 3D scenes. By learning the relationships between these pairs, the network can convert a noisy image generated with fewer samples into a high quality, noiseless image. The assumption is that a strong correlation exists between noisy and noiseless images, and by incorporating the consistency of neighboring pixels during training, the network can rapidly produce high-quality images that account for global illumination.

In Sect. 2.4, we discussed a fast method using basis functions for intensity calculation with precomputation. A method that incorporates deep learning into this approach has also been proposed [36]. The core idea is to train a neural network to predict the intensity of an object under various lighting conditions for a given scene. However, direct illumination often results in sharp, discontinuous changes in shadows and shading as the light source or viewpoint moves, making efficient learning challenging. To address this, the method trains the network to separately learn the relationship between direct and indirect light components. Direct light can be calculated relatively quickly and inexpensively, while the indirect component is estimated through simple multiplication and addition operations within the neural network. This allows for the rapid generation of realistic images that account for global illumination.

The same idea has been applied to rendering light scattering phenomena [37]. In this approach, a neural network is trained to predict the effects of multiple scattering based on intensity distributions computed using only single scattering. This method has been particularly successful in rendering realistic clouds. A database is constructed with pairs of intensities for clouds with varying density distributions, capturing both single and multiple scattering effects. The network is then trained to predict the multiple scattering intensity from the single scattering data, allowing highly realistic cloud images to be generated within a few seconds.

Deep learning functions as a black box, capable of representing complex, high-dimensional relationships when provided with sufficient data. Once the model is trained, it can be utilized to solve inverse problems as well. For instance, a trained network can estimate parameters of the BRDF needed to achieve a desired appearance. Deep learning is being applied to various challenges in computer graphics, beyond just rendering, and is increasingly replacing traditional mathematical approaches. With the rapid advancements in computational power, it is expected to become a fundamental technology in the future.

2.6.2 Differential Rendering

Differential rendering is a technique that generates *differential images* with respect to the parameters involved in rendering processes. These parameters may include the position and orientation of the camera or the position and intensity of the light source. By calculating the rate of change in pixel intensity as these parameters vary, differential rendering outputs the result as an image. In computer graphics, however, the term generally refers to methods that compute differential images using path tracing, accounting for global illumination.

In differential rendering, instead of differentiating the function representing the intensity of each pixel through symbolic or numerical operations, a technique called automatic differentiation is employed. *Automatic differentiation* differentiates functions represented as programs or procedures. This approach gained significant attention following the development of the differentiable path tracer, called Mitsuba2, by

Jakob's group [38]. It has been continuously updated, with the latest version being Mitsuba3, as of the publication data of this book.

In the Mitsuba series, a graph representation is utilized for calculating differentiation. When a specific light path is determined, a graph is generated to represent the input-output relationship of the functions used to calculate its contribution. The edges of the graph represent each function, with the differential value of its input assigned as a weight. By traversing the graph and applying the product and chain rules of differentiation, the overall differential value can be computed. However, for light paths involving multiple reflections or complex BRDFs, calculations can become intricate, leading to large graphs that decrease memory and computational efficiency. To address this, efforts have been made to reduce the number of nodes in the graph through partial calculations. Automatic differentiation supports both forward (calculating from input to output) and backward (calculating from output to input) methods, and both are implemented in the Mitsuba series. Furthermore, acceleration is achieved by leveraging parallel computation on a GPU.

With the differential renderer, solving optimization problems becomes more straightforward. A typical optimization problem involves finding parameters that generate a reference image provided by the user. In such cases, the objective function is often defined as the sum of the squares of the intensity differences between the reference and rendered images. The parameters are then updated sequentially to minimize this objective function. To update the parameters, the gradient of the objective function must be calculated, which requires differentiating the objective function with respect to the parameters, including the differentiation of the rendered image by those parameters. The differential renderer facilitates this process. Unlike numerical differentiation, which can introduce errors, the exact differential value is obtained, allowing for accurate calculation of the gradient for the objective function and enabling more precise solutions to the optimization problem.

The parameters to be optimized can include not only the information about the camera and light source but also the material of the object and even the object's shape. Figure 2.38 illustrates an example of simultaneous optimization of an object's shape

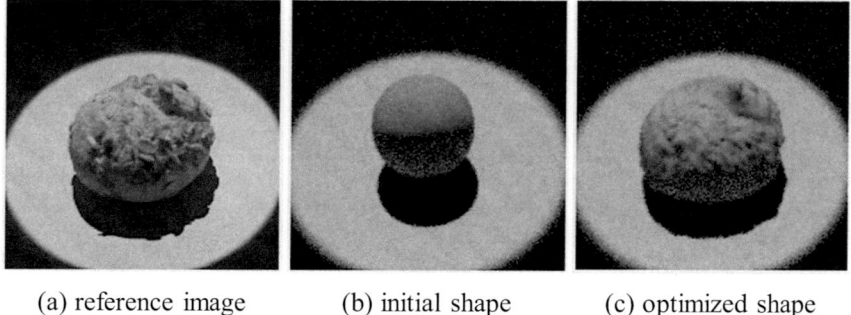

(a) reference image   (b) initial shape   (c) optimized shape

Fig. 2.38 Optimization with Differential Rendering. Images courtesy of Wenzel Jakob

and texture using differential rendering. Figure (a) serves as the reference image. The optimization process begins with the sphere shown in figure (b), and the resulting optimized image is shown in figure (c). While figure (a) is a static reference image, figure (c) is generated using the 3D shape and texture obtained through optimization. Since differential rendering relies on path tracing, the optimization of shape and texture accounts for global illumination effects, resulting in an image that closely resembles the reference image.

Differential rendering is also compatible with the deep learning techniques discussed in the previous section. In deep learning, optimizing the network based on training data is essential, and this can be achieved by linking the differential renderer to the network to generate differential images that minimize errors. The integration of differential rendering with deep learning will be an indispensable technology for the future advancement of computer graphics.

2.7 Conclusion

This chapter has focused on the intensity calculation of objects to generate realistic images. In the real world, when light is activated, it propagates instantaneously and influences the intensity perceived by an observer. I hope readers have gained insight into the propagation process and the computer simulation methods involved. I introduced some definitions of the governing equations related to light simulation (rendering equations) and their typical solutions. Methods based on path tracing can produce extremely realistic images by accounting for all light paths. Additionally, techniques utilizing precomputation enable real-time image generation. Approaches that simulate the scattering of light significantly enhance the realism of synthetic images. These techniques can be employed individually or in combination, depending on the characteristics and objectives of the target to be displayed.

Many people associate computer graphics primarily with entertainment applications, such as movies and video games. However, its applications extend much wider, including industries such as medicine, architecture, and cosmetics. In these industrial contexts, computer graphics is not only used to generate realistic images but also to identify physical parameters necessary for achieving desired appearances, textures, lighting, and more. This process is often referred to as the inverse problem as mentioned in the previous section. The combination of differential rendering and deep learning is undoubtedly a crucial foundational technology for addressing such inverse problems. While deep learning necessitates a substantial amount of training data, computer graphics can generate this data effectively. Therefore, further advancements in the fundamental rendering technologies required for generating the necessary training images are essential. Additionally, with the recent expansion of cyberspace, the demand and expectations for rendering technologies capable of producing highly realistic images will undoubtedly continue to grow.

References

1. Bui Tuong Phong, Illumination for computer generated pictures, Communications of ACM 18 (1975), no. 6, 311–317.
2. R. Cook and K. Torrance. "A reflectance model for computer graphics". Computer Graphics (SIGGRAPH '81 Proceedings), Vol. 15, No. 3, July 1981, pp. 301–316.
3. Bruce Walter, Stephen Robert Marschner, Hongsong Li, Kenneth E. Torrance, Microfacet models for refraction through rough surfaces, Proceedings of the 18th Eurographics conference on Rendering TechniquesJune 2007 Pages 195–206
4. Pierre Poulin, Alain Fournier A model for anisotropic reflection, ACM SIGGRAPH Computer Graphics, Vol. 24, No. 4, 1990
5. J. T. Kajiya, Anisotropic reflection models, ACM SIGGRAPH Computer Graphics, Vol. 19, No. 3, 1985
6. Steve Marschner, Henrik Wann Jensen, Mike Cammarano, Steve Worley, Pat M Hanrahan, Light scattering from human hair fibers, Vol. 22, No. 3, ACM Transactions on Graphics
7. James T. Kajiya, "The Rendering Equation", Proc. ACM SIGGRAPH 1986, pp. 143–150 (1986).
8. Tomoyuki Nishita, Eihachiro Nakamae, "Continuous tone representation of three-dimensional objects taking account of shadows and interreflection," Proc. ACM SIGGRAPH 1985, pp. 23–30 (1985).
9. Michael F. Cohen, Shenchang Eric Chen, John R. Wallace, Donald P. Greenberg, "A progressive refinement approach to fast radiosity image generation," Proc. ACM SIGGRAPH 1988, pp. 75–84 (1988).
10. David S. Immel, Michael F. Cohen, Donald P. Greenberg, "A radiosity method for non-diffuse environments," ACM SIGGRAPH Computer Graphics, Vol. 20, Issue 4, 1986, pp. 133–142 (1986).
11. Françis X. Sillion, James R. Arvo, Stephen H. Westin, Donald P. Greenberg, "A global illumination solution for general reflectance distributions," SIGGRAPH '91: Proceedings of the 18th annual conference on Computer graphics and interactive techniquesJuly 1991 Pages 187–196 (1991).
12. Carsten Dachsbacher, Marc Stamminger, George Drettakis, Frédo Durand, "Implicit visibility and antiradiance for interactive global illumination," ACM Transactions on Graphics, Vol. 26, No. 3, Article 61 (2007).
13. E. Lafortune and Y. Willems, "Bi-directional path tracing," Proceedings of CompuGraphics, (Alvor, Portugal), pp. 145–153, Dec. 1993 (1993).
14. Eric Veach and Leonidas J. Guibas, "Metropolis light transport," SIGGRAPH '97: Proceedings of the 24th annual conference on Computer graphics and interactive techniquesAugust 1997 Pages 65–76 (1997).
15. Henrik Wann Jensen, "Global Illumination using Photon Maps," In "Rendering Techniques '96". Eds. X. Pueyo and P. Schröder. Springer-Verlag, pp. 21–30 (1996).
16. Bentley, Jon Louis: "Multidimensional Binary Search Trees Used for Associative Searching," Comm. of the ACM 18 (9), pp. 509–517 (1975).
17. Toshiya Hachisuka, Shinji Ogaki, and Henrik Wann Jensen, "Progressive Photon Mapping, " ACM Transactions on Graphics, Vol. 27, Issue 5, Article No.: 130, pp 1–8 (2008).
18. Paul E. Debevec, "Rendering Synthetic Objects into Real Scenes: Bridging Traditional and Image-Based Graphics with Global Illumination and High Dynamic Range Photography," Proceedings of ACM SIGGRAPH 1998, Pages 189–198 (1998).
19. Y.Dobashi, K.Kaneda, H.Yamashita, T. Nishita, "Method for Calculation of Sky Light Luminance Aiming at an Interactive Architectural Design," Computer Graphics Forum (Proc. EUROGRAPHICS'96), Vol.15, No.3, pp. 112–118 (1996).
20. Peter-Pike Sloan, Jan Kautz, John Snyder, "Precomputed radiance transfer for real-time rendering in dynamic, low-frequency lighting environments," ACM Transactions on Graphics, Vol. 21, Issue 3, pp. 527–536 (2002).

21. Y.Dobashi, K.Kaneda, E.Nakashima, H.Yamashita, T. Nishita, "A Quick Rendering Method using Basis Functions for Interactive Lighting Design," Computer Graphics Forum, Vol.14, No.3, pp. 229–240 (1995).

22. R. Ng, R. Ramamoorthi, P. Hanrahan, All-frequency shadows using non-linear wavelet lighting approximation, ACM Trans. on Graph., Vol. 22, No. 3, pp. 376–381 (2003).

23. Y.-T. Tsai, Z.-C. Shih, "All-frequency precomputed radiance transfer using spherical radial basis functions and clustered tensor approximation," ACM Trans. on Graph., Vol. 25, No. 3, pp. 967–976 (2006).

24. Y.Dobashi, T. Yamamoto , T.Nishita, "Interactive Rendering Method for Displaying Shafts of Light," Proc.Pacific Graphics 2000, pp. 31–37 (2000).

25. Eric P. Lafortune and Yves D. Willems, "Rendering participating media with bidirectional path tracing," Proceedings of the eurographics workshop on Rendering techniques '96, pp. 91–100 (1996).

26. Henrik Wann Jensen and Per H. Christensen, "Efficient Simulation of Light Transport in Scenes with Participating Media using Photon Maps," Proceedings of SIGGRAPH'98, pages 311–320 (1998).

27. Y. Yue, K. Iwasaki, B.-Y. Chen, Y.Dobashi, T. Nishita, "Unbiased, Adaptive Stochastic Sampling for Rendering Inhomogeneous Participating Media," ACM Trans. on Graphics, Vol. 29, No. 5 (Proc. SIGGRAPH Asia 2010), Article 177 (2010).

28. Y.Dobashi, K.Kaneda, H.Yamashita, T. Nishita "Fast Display Method of Sky Color Using Basis Functions," Proc. Pacific Graphics'95, pp. 194–208 (1995).

29. T. Nishita, Y.Dobashi, K.Kaneda, H.Yamashita, "Display Method of the Sky Color Taking into Account Multiple Scattering," Proc. Pacific Graphics'96, pp.66–79 (1996).

30. T. Nishita and E. Nakamae, "A Shading Model for Atmosphere Scattering Considering Luminous Intensity Distribution of Light Sources," Computer Graphics, Vol.21, No.3, 1987-7, pp.303–310 (1987).

31. Y.Dobashi, K.Kaneda, H.Yamashita, T.Okita, T.Nishita, "A Simple, Efficient Method for Realistic Animation of Clouds," Proc. SIGGRAPH2000, 2000-7, pp. 19–28 (2000).

32. Y.Dobashi, T. Yamamoto , T.Nishita, "Interactive Rendering Method for Displaying Shafts of Light," Proc.Pacific Graphics 2000, pp. 31–37 (2000).

33. K. Iwasaki, Y.Dobashi, T.Nishita, "Efficient Rendering of Optical Effects within Water Using Graphics Hardware," Proc. Pacific Graphics 2001, pp. 374–383 (2001).

34. Henrik Wann Jensen, Stephen R. Marschner, Marc Levoy, Pat Hanrahan, "A practical model for subsurface light transport," Proceedings of the 28th annual conference on Computer graphics and interactive techniquesAugust 2001 (SIGGRAPH 2001) pp. 511–518 (2001).

35. Yuchi Huo, Sung-eui Yoon, A survey on deep learning-based Monte Carlo denoising," Computational Visula Media, Vol. 7, No. 2, pp. 169–185 (2021).

36. Gilles Rainer, Adrien Bousseau, Tobias Ritschel, George Drettakis, "Neural Precomputed Radiance Transfer", Computer Graphics Forum (Proceedings of the Eurographics conference), Vol. 41, No. 2 (2022).

37. S. Kallweit, T. Müller, B. McWilliams, M. Gross, J. Novák, "Deep scattering: Rendering atmospheric clouds with radiance-predicting neural networks," ACM Transactions on Graphics Vol. 36, No. 6, Article No. 231 (2017).

38. Merlin Nimier-David, Delio Vicini, Tizian Zeltner, Wenzel Jakob, "Mitsuba 2: a retargetable forward and inverse renderer," ACM Transactions on Graphics, Vol. 38, Issue 6, Article No. 203 (2019).

Chapter 3
Character Animation

Tomohiko Mukai[ID]

Abstract This chapter explains animation editing techniques for 3D character models, especially human-like characters. First, we explain the skeleton-based method, which is a de facto standard technique in character animation production. Next, we explain several approaches to editing a static pose of a character, known as inverse kinematics, and editing character motion represented as time-series data of pose changes. We then introduce a data-driven motion generation approach, which generates new motions based on multiple pre-created motion samples, and finally summarize future prospects. Note that reading this chapter requires a basic knowledge of three-dimensional geometry and numerical optimization techniques such as least squares methods.

3.1 Introduction

In the field of visual content and computer graphics, *animation* refers to the temporal movement of objects in a video or the moving image itself. Since the etymology of the word *animate* means "to bring to life" or "to activate," animation is content that brings shape models to life as if they were alive.

The character animation techniques determine the behavior of the human-like model and bring it to life. Character animation often involves full-body animation, which changes the silhouette of the entire character, such as the torso, limbs, head, fingers, and toes, and facial animation, which includes changes in facial expressions and eye movements. Furthermore, full-body animation techniques include various methods, such as deforming the character's pose and movement, synthesizing a new motion using an existing dataset, editing multiple animation data, and moving the character body according to physical laws. The field of research includes not only 3DCG but also robotics, biomechanics, and computer vision.

This chapter mainly summarizes techniques for editing full-body animation data of human-like characters that have been researched in the field of 3DCG. In Sect. 3.2, we explain the basics of the skeleton-based method, a standard technique in character animation production, including the definition of coordinate transformation and joint pose, and the computation of forward kinematics.

J. Mitani et al., *Mathematics and Applications of Computer Graphics*,
https://doi.org/10.1007/978-981-96-2933-6_3

In Sect. 3.3, we summarize inverse kinematics, a computational technique for editing a static pose. In particular, we explain analytical techniques suitable for humanoid character limbs, the gradient descent method, a typical numerical computation method, and its extension. We also explain a heuristic technique called the FABRIK algorithm.

In Sect. 3.4, we summarize computational techniques for editing character motion represented as time-series data of pose changes. In particular, we introduce motion editing methods using signal processing techniques, inverse kinematics, and motion deformation based on spacetime optimization.

Finally, in Sect. 3.5, we introduce the concept of motion editing techniques using machine learning, which is an approach to generate new motions based on multiple pre-created motion samples, and summarize future prospects in Sect. 3.6.

3.2 Basics of Character Animation

3.2.1 Skeleton Method

Character animation is created by deforming a shape model that represents the surface of a character, such as skin and clothing. For example, if a polygon mesh represents a character shape, the animation is expressed by changing the position, orientation, and size of each polygon over time. The simplest method is to play back pre-created time-series data of each vertex coordinate or automatically modify each polygon coordinate according to the character's movement or environmental changes. However, manipulating thousands to tens of thousands of polygons individually burdens the animator, and the data size and computational load also become enormous.

An internal mechanism called a *rig* or character rig is therefore introduced to deform the character model efficiently. A rig is a general term for an internal mechanism and user interface that allows animators to intuitively manipulate the character shape through a small number of parameters. In building a rig, appropriate shape deformation algorithms for each part of the character must be combined while providing an intuitive interface that does not make the animator aware of the internal mechanisms. Such rigging techniques can reduce production costs and data sizes while improving animation quality and computational efficiency.

The *skeleton* is the standard rig for producing full-body animations of humanoid characters. A skeleton is a structure that connects multiple *joints* with *bones*, as shown in Fig. 3.1a. This structure mimics articulated bodies such as humans, vertebrates, and robots. For example, a humanoid model is constructed by connecting rotating joints that mimic movable joints such as the spine, shoulders, elbows, wrists, knees, and ankles to rigid bones of fixed length that correspond to bones. Then, by rotating the joints over time, the character's surface, called *skin*, deforms according to the skeleton pose, as shown in Fig. 3.1b.

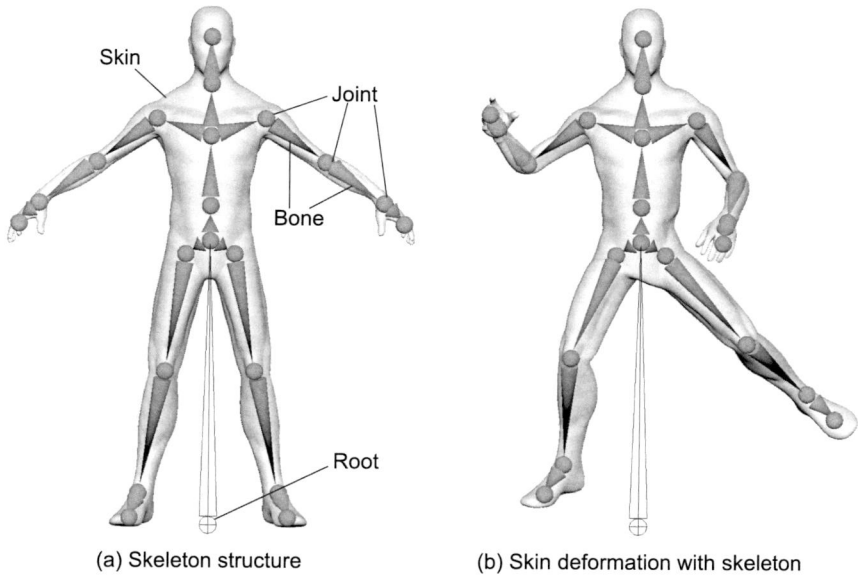

(a) Skeleton structure   (b) Skin deformation with skeleton

Fig. 3.1 Overview of the skeleton method

The skin model can contain not only the shape of the character's skin, but also clothing and even tufts of hair. The construction procedure of a skin model by binding a skeleton to the skin mesh is called *skinning*. Various skinning models have been proposed to deform the skin shape according to the skeleton pose change, such as the linear blend skinning method [1], dual quaternion skinning method [2], joint deformer model [3], and delta mush models [4, 5].

3.2.2 Joint Hierarchy

The skeleton of a humanoid character consists of a branching structure of an upper body that extends from the hip joint to both arms and the head, and a lower body branching structure that extends from the hip joint to both legs. In addition, a virtual joint called the *root* is often placed on the ground surface below the hip joint. The root is a joint introduced to manipulate the position, orientation, and overall scale of the character in world space. On the other hand, joints at the ends of the skeleton, such as the top of the head and the tips of the hands and feet, are called end-effectors or *effectors*.

In a general skeleton structure, joints other than the root are always connected to a parent joint by a bone, and joints other than the effector are always connected to one or more child joints. The two joints connected by a bone have an asymmetric parent-child relationship; changing the pose of the parent joint affects the pose of

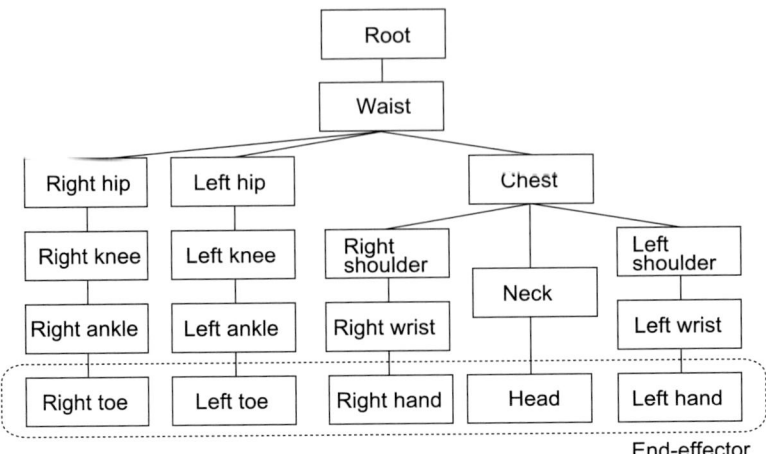

Fig. 3.2 Joint hierarchy structure

its child joint and, thus, all of its descendant joints. On the other hand, changing the pose of the child joint does not affect the parent or ancestor joints.

Such parent-child relationships between joints are represented by a tree structure called a *joint hierarchy*. The root joint is the top level of the joint hierarchy, and the leaf nodes at the lowest level correspond to the effectors. Its subtree also shows the pose inheritance relationship, i.e., how the top-level joint's pose change affects the descendant joints and in what order. As a concrete example, the joint hierarchy structure of the skeleton of Fig. 3.1 is shown in Fig. 3.2. Looking at this hierarchical structure, the rotation of the hip joint changes the tilt of the entire character, and the pose change of the left thigh only affects the pose of the left leg, but not any other parts.

3.2.3 Joint Coordinate System

The position and orientation of each part of the skeleton are determined by propagating the rotation of each joint according to the hierarchical structure. Here we summarize the notations for such joint poses using a simple skeleton shown in Fig. 3.3. First, the position and orientation in three-dimensional space are described using the *world coordinate system*, with $\mathbf{O}_W$ as the origin and x_W, y_W, z_W as the axis directions. The world coordinate system is also called the reference coordinate system or the absolute coordinate system because the position of $\mathbf{O}_W$ and the directions of x_W, y_W, z_W remain unchanged regardless of the time in the animation or changes in the scene. In this world coordinate system, the skeleton has joint A at position $\mathbf{O}_A$, which is $[1\ 1\ 0]^T$ away from $\mathbf{O}_W$, and joint B is connected by a bone of length 1, which extends in direction $-y_W$.

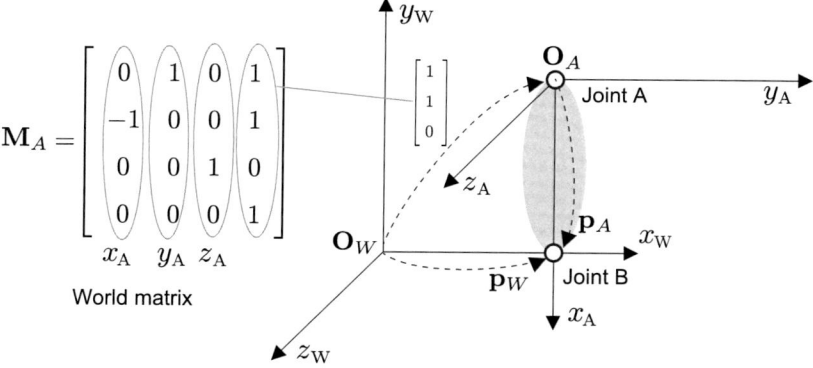

Fig. 3.3 Relative relationship of joint pose and coordinate transformation

These two joints each have their own coordinate system called the joint coordinate system or *local coordinate system*. The local coordinate system is also called the moving coordinate system because it translates and rotates within the world coordinate system in response to changes in the skeleton pose. In the example of Fig. 3.3, the origin of the local coordinate system of joint A is at $\mathbf{O}_A$, and it is rotated $-90°$ around the axis parallel to the z_W axis of the world coordinate system. Thus, the direction of the z_A axis coincides with the z_W direction, and the directions of the x_A and y_A axes correspond to the $-y_W$ and x_W axes, respectively. At this point, the position of joint B from the local coordinate system of joint A is $\mathbf{p}_A = [p_{A,x} \; p_{A,y} \; p_{A,z}]^T = [1\ 0\ 0]^T$, and it remains unchanged no matter how joint A translates or rotates. On the other hand, the position of joint B from the world coordinate system is $\mathbf{p}_W = [p_{W,x} \; p_{W,y} \; p_{W,z}]^T = [1\ 0\ 0]^T$, and it changes with the translation or rotation of joint A.

3.2.4 Coordinate Transformation and World Pose

The differences in coordinate values and axis directions between these two coordinate systems are referred to as a *coordinate transformation*. A coordinate transformation is a calculation that converts a pose expressed in one coordinate system to a pose viewed from another. Linear coordinate transformations in three-dimensional space are represented by a 4×4 *homogeneous transformation matrix*. Three-dimensional coordinates are represented by a four-dimensional vector $[x \; y \; z \; w = 1]^T$, called the *homogeneous coordinates*, which adds a fourth component $w = 1$.

As a concrete example, consider the coordinate transformation from the homogeneous coordinates $\mathbf{p}_A \in \mathfrak{R}^4$ viewed from the local coordinate system in Fig. 3.3 to the homogeneous coordinates $\mathbf{p}_W \in \mathfrak{R}^4$ in the world coordinate system. When the homogeneous transformation matrix is represented as $\mathbf{M}_A \in \mathfrak{R}^{4 \times 4}$, the coordinate transformation is given by Eq. 3.1.

$$
\mathbf{p}_W = \begin{bmatrix} p_{W,x} \\ p_{W,y} \\ p_{W,z} \\ 1 \end{bmatrix} = \mathbf{M}_A \mathbf{p}_A
$$

$$
= \begin{bmatrix} 0 & 1 & 0 & 1 \\ -1 & 0 & 0 & 1 \\ 0 & 0 & 1 & 0 \\ 0 & 0 & 0 & 1 \end{bmatrix} \begin{bmatrix} p_{A,x} \\ p_{A,y} \\ p_{A,z} \\ 1 \end{bmatrix}, \qquad (3.1)
$$

where the first to third columns of $\mathbf{M}_A$ represent the directions of the x_A axis, y_A axis, and z_A axis viewed from the world coordinate system, respectively. The upper left 3×3 submatrix of $\mathbf{M}_A$ corresponds to a rotation of $-90°$ around the z_W axis to align the axis directions of the world coordinate system with those of the local coordinate system of joint A. The fourth column represents the translation from $\mathbf{O}_W$ to $\mathbf{O}_A$ as seen from the world coordinate system. Using this coordinate transformation, $\mathbf{p}_A = [1\ 0\ 0\ 1]^T$ is transformed into $\mathbf{p}_W = [1\ 0\ 0\ 1]^T$, and $\mathbf{p}_A = [0\ 1\ 0\ 1]^T$ becomes $\mathbf{p}_W = [2\ 1\ 0\ 1]^T$.

Furthermore, the coordinate transformation from these joint coordinate systems to the world coordinate system is called *world coordinate transformation*. The homogeneous transformation matrix $\mathbf{M}$ representing the world coordinate transformation is called *world matrix*. This is because it represents the pose of the joint in the world coordinate system, so we will also call it *world pose*.

3.2.5   Local Pose

The world pose of each part of the skeleton is determined based on the *local coordinate transformation* between two joint coordinate systems connected by a bone. In particular, the coordinate transformation from the child joint coordinate system to the parent joint coordinate system, the *local pose* of the child joint based on the parent joint, is a fundamental element of character animation technologies. The homogeneous transformation matrix representing the local pose is called the *local matrix*.

In humanoid character animation, the local coordinate transformation of the joint is often considered to be represented by a rigid transformation when any body parts are not scaled. The local matrix is represented as a composition of translation and rotation components. Specifically, the coordinate transformation $\mathbf{T}$ representing the translation $[t_x\ t_y\ t_z]^T$ from the origin of the parent joint coordinate system to the origin of the child joint coordinate system, as seen from the parent joint coordinate system, is given by Eq. 3.2. The coordinate transformations $\mathbf{R}_x(\theta_x)$, $\mathbf{R}_y(\theta_y)$, and $\mathbf{R}_z(\theta_z)$ that give rotations of θ_x, θ_y, and θ_z about each axis of the parent joint coordinate system are represented by the homogeneous transformation matrices given by Eqs. 3.3–3.5.

$$
\mathbf{T} = \begin{bmatrix} 1 & 0 & 0 & t_x \\ 0 & 1 & 0 & t_y \\ 0 & 0 & 1 & t_z \\ 0 & 0 & 0 & 1 \end{bmatrix} \in \mathfrak{R}^{4\times4} \,, \tag{3.2}
$$

$$
\mathbf{R}_x(\theta_x) = \begin{bmatrix} 1 & 0 & 0 & 0 \\ 0 & \cos\theta_x & -\sin\theta_x & 0 \\ 0 & \sin\theta_x & \cos\theta_x & 0 \\ 0 & 0 & 0 & 1 \end{bmatrix} \in \mathfrak{R}^{4\times4} \,, \tag{3.3}
$$

$$
\mathbf{R}_y(\theta_y) = \begin{bmatrix} \cos\theta y & 0 & \sin\theta_y & 0 \\ 0 & 1 & 0 & 0 \\ -\sin\theta_y & 0 & \cos\theta_y & 0 \\ 0 & 0 & 0 & 1 \end{bmatrix} \in \mathfrak{R}^{4\times4} \,, \tag{3.4}
$$

$$
\mathbf{R}_z(\theta_z) = \begin{bmatrix} \cos\theta_z & -\sin\theta_z & 0 & 0 \\ \sin\theta_z & \cos\theta_z & 0 & 0 \\ 0 & 0 & 1 & 0 \\ 0 & 0 & 0 & 1 \end{bmatrix} \in \mathfrak{R}^{4\times4} \,. \tag{3.5}
$$

And the joint local matrix $\mathbf{L} \in \mathfrak{R}^{4\times4}$ is given by the matrix product given by Eq. 3.6.

$$
\mathbf{L} = \mathbf{TR} \,, \tag{3.6}
$$

where the rotation matrix $\mathbf{R}$ is either $\mathbf{R}_x$, $\mathbf{R}_y$, $\mathbf{R}_z$, or a combination of these. Looking again at Eq. 3.1, it can be seen that the homogeneous transformation matrix $\mathbf{M}_A$ can be decomposed into a combination of translation and rotation as shown in Eq. 3.7.

$$
\begin{aligned}
\mathbf{p}_W &= \mathbf{T}_A \mathbf{R}_A \mathbf{p}_A \\
&= \mathbf{T}_A \mathbf{R}_z \left(-\frac{\pi}{2}\right) \mathbf{p}_A \\
&= \begin{bmatrix} 1 & 0 & 0 & 1 \\ 0 & 1 & 0 & 1 \\ 0 & 0 & 1 & 0 \\ 0 & 0 & 0 & 1 \end{bmatrix} \begin{bmatrix} 0 & 1 & 0 & 0 \\ -1 & 0 & 0 & 0 \\ 0 & 0 & 1 & 0 \\ 0 & 0 & 0 & 1 \end{bmatrix} \mathbf{p}_A \,.
\end{aligned} \tag{3.7}
$$

The local pose $\mathbf{L}_j$ of the j-th joint is represented by a three-dimensional vector $\mathbf{t}_j \in \mathfrak{R}^3$ representing the translation component and the Euler angles $\{\theta_{j,x}, \theta_{j,y}, \theta_{j,z}\}$ represent the rotation component, and the rotation matrix is composed in the order $\mathbf{R}_j = \mathbf{R}_x(\theta_{j,x})\mathbf{R}_y(\theta_{j,y})\mathbf{R}_z(\theta_{j,z})$. However, for characters where all bone lengths are fixed and do not stretch, the local translation component $\mathbf{t}_j$ of each joint and the corresponding $\mathbf{T}_j$ is considered time-invariant.

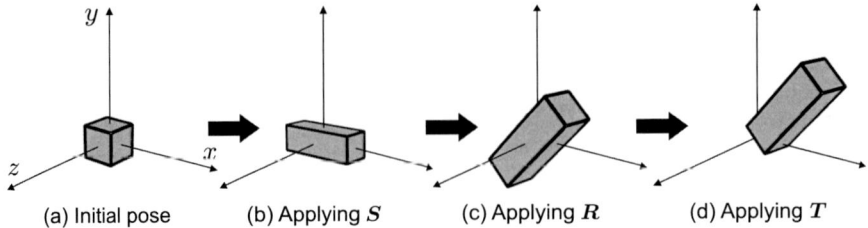

Fig. 3.4 Joint local pose

For characters whose body parts stretch, the translation component **t** is considered to be time-variant, or a matrix $\mathbf{S} \in \Re^{4 \times 4}$ representing the scaling along each axis is introduced to extend the calculation of the local matrix to $\mathbf{L} = \mathbf{TRS}$. When using the skeleton method, animations can be created using the translational and scaling components in addition to the rotation component, especially for models other than articulated bodies, such as facial animation and soft-body characters.

For example, if a coordinate transformation represented by a local matrix $\mathbf{L} = \mathbf{TRS}$ including scaling is applied to a cube as shown in Fig. 3.4a, a rectangular box that is stretched along each axis by the scale component $\mathbf{S}$ is obtained as shown in Fig. 3.4b. Then, the orientation of the rectangular box is determined by the rotation component $\mathbf{R}$ as shown in Fig. 3.4c. Finally, the center of the box is translated to the position corresponding to $\mathbf{T}$ to obtain the pose in Fig. 3.4d. Note that due to the non-commutativity of matrix multiplication, changing the multiplication order to $\mathbf{TRS}$ can cause distortion in the coordinate transformation result.

3.2.6 Forward Kinematics

The skeleton poses with all bone lengths fixed are operated by specifying the local rotation of each joint individually. For example, the pose of the arm-like skeleton is determined by specifying the shoulder rotation, the elbow flexion, and the wrist rotation, respectively. In this case, the position and orientation of the wrist in the world coordinate system must be calculated to determine the distance between the character and an external object. Such a calculation procedure to determine the world pose of each joint based on the local pose of all joints is called *forward kinematics* or *FK* for short.

To explain the specific computation procedure of FK, we use a skeleton that connects joints 1 to 3 in series through two bones, as shown in Fig. 3.5. First, the local coordinate system of joint 1 coincides with the world coordinate system. That is, for any coordinate **p** viewed from the local coordinate system of joint 1, the coordinate $\mathbf{M}_1\mathbf{p}$ after the world coordinate transformation is always equal to **p**, so it can be seen that the world pose $\mathbf{M}_1$ of joint 1 is the unit matrix **I**. Since joint 1 is the root, the local matrix $\mathbf{L}_1$ holds that $\mathbf{L}_1 = \mathbf{M}_1 = \mathbf{I}$.

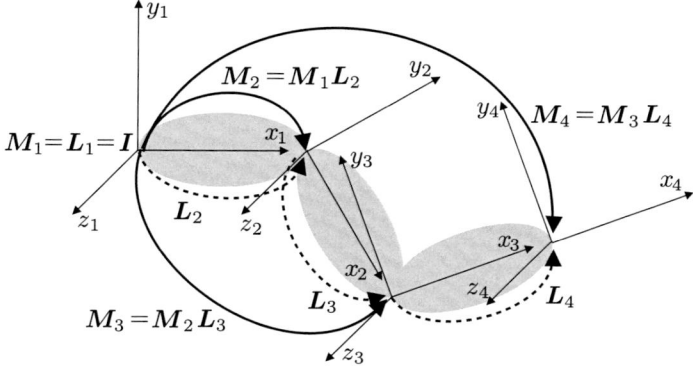

Fig. 3.5 Forward kinematics of a 3-bone skeleton

Next, looking at the local coordinate system of joint 2, the origin is on the x_1 axis of the local coordinate system of joint 1, and it rotates in the negative direction around the axis parallel to the z_1 axis. Therefore, the local matrix $\mathbf{L}_2$ of joint 2 is represented as the composite transformation $\mathbf{L}_2 = \mathbf{T}_2\mathbf{R}_2$ of the negative rotation $\mathbf{R}_2$ around the z_1 axis and the translation $\mathbf{T}_2$ in the positive direction of the x_1 axis. At this point, the world pose $\mathbf{M}_2$ of joint 2 is obtained as the coordinate transformation $\mathbf{M}_2 = \mathbf{M}_1\mathbf{L}_2$ of the local pose $\mathbf{L}_2$ by the world matrix $\mathbf{M}_1$ of joint 1. Similarly, the local pose of joint 3 $\mathbf{L}_3 = \mathbf{T}_3\mathbf{R}_3$ is determined by the translation and rotation with respect to the coordinate system of joint 2. The world pose is obtained as $\mathbf{M}_3 = \mathbf{M}_2\mathbf{L}_3 = \mathbf{L}_1\mathbf{L}_2\mathbf{L}_3$ using the world matrix $\mathbf{M}_2$ of its parent joint.

In this way, the world coordinate transformation of any joint can be determined by sequentially accumulating all local coordinate transformations of joints from the root to that joint. To organize the above relationship, the world matrix $\mathbf{M}_j$ of joint j is expressed as the product of the world matrix $\mathbf{M}_{\rho(j)}$ of the parent joint $\rho(j)$ and the local matrix $\mathbf{L}_j$, as shown in Eq. 3.8.

$$\begin{aligned} \mathbf{M}_j &= \mathbf{M}_{\rho(j)}\mathbf{L}_j \\ &= \mathbf{M}_{\rho(j)}\mathbf{T}_j\mathbf{R}_j \ . \end{aligned} \tag{3.8}$$

Since there is no parent joint at the root, its world matrix is equal to the local matrix, and $\mathbf{M}_{\text{root}} = \mathbf{T}_{\text{root}}\mathbf{R}_{\text{root}}$ holds, where $\mathbf{T}_{\text{root}}$ and $\mathbf{R}_{\text{root}}$ represent the position and orientation of the character in the world coordinate system, respectively, both of which can change over time.

3.2.7 Pose and Motion

The skeleton pose of a humanoid character, excluding the root, is determined only by the rotation component $\mathbf{R}_j$, and thus by the local rotation angles $\{\theta_{j,x}, \theta_{j,y}, \theta_{j,z}\}$, if all translation components $\mathbf{T}_j$ are constant. In the following sections of this chapter, the vector of all local rotation angles is called *pose vector* $\boldsymbol{\theta}$.

$$\boldsymbol{\theta} = [\theta_1 \ \theta_2 \ \theta_3 \ \cdots \ \theta_{3J}]^T \in \mathfrak{R}^{3J} \ , \tag{3.9}$$

where J denotes the number of joints, and the joint rotation angles $\{\theta_{j,x}, \theta_{j,y}, \theta_{j,z}\}$ correspond to the $(3j-2)$-th, $(3j-1)$-th, and $(3j)$-th components, respectively. The world matrix $\mathbf{M}_j$ of each joint is obtained by FK computation with respect to the pose vector $\boldsymbol{\theta}$.

Animation based on the skeleton method is created by specifying poses that change over time. We will refer to the animation represented as a time series of the pose vector as *motion*, and the time series of each local rotation parameter as an *animation curve*. In other words, motion is a multidimensional time series composed of animation curves proportional to the number of joints.

Computer animation is usually represented by temporally discretized data. For example, in an animation video with a frame rate of 30 fps, the number of frames F to be displayed equals 30 times the playback time in seconds. Therefore, if the pose is specified for each frame, the motion data is represented as a $3J \times F$ matrix as shown in Eq. 3.10, where the pose vector at the f-th frame is $\boldsymbol{\theta}_f$.

$$[\boldsymbol{\theta}_1 \ \boldsymbol{\theta}_2 \ \cdots \ \boldsymbol{\theta}_F] = \begin{bmatrix} \theta_{1,1} & \theta_{2,1} & \cdots & \theta_{F,1} \\ \theta_{1,2} & \ddots & \ddots & \vdots \\ \vdots & \ddots & \ddots & \vdots \\ \theta_{1,3J} & \theta_{2,3J} & \cdots & \theta_{F,3J} \end{bmatrix} \in \mathfrak{R}^{3J \times F} \ , \tag{3.10}$$

where $\theta_{f,j}$ represents the j-th rotation parameter at the f-th frame. Furthermore, the matrix shown in Eq. 3.10 can be represented by the $3JF$ dimensional vector shown in Eq. 3.11.

$$\begin{aligned} \boldsymbol{\Theta} &= \begin{bmatrix} \boldsymbol{\theta}_1^T & \cdots & \boldsymbol{\theta}_F^T \end{bmatrix}^T \\ &= \begin{bmatrix} \theta_{1,1} \ \theta_{1,2} & \cdots & \theta_{1,3J} \ \theta_{2,1} & \cdots & \theta_{F,3J} \end{bmatrix}^T \in \mathfrak{R}^{3JF} \ , \end{aligned} \tag{3.11}$$

where $\boldsymbol{\Theta}$ is referred to as a *motion vector*.

This method of digitizing pre-created poses for all frames is intuitive and has the advantage of being played back by a simple mechanism. However, hundreds of poses must be created for even a few seconds of motion, which can easily increase both labor and data size. Furthermore, in applications where a constant frame rate cannot be guaranteed, the pose must be determined at any time between adjacent frames. Therefore, the *keyframe animation* technique is widely used to create the joint pose only at some important moments during the motion. In skeleton animation, a *keyframe* refers to the time when the joint pose is specified, and the joint pose is called a key pose or simply a key. The pose at any given time is computed by *sampling*, which can be achieved by interpolating the discrete set of keyframes.

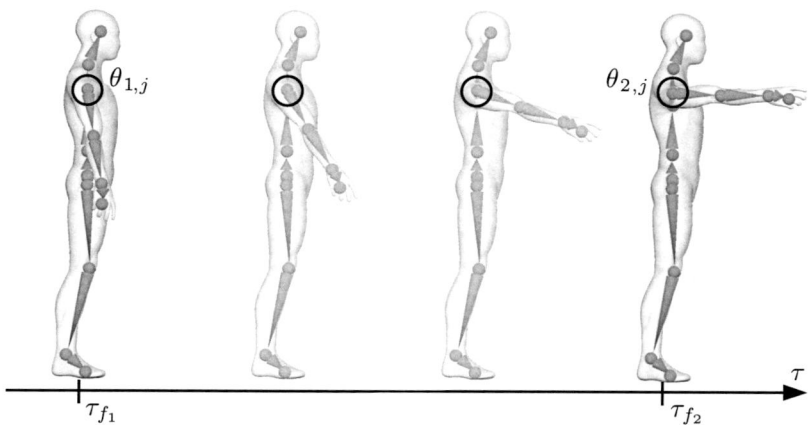

Fig. 3.6 Motion production by the keyframe method

The specific calculation procedure of keyframe interpolation is explained using the right arm swing motion shown in Fig. 3.6. In this example, the keys for the right shoulder joint j are set at frames f_1 and f_2, and the time at each frame is τ_{f_1} and τ_{f_2}, and the rotation angle of the right shoulder is $\theta_{1,j}$ and $\theta_{2,j}$, respectively. The simplest method is to sample the joint angle $\theta_j(\tau)$ at given time τ ($\tau_{f_1} \le \tau \le \tau_{f_2}$) by linearly interpolating two adjacent keyframes, that is, the angle $\theta_j(\tau)$ in the interval $[\tau_{f_1}, \tau_{f_2}]$ is determined by piecewise linear interpolation shown by Eq. 3.12.

$$\theta_j(\tau) = \frac{\tau_{f_2} - \tau}{\tau_{f_2} - \tau_{f_1}}\theta_{1,j} + \frac{\tau - \tau_{f_1}}{\tau_{f_2} - \tau_{f_1}}\theta_{2,j} \tag{3.12}$$

This piecewise linear interpolation is often used in interactive animations such as games because it can be processed quickly with simple calculations, although it causes discontinuous velocity changes at keyframes. Various spline interpolation algorithms are used to interpolate three or more keyframes smoothly and control the gradient of the animation curve at keyframes.

3.3 Inverse Kinematics

Inverse kinematics or *IK* for short, is used to compute the local pose of each joint to satisfy the world pose specified for one or more joints. IK comes from the inverse problem of forward kinematics, which derives the world pose from the local pose. In this section, we introduce the IK algorithm for determining the local rotation of each joint to satisfy the joint pose specified in the world coordinate system. Also in this section, we conveniently denote the operation to obtain the position vector representing the world coordinates from the world matrix $\mathbf{M}_j$ as $\mathrm{pos}\left(\mathbf{M}_j\right) = \mathbf{p}_j$, and the operation to obtain the rotation matrix representing the orientation in the world coordinate system as rot $(\mathbf{M}_j) = \mathbf{R}_j$.

The typical IK problem can be defined as an optimization problem, as shown in Eq. 3.13.

$$\min_{\theta} E(\theta, \overline{\theta})$$

$$\text{subject to } \forall b, \ C_b(\theta) = 0 \ , \tag{3.13}$$

where the objective function $E(\theta, \overline{\theta})$ is a scalar function that evaluates the amount of change from the source pose $\overline{\theta}$ to the pose θ corrected by IK. By finding a solution that minimizes this objective function, we aim to reduce the correction by IK and preserve the source pose. $\{C_b|b \in \{1, \ldots, B\}\}$ correspond to the constraint functions for the B conditions that the deformed pose should satisfy. For example, the constraint function to fit the head to the specified position $\mathbf{p}_{\text{head}}$ is expressed as $C(\theta) = \|\mathbf{p}_{\text{head}} - \text{pos}(\mathbf{M}_{\text{head}}(\theta))\|$ where $\| \cdot \|$ is the Euclidean norm.

This formulation shows that IK is often used to correct a given pose. The pose is corrected to satisfy constraints on joint position and orientation while minimizing the amount of change from the reference pose. For example, a standing pose on uneven ground can be synthesized by correcting the foot position of a standing pose on a flat plane. Similarly, suppose a pose is given with the right fingertip pointing at a target. In that case, IK can be used to correct the direction of the fingertip so that it follows the movement of the target position while maintaining the original whole-body pose as much as possible.

However, there may be no solution for a given set of constraints. For example, if both hand positions are constrained simultaneously, no pose satisfies both constrained positions if the target position is farther than the body size. The constraint function can be relaxed as an objective function to avoid such computational infeasibility, as shown in Eq. 3.14.

$$\min_{\theta} \left[E(\theta, \overline{\theta}) + \sum_b w_b C_b(\theta) \right] , \tag{3.14}$$

where w_b represents the importance of each constraint. For example, if both hand positions are constrained to a point farther than the body size, increasing the weight associated with the right-hand constraint will prioritize, the right hand to approach the constraint point. On the other hand, the error of the left hand is not emphasized, resulting in a significant deviation from the target position. Increasing w_b emphasizes the achievement of the constraints, allowing large deformations from the source pose.

3.3.1 Analytical IK Methods for Limbs

One of the typical uses of IK is to correct the position and orientation of the effectors, and correcting only the pose of the arms and legs is sufficient in many cases. As an IK technique targeting only such limbs, an analytical algorithm has been proposed for a 7-degree-of-freedom skeleton [6]. This method makes two assumptions: the arm skeleton consists of the shoulder, elbow, and wrist, and the leg skeleton consists of the hip, knee, and ankle. First, the elbow and knee perform only one-axis bending and can only rotate in the range of 0 to 180° from the state where the arm is extended in a straight in both directions. Then, joints other than the elbow and knee can rotate about three axes. For a skeleton with a total of 7 degrees of freedom, the local rotation of the three joints is determined analytically by specifying the position of the wrist and the orientation of the hand based on the coordinate system of the shoulder joint or the position of the ankle and the orientation of the foot in the coordinate system of the hip joint.

The specific calculation procedure is explained using the left arm of the character shown in Fig. 3.7a. In the world coordinate system, the local coordinate system of the left shoulder joint is assumed to have the x axis to the left, the y axis vertically up, and the z axis toward the front of the body. The initial pose of the skeleton is such that the upper arm, forearm, and hand are all extended in a straight line in the horizontal left direction, i.e., on the x-axis of the shoulder joint, and the local rotations of the three joints at this time are all $\mathbf{R}_1 = \mathbf{I}$, $\mathbf{R}_2 = \mathbf{I}$, and $\mathbf{R}_3 = \mathbf{I}$. The translation matrix corresponding to the length l_1 of the upper arm is $\mathbf{T}_2$, the translation matrix corresponding to the length l_2 of the forearm is $\mathbf{T}_3$, and the positions of the shoulder, elbow, and wrist are denoted as $\mathbf{p}_1$, $\mathbf{p}_2$, and $\mathbf{p}_3$, respectively. The world matrix of the target wrist is denoted as $\mathbf{G}$, and the world coordinates as $\mathbf{g} = \mathrm{pos}(\mathbf{G})$.

First, the elbow bending angle θ_2, i.e., the local rotation angle around the y axis, is determined. Given a triangle composed of a vector of length l_1 representing the upper arm, a vector of length l_2 representing the forearm, and a vector connecting the shoulder and the target position of the wrist $\mathbf{g} - \mathbf{p}_1$, the angle θ_2 at the vertex corresponding to the elbow can be uniquely determined using the law of cosines.

$$\theta_2 = \pi - \arccos\left(\frac{l_1^2 + l_2^2 - d_{1 \to g}^2}{2 l_1 l_2}\right), \tag{3.15}$$

where $d_{1 \to g} = \|\mathbf{g} - \mathbf{p}_1\|$. Note that if the numerator is greater than the denominator inside arccos, i.e., if the target position is further away than the length of the upper arm and forearm, the calculation becomes infeasible because it exceeds the range of the inverse cosine. This corresponds to the structural limitation that the character cannot reach the target position no matter how far the arm is extended.

Next, the shoulder rotation $\mathbf{R}_1$ is determined in two steps. In the first step, the rotation $\theta_{1,y}$ around the y-axis to align the wrist with the x-axis (Fig. 3.7c) is determined from the pose with the elbow bent by θ_2 (Fig. 3.7b). The angle $\theta_{1,y}$ of the upper

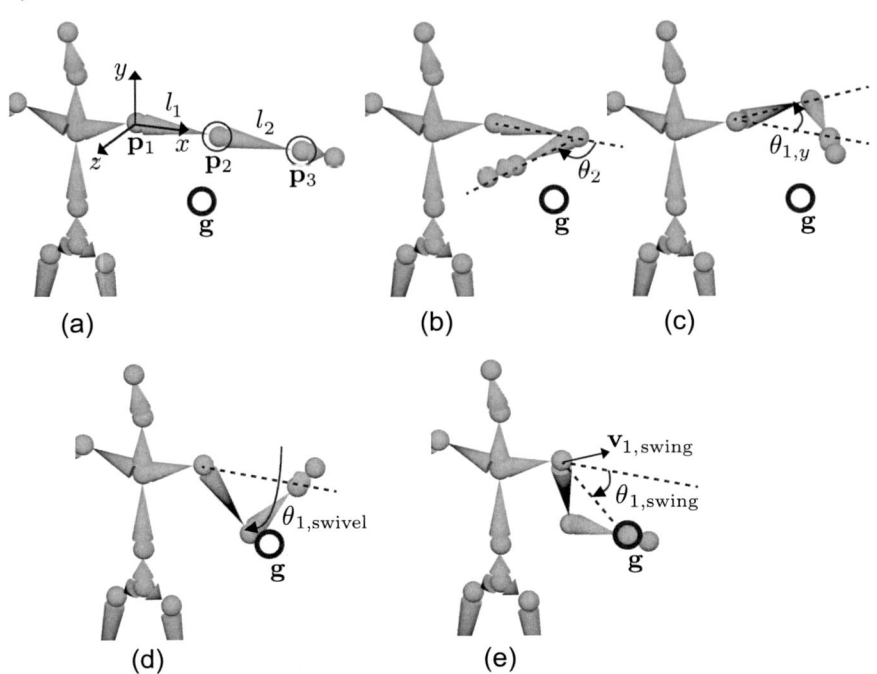

Fig. 3.7 Analytical IK for 7-DOF skeleton

arm with respect to the line segment from the shoulder to the wrist can be uniquely calculated using the law of cosines.

$$\theta_{1,y} = \arccos\left(\frac{l_1^2 + d_{1\to g}^2 - l_2^2}{2l_1 d_{1\to g}}\right). \tag{3.16}$$

In the following second step, as shown in Fig. 3.7e, a rotation is determined to align the wrist $\mathbf{p}_3$ with the target position $\mathbf{g}$. Since the wrist is on a line parallel to the x-axis due to the previous calculations, the rotation axis $\mathbf{v}_{1,\text{swing}}$ and the rotation angle $\theta_{1,\text{swing}}$ around the axis can be determined to match the target position using the dot product and cross product, as shown in Eq. 3.18.

$$\mathbf{v}_{1,\text{swing}} = \frac{\mathbf{v}_x \otimes (\mathbf{g} - \mathbf{p}_1)}{\|\mathbf{v}_x \otimes (\mathbf{g} - \mathbf{p}_1)\|}, \tag{3.17}$$

$$\theta_{1,\text{swing}} = \arccos\left(\frac{\mathbf{v}_x \odot (\mathbf{g} - \mathbf{p}_1)}{d_{1\to g}}\right), \tag{3.18}$$

where $\otimes$ and $\odot$ represent the cross product and dot product of the 3D vectors, respectively. By setting the composite rotation obtained by these two-step calculations, $\mathbf{R}(\mathbf{v}_{1,\text{swing}}, \theta_{1,\text{swing}})\mathbf{R}_y(\theta_1)$, as the local rotation of the shoulder joint, the wrist can be adjusted to the target position.

Furthermore, even if the positions of the shoulder and wrist are fixed, there remains a degree of rotation about the line passing through them that allows the elbow to move. This *swivel angle* $\theta_{1,\text{swivel}}$/can be specified arbitrarily to determine the position of the elbow. Precisely, the rotation around the x-axis in the pose shown in Fig. 3.7d corresponds to the swivel angle. An arm pose can be computed that aligns the wrist with the target position, while the swivel angle θ_{swivel} can be obtained by determining the rotation of the shoulder joint in the manner of Eq. 3.19.

$$\mathbf{R}_1 = \mathbf{R}(\mathbf{v}_{1,\text{swing}}, \theta_{1,\text{swing}})\mathbf{R}_x(\theta_{1,\text{swivel}})\mathbf{R}_y(\theta_{1,y}) \ . \tag{3.19}$$

Finally, the local rotation of the wrist $\mathbf{R}_3$ is determined so that the world matrix of the wrist joint matches the specified value $\mathbf{G}$.

$$\mathbf{R}_3 = (\mathbf{R}_1\mathbf{T}_2\mathbf{R}_2\mathbf{T}_3)^{-1}\mathbf{G} \ . \tag{3.20}$$

Consequently, the limb pose can be calculated analytically using the arccosine when determining the elbow angle and basic geometric operations such as dot products and cross products.

In addition, when correcting a given pose in advance, the swivel angle calculated from the original arm pose is used to minimize the appearance of pose changes. However, the world pose of the elbow changes not only by the swivel angle but also by $\mathbf{R}(\mathbf{v}_{1,\text{swing}}, \theta_{1,\text{swing}})$. Therefore, a result similar to the source pose is not necessarily obtained if a target position far from the original wrist position is specified.

3.3.2 Gradient Descent Method-Based IK

The world pose of the skeletal joints changes nonlinearly with respect to the changes in the pose vector $\boldsymbol{\theta}$. In particular, deeper joint hierarchy makes the relationship between $\boldsymbol{\theta}$ and the world pose more complex. However, the joint world poses, and the angular displacement can be considered to have a locally linear relationship when the angular displacement of each joint rotation is small. Based on this differential relationship, a gradient-based method gradually corrects the pose to bring the specified joint closer to the target world pose by repeating linear operations. This approach is a type of numerical optimization called the *gradient descent method* and is known in IK as the *Jacobi method*.

For example, if we denote the world position of the i-th joint as $\text{pos}(\mathbf{M}_j) = \mathbf{p}_j = [p_{j,x} \ p_{j,y} \ p_{j,z}]^T \in \mathfrak{R}^3$, the small displacement $\delta\mathbf{p}_i \in \mathfrak{R}^3$ with respect to the small angular change $\delta\boldsymbol{\theta} \in \mathfrak{R}^{3J}$ is expressed as in Eq. 3.21 using the gradient $\frac{\partial \mathbf{p}_i}{\partial \boldsymbol{\theta}}$ of the joint position $\mathbf{p}_i$ with respect to the pose vector $\boldsymbol{\theta}$.

$$\delta\mathbf{p}_i = \frac{\partial\mathbf{p}_i}{\partial\boldsymbol{\theta}}\delta\boldsymbol{\theta} \ . \tag{3.21}$$

This partial differential matrix $\frac{\partial \mathbf{p}_i}{\partial \boldsymbol{\theta}}$ is called the *Jacobian matrix*, and it represents the relationship between the small changes in each joint angle and the small changes in each component of the joint coordinates. Specifically, as shown in Eq. 3.22, it is composed of the partial derivatives of each joint coordinate with respect to each joint angle.

$$\frac{\partial\mathbf{p}_i}{\partial\boldsymbol{\theta}} = \begin{bmatrix} \frac{\partial p_{j,x}}{\partial\theta_1} & \frac{\partial p_{j,x}}{\partial\theta_2} & \cdots & \frac{\partial p_{j,x}}{\partial\theta_{3J}} \\ \frac{\partial p_{j,y}}{\partial\theta_1} & \frac{\partial p_{j,y}}{\partial\theta_2} & \cdots & \frac{\partial p_{j,y}}{\partial\theta_{3J}} \\ \frac{\partial p_{j,z}}{\partial\theta_1} & \frac{\partial p_{j,z}}{\partial\theta_2} & \cdots & \frac{\partial p_{j,z}}{\partial\theta_{3J}} \end{bmatrix} \in \mathfrak{R}^{3\times 3J} \ . \tag{3.22}$$

The partial derivative of the coordinate value of joint i $(i \geq j)$ with respect to the rotation $\theta_{j,x} = \theta_{3j-2}$ about the x-axis of any joint j can be obtained by Eq. 3.23.

$$\begin{bmatrix} \frac{\partial p_{i,x}}{\partial\theta_{3j-2}} \\ \frac{\partial p_{i,y}}{\partial\theta_{3j-2}} \\ \frac{\partial p_{i,z}}{\partial\theta_{3j-2}} \\ 0 \end{bmatrix} = \mathbf{T}_1\mathbf{R}_1\cdots\mathbf{T}_j\left(\frac{\partial\mathbf{R}_x(\theta_{3j-2})}{\partial\theta_{3j-2}}\mathbf{R}_y(\theta_{3j-1})\mathbf{R}_z(\theta_{3j})\right)\cdots\mathbf{T}_i\mathbf{R}_i\begin{bmatrix} 0 \\ 0 \\ 0 \\ 1 \end{bmatrix} \ . \tag{3.23}$$

On the other hand, if $i < j$, joint j is a descendant of joint i and does not affect $\mathbf{p}_i$, so $\frac{\partial\mathbf{p}_i}{\partial\theta_{3j-2}} = \mathbf{0}$. This relation holds for the world coordinates of any joint i with respect to the rotation θ_{3j-1} around the y-axis and the rotation θ_{3j} around the z-axis of joint j. In the following, the Jacobian matrix $\frac{\partial\mathbf{p}_i}{\partial\boldsymbol{\theta}}$ will be denoted as $\mathbf{P}'_i$.

The geometric interpretation of the Jacobian matrix is shown in Fig. 3.8a. In this example, if the root is rotated by $\delta\theta_1$, infinitesimal displacement of the effector $\frac{\partial\mathbf{p}}{\partial\theta_1}$ occurs perpendicular to the line segment connecting the root and the effector. Similarly, $\delta\theta_2$ and $\delta\theta_3$ also cause displacement in the effector, but the direction varies depending on the skeleton pose. Furthermore, if the angular displacement of the three joints is of the same magnitude, it is obvious that the joints further away from the effector will cause a larger displacement. The Jacobian matrix contains the multidimensional gradient information of the joint position with respect to the pose vector in a single matrix. The Jacobian matrix $\mathbf{P}'_i$ provides a linear transformation from the infinitesimal change of the pose vector to the infinitesimal displacement of the i-th joint. Therefore, the displacement of the pose vector that satisfies the specified small change of the joint coordinate can be calculated using the inverse transformation, as shown in Fig. 3.8b.

However, since $\mathbf{P}'_i$ is a non-square matrix, its inverse does not exist. Therefore, we use the *pseudoinverse matrix*, also called the Moore-Penrose pseudoinverse matrix

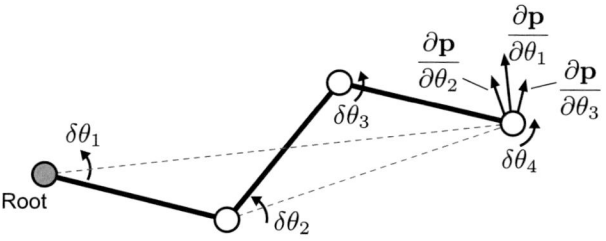

(a) Derivative of effector displacement w.r.t. joint angles

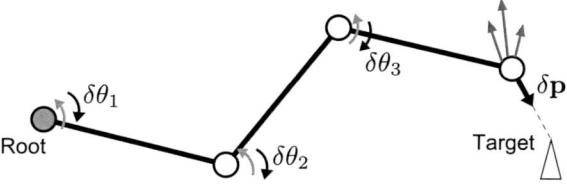

(b) Angular displacement satisfying target displacement of effector

Fig. 3.8 Geometric interpretation of the Jacobian matrix and its application to IK

or the generalized inverse matrix. The Jacobian matrix $\mathbf{P}'_i$ discussed in this chapter is a wide matrix, so its pseudoinverse matrix pinv$(\mathbf{P}'_i)$ is defined by Eq. 3.24.

$$\text{pinv}\left(\mathbf{P}'_i\right) = \mathbf{P}_i'^{T}\left(\mathbf{P}'_i\mathbf{P}_i'^{T}\right)^{-1} . \tag{3.24}$$

The IK calculation to find the pose displacement from the infinitesimal displacement of the joint coordinates using pinv $\left(\mathbf{P}'_i\right)$ is represented by Eq. 3.25.

$$\delta\boldsymbol{\theta} = \text{pinv}\left(\mathbf{P}'_i\right)\delta\mathbf{p}_i . \tag{3.25}$$

From the definition of Eq. 3.24, it is obvious that the pseudoinverse matrix satisfies $\mathbf{P}'_i\,\text{pinv}\left(\mathbf{P}'_i\right) = \mathbf{I}$. Therefore, multiplying $\mathbf{P}'_i$ from the left on both sides of Eq. 3.25 gives the same equation as the FK calculation (Eq. 3.21), as shown in Eq. 3.26.

$$\mathbf{P}'_i\delta\boldsymbol{\theta} = \mathbf{P}'_i\text{pinv}\left(\mathbf{P}'_i\right)\delta\mathbf{p}_i ,$$
$$\mathbf{P}'_i\delta\boldsymbol{\theta} = \delta\mathbf{p}_i . \tag{3.26}$$

The pose displacement $\delta\boldsymbol{\theta}$ obtained using such a pseudoinverse matrix is one of the feasible solutions that satisfy the joint coordinate displacement $\delta\mathbf{p}$ while minimizing the L^2-norm $\|\delta\boldsymbol{\theta}\|^2$. This is a desirable property in CG animation production. For example, it is used for pose correction to ensure that the character's feet are firmly planted on the ground or to correct for minor positional deviations in various parts of the body. The amount of change from the source pose should be minimized to preserve the original content and style of the source motion.

With the method described above, the infinitesimal displacement of the pose vector can be obtained from the infinitesimal displacement of the joint coordinates. However, the displacement from the joint coordinates to the target position is often large. Therefore, as shown in the procedure from Eq. 3.27 to 3.29, the Jacobian IK iteratively makes small adjustments to the pose vector so that the joint gradually approaches the target position.

$$\delta \mathbf{p}_i \leftarrow \beta_i \left(\mathbf{g}_i - \mathbf{p}_i \right) , \tag{3.27}$$

$$\delta \theta \leftarrow \text{pinv} \left(\mathbf{P}'_i \right) \delta \mathbf{p}_i , \tag{3.28}$$

$$\theta \leftarrow \theta + \delta \theta , \tag{3.29}$$

where β_i $(0 < \beta_i \leq 1)$ is a coefficient that determines the target displacement from the current position of the i-th joint to the target position. Thus, the Jacobian IK requires iterative computations, and each iteration process involves the inverse of a high-dimensional matrix, which is computationally expensive.

Depending on the pose, the square matrix $\mathbf{P}'_i \mathbf{P}'_i{}^T \in \mathfrak{R}^{3 \times 3}$ in the formula for computing the pseudoinverse matrix may become rank deficient, making it impossible to calculate the inverse. A method adds an appropriate constant α to all diagonal elements in such cases.

$$\text{pinv} \left(\mathbf{P}'_i, \alpha \right) = \mathbf{P}'_i{}^T \left(\mathbf{P}'_i \mathbf{P}'_i{}^T + \alpha \mathbf{I} \right)^{-1} . \tag{3.30}$$

This method is called *damped pseudoinverse matrix* and is used to solve IK stably. Note that this method is also called the damped least squares (DLS) or Levenberg-Marquardt method.

The Jacobi method can also be extended to problems with multiple constraints. For example, for a problem that simultaneously constrains joints i and k, the IK solution given by Eq. 3.31 can be obtained by vertically aligning the Jacobian matrix $\mathbf{P}'_i$ for joint i and $\mathbf{P}'_k$ for joint k, and the target displacement amount $\delta \mathbf{p}_i$ for joint i and $\delta \mathbf{p}_k$ for joint k.

$$\delta \theta = \text{pinv} \left(\begin{bmatrix} \mathbf{P}'_i \\ \mathbf{P}'_k \end{bmatrix} \right) \begin{bmatrix} \delta \mathbf{p}_i \\ \delta \mathbf{p}_k \end{bmatrix} . \tag{3.31}$$

3.3.3 Formulation as Quadratic Programming Problem

In the gradient descent method using the pseudoinverse matrix, we seek a pose vector displacement that minimizes the sum of squares of the joint angle changes. This optimization problem can be formulated as a constrained minimization problem, as shown in Eq. 3.32.

$$\min_{\delta\theta} \frac{1}{2}\|\delta\theta\|^2$$

$$\text{subject to } \mathbf{P}'_i\delta\theta = \delta\mathbf{p} \; . \tag{3.32}$$

This problem can be further extended by adding various constraints related to pose changes. A representative method is the IK method, which introduces constraints expressed by linear inequalities [7]. This method relaxes the constraint of Eq. 3.32 as an objective function expressed as the unconstrained minimization problem shown in Eq. 3.33.

$$\min_{\delta\theta} \frac{1}{2}\left\{\|\delta\theta\|^2 + \|\delta\mathbf{p} - \mathbf{P}'_i\delta\theta\|^2\right\} \; . \tag{3.33}$$

This method introduces an inequality constraint $\mathbf{c}^l \leq \mathbf{C}\delta\theta \leq \mathbf{c}^u$, where $\mathbf{C}$ is a coefficient matrix associated with the constraint, $\mathbf{c}^l$ and $\mathbf{c}^u$ are the lower and upper bounds of $\mathbf{C}\delta\theta$, and the inequality $\mathbf{v}_1 \leq \mathbf{v}_2$ about two vectors implies that all elements of $\mathbf{v}_1$ are equal to or less than the corresponding elements of $\mathbf{v}_2$, respectively. By extending Eq. 3.33 and omitting the constant term, we derive the inequality-constrained least squares problem shown in Eq. 3.34.

$$\min_{\delta\theta} \frac{1}{2}\delta\theta^T \left(\mathbf{I} + \mathbf{P}'_i{}^T \mathbf{P}'_i\right)\delta\theta - \left(\delta\mathbf{p}^T\mathbf{P}'_i\right)\delta\theta$$

$$\text{subject to } \mathbf{c}^l \leq \mathbf{C}\delta\theta \leq \mathbf{c}^u \; . \tag{3.34}$$

This optimization problem, which consists of an objective function expressed as a quadratic equation in $\delta\theta$ and constraints expressed as linear inequalities, is a typical *quadratic programming* problem, for which efficient numerical algorithms have been proposed [8].

A typical example of a linear inequality used as a constraint function is the range of joint rotation. For example, if the valid ranges of two rotation parameters θ_1 and θ_2 are $[\theta_1^l, \theta_1^u]$ and $[\theta_2^l, \theta_2^u]$ respectively, both $\theta_1^l \leq \theta_1 + \delta\theta_1 \leq \theta_1^u$ and $\theta_2^l \leq \theta_2 + \delta\theta_2 \leq \theta_2^u$ must be satisfied at each iteration step. The constraints are expressed as follows.

$$\begin{bmatrix} \theta_1^l - \theta_1 \\ \theta_2^l - \theta_2 \end{bmatrix} \leq \begin{bmatrix} 1 & 0 \\ 0 & 1 \end{bmatrix}\begin{bmatrix} \delta\theta_1 \\ \delta\theta_2 \end{bmatrix} \leq \begin{bmatrix} \theta_1^u - \theta_1 \\ \theta_2^u - \theta_2 \end{bmatrix} \; . \tag{3.35}$$

If the j-th joint position is constrained within $[\mathbf{p}^l, \mathbf{p}^u]$, the approximated coordinates after correction $\mathbf{p} + \mathbf{P}'_j\delta\theta$ should be within the specified range. This inequality constraint is expressed as follows.

$$\mathbf{p}^l - \mathbf{p}_j \leq \mathbf{P}'_j\delta\theta \leq \mathbf{p}^u - \mathbf{p}_j \; . \tag{3.36}$$

Furthermore, the constraint when limiting the range of the j-th joint within $[\mathbf{p}^l, \mathbf{p}^u]$ while setting the rotation range $[\theta^l, \theta^u]$ for all joints is expressed by Eq. 3.37, which combines Eqs. 3.35 and 3.36.

$$\begin{bmatrix} \boldsymbol{\theta}^l - \boldsymbol{\theta} \\ \mathbf{p}_l - \mathbf{p}_i \end{bmatrix} \leq \begin{bmatrix} \mathbf{I} \\ \mathbf{P}'_i \end{bmatrix} \delta\boldsymbol{\theta} \leq \begin{bmatrix} \boldsymbol{\theta}^u - \boldsymbol{\theta} \\ \mathbf{p}_u - \mathbf{p}_i \end{bmatrix}. \qquad (3.37)$$

By designing appropriate inequality constraints, it is possible to compute pose displacements that satisfy various conditions. The final pose can be obtained using the optimized $\delta\boldsymbol{\theta}$ by iteratively updating $\boldsymbol{\theta} \leftarrow \boldsymbol{\theta} + \delta\boldsymbol{\theta}$ in the same procedure as the gradient descent method. However, it is difficult to apply to real-time computation because solving the quadratic programming problem multiple times to obtain a deformed pose requires a significant computational cost. In addition, the specified range is not necessarily strictly satisfied because the displacement constraint is a linear approximation in gradient space.

3.3.4 Heuristic Methods

The gradient descent method and quadratic programming have been widely studied in the field of numerical computation and thoroughly verified in terms of computational accuracy and complexity. However, such a general-purpose numerical method requires redundant computation and memory consumption in character animation. On the other hand, various techniques, referred to as *heuristic methods* or *heuristics*, have been proposed that are specialized for character IK problems. Many heuristic methods do not necessarily have theoretical guarantees regarding computational accuracy, but they are known to achieve empirically sufficient animation quality. Many of these techniques aim at fast computation and are suitable for real-time systems and simple implementation. They are powerful techniques for applications that do not require high accuracy. Several heuristic IK methods use *greedy algorithms*, which quickly find approximate optimal solutions by iteratively finding local optimal solutions. For example, the cyclic coordinate descent (*CCD*) algorithm [9, 10] and the particle *IK* [11] method are widely used.

This chapter introduces the *FABRIK* (Forward And Backward Reaching Inverse Kinematics) algorithm [12], which is used in real-time 3DCG applications. This iterative algorithm is simple to implement and fast to compute. It is stably computed even when multiple constraints are specified for skeletons with branching structures. In FABRIK, two types of computations, backward and forward processes, are repeated alternately. First, in the backward process, all joint positions from the effector to the root are evaluated to satisfy the bone length constraints after the effector is aligned with the target position. In the subsequent forward process, after the root is moved back to its initial position, each joint position from the root to the effector is corrected to satisfy the bone length constraints. This iterative computation results in a pose where the root is always fixed at the initial position, and the effector is closest to the target position. Both of these processes directly manipulate the world position of the joint and apply corrections to satisfy structural constraints such as bone length and joint rotation. In this respect, it is similar to the approach of the particle IK method, but it proposes a more sophisticated computational procedure.

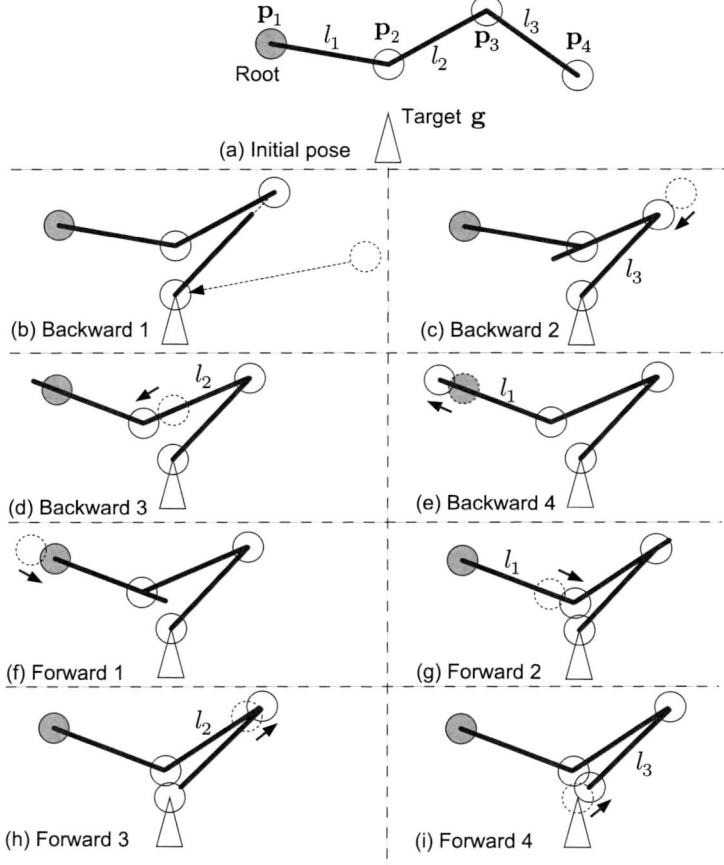

Fig. 3.9 Example of FABRIK calculation procedure

As a simple example, consider a skeleton that connects four joints in series with three bones, as shown in Fig. 3.9a. The points $\mathbf{p}_1$ through $\mathbf{p}_4$ represent the world positions of each joint, and the lengths of the bones are represented as l_1 through l_3. The goal of the IK is to move the effector to the target position $\mathbf{g}$ while keeping the root at its initial position. At the beginning of the backward process, as shown in Fig. 3.9b, the point $\mathbf{p}_4$ is matched to the target position $\mathbf{g}$. As a result, the distance between the points $\mathbf{p}_4$ and $\mathbf{p}_3$ becomes longer than the bone length l_3, so the point $\mathbf{p}_3$ is moved closer to satisfy the bone length l_3 according to Eq. 3.38 (Fig. 3.9c).

$$\mathbf{p}_3 \leftarrow \mathbf{p}_4 + l_3 \frac{\mathbf{p}_3 - \mathbf{p}_4}{\|\mathbf{p}_3 - \mathbf{p}_4\|} \ . \tag{3.38}$$

Then, point $\mathbf{p}_2$ is moved away because the distance between points $\mathbf{p}_2$ and $\mathbf{p}_3$ becomes shorter than l_2, as shown in Fig. 3.9d. The backward process is completed by moving the root $\mathbf{p}_1$ to satisfy the bone length l_1. The correction procedure for the joint coordinates at each step of this backward process can be summarized as in Eq. 3.39.

$$\mathbf{p}_j \leftarrow \mathbf{p}_{j+1} + l_j \frac{\mathbf{p}_j - \mathbf{p}_{j+1}}{\|\mathbf{p}_j - \mathbf{p}_{j+1}\|} \quad , \quad j = J-1, J-2, \ldots, 1 \qquad (3.39)$$

In the following forward process, the root $\mathbf{p}_1$ is first adjusted to the initial position, as shown in Fig. 3.9f. Then, the coordinates of each point are corrected from the root to the effector to satisfy the bone length constraint.

$$\mathbf{p}_j \leftarrow \mathbf{p}_{j-1} + l_{j-1} \frac{\mathbf{p}_j - \mathbf{p}_{j-1}}{\|\mathbf{p}_j - \mathbf{p}_{j-1}\|} \quad , \quad j = 2, 3, \ldots, J \qquad (3.40)$$

Each time these backward and forward processes are performed iteratively, the pose converges so that the effector approaches the target position.

Note that the above explanation is only a summary of the basic concepts. In reality, processes such as calculating local rotations based on joint positions, dealing with joints such as elbows and knees where the axis of rotation is limited, and adjusting joint coordinates according to structural constraints such as the range of joint rotation are necessary. For details on these calculations, please see the original paper [12] and the follow-up paper [13].

3.4 Motion Deformation

This section will summarize the *motion deformation* method for editing a source motion to satisfy geometric and temporal constraints while preserving as much of the original content and style as possible. The simplest motion deformation is to modify each key pose by FK or IK. However, manual editing of densely arranged keyframes, such as motion capture data, requires enormous effort due to the many poses that need to be deformed. Therefore, several techniques have been investigated to naturally deform the entire motion by operations on only a few key frames, taking advantage of the characteristic of motion that poses change smoothly over time. This section describes methods for deforming animation curves by applying time-series processing and numerical optimization techniques to satisfy arbitrary constraints.

3.4.1 Animation Curve Editing

Motion is a collection of time-series data of local rotation parameters of each joint, i.e., animation curves. Various time-series processing techniques are applied to the animation curves, considering each curve as one-dimensional waveform data. In particular, several signal processing techniques are applied to edit the animation curves [14]. For example, in a motion where the character is saying goodbye and vigorously waving their forehand, the animation curve corresponding to the elbow angle would likely be close to a sine wave. Such waveforms can be edited to make the arm swing harder by increasing the amplitude of the sine wave or to make the hand swing softer by increasing the period of the oscillation. Here we summarize four representative techniques based on signal processing techniques.

Motion Displacement Mapping

Motion displacement mapping modifies the source animation curve by adding a displacement curve. In other words, a differential motion $\Delta\boldsymbol{\theta}(\tau)$ is added to the source motion $\boldsymbol{\theta}(\tau)$ to synthesize a deformed curve as $\boldsymbol{\theta}(\tau) + w\Delta\boldsymbol{\theta}(\tau)$, with the addition coefficient w changing over time. Multiple differential motions can also be added to the source motion simultaneously as

$$\boldsymbol{\theta}(\tau) + \sum_b w_b\Delta\boldsymbol{\theta}_b(\tau) , \tag{3.41}$$

where w_b represents the blend coefficient for b-th differential motion $\Delta\boldsymbol{\theta}_b(\tau)$.

This process is also called *additive motion* and adds different variations to a single source motion. These techniques have been used to transform motion smoothly [15] and by reference to joint trajectories given as 2D sketch inputs [16].

Motion Filtering

Motion filtering calculates a linear combination of the poses within a time interval centered on a target frame. For example, motion smoothing can be computed by averaging the poses around a target frame to suppress sudden pose changes. A representative method uses the *convolutional filter* to linearly blend the poses of K frames before and after the target f-th frame as

$$\boldsymbol{\theta}_f + \sum_{i=-K}^{K} k_i\boldsymbol{\theta}_{f+i} , \tag{3.42}$$

where the set of coefficients $\{k_i | i = \{-K, \ldots, 0, \ldots, K\}\}$ are called filters and represent the blend ratio for each frame. For example, a filter that averages $2K + 1$ frames of poses is represented as $\forall i, k_i = 1/(2K + 1)$, and works to smooth the motion. In the example shown in Fig. 3.10, applying the averaging filter to the animation curve shown by the dashed line has suppressed the steep changes in the curve shown by the bold line. Other motion smoothing methods, such as the Gaussian filter, are also used. A method of exaggerating motion changes using the LoG (Laplacian of the Gaussian) filter has also been proposed [17].

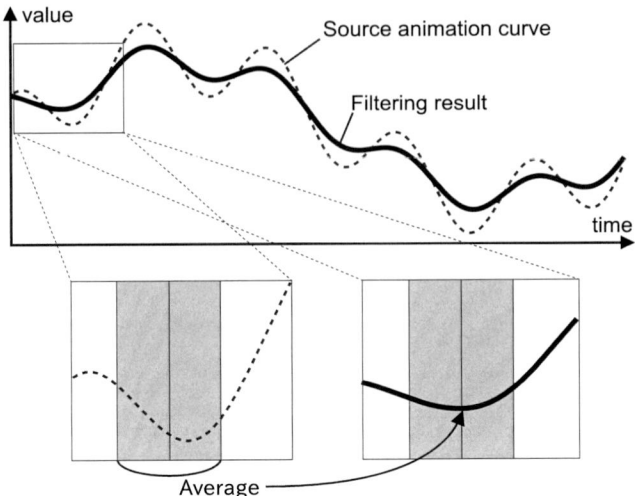

Fig. 3.10 Example of smoothing by convolutional filtering

Note that when filtering for animation curves represented in Euler angles, unintended problems such as gimbal lock and 2π ambiguity can cause problems such as rotation inversion. To avoid such problems, a convolution filter algorithm for quaternions has been proposed [18].

Time Warping

Motion time warping changes the playback speed of the motion or the appearance time of each frame without modifying the poses contained in the motion data. For example, time warping includes slow playback of the entire motion and double-speed playback of only a specific portion. In keyframe animation, changing the time of each keyframe can also be considered a form of time warping.

Time warping is achieved by changing the sampling interval each time. Specifically, when the sampling interval at the i-th display frame is $\Delta\tau_i$, the reference time τ_f corresponding to the f-th display frame is obtained by summing $\tau_f = \sum_{i=1}^{f} \Delta\tau_i$. Then, the pose vector $\theta(\tau_f)$ corresponding to the reference time τ_f is obtained from the motion data by keyframe interpolation. For example, the animation duration equals that of the motion data if all $\Delta\tau_i$ are 1, and $\Delta\tau_i > 1$ results in a shorter duration and faster playback.

In Fig. 3.11, the sampling interval at each frame is represented by a white arrow. In this case, the sampling interval for the input motion changes each time the display frame is updated. For example, the display pose at the fourth frame is sampled at the reference time τ_f in the motion data. This reference time is determined by the sum of the sampling intervals of four frames $\tau_4 = \sum_{i=1}^{4} \Delta\tau_i$, and the pose at this time is sampled by interpolating the two adjacent keyframes. The animation data is thus played back slowly at the beginning, and the sampling interval is expanded to gradually increase the playback speed, as shown in Fig. 3.11.

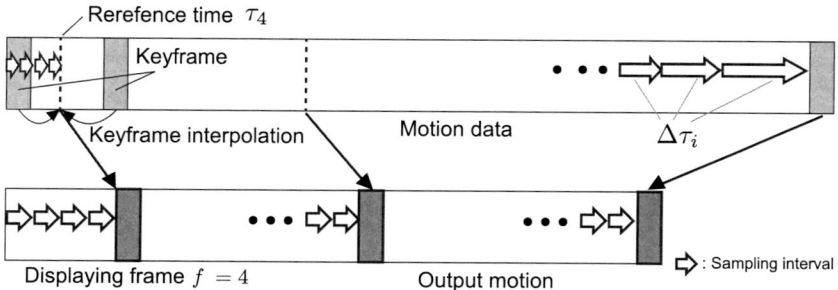

Fig. 3.11 Motion time warping

Using such time warp processing, controlling time-domain expressions such as timing and speed is possible. It is also applied to automatic synchronization of two motions using the dynamic time warping method [19] and example-based retiming techniques [20].

Deformation in the Frequency Domain

Discrete Fourier or discrete cosine transform deform animation curves in the frequency analysis. A representative technique is the application of band-pass filters to motion data [14]. For example, fine fluctuations and abrupt changes in motion can be eliminated by removing high-frequency components. By emphasizing only low-frequency components, the overall action can be exaggerated while preserving the fine behavior of the joints. The frequency domain is also used in motion control techniques by emotional parameters [21] and in motion style translation techniques [22].

3.4.2 Application of Inverse Kinematics

Signal processing techniques can generate a variety of deformed motions by adjusting a small number of control parameters. However, it is unsuitable for deformations that specify geometric constraints, such as joint angles or positions at specific frames. Therefore, an IK technique is used to edit the pose at the specified frame and the surrounding frames to connect smoothly to the deformed frame.

For example, consider motion capture data that records a motion starting from a standing pose and grasping a sphere with the right hand, as shown in the upper left of Fig. 3.12. The purpose of the deformation is to make the character grasp a sphere in a different position. IK is first applied to move the right hand onto the sphere in the time interval when the character must be in contact with the sphere. However, IK cannot be applied to the other time intervals since the path from the upright pose to the sphere is not obvious. This causes a discontinuous pose change at the boundary between the intervals.

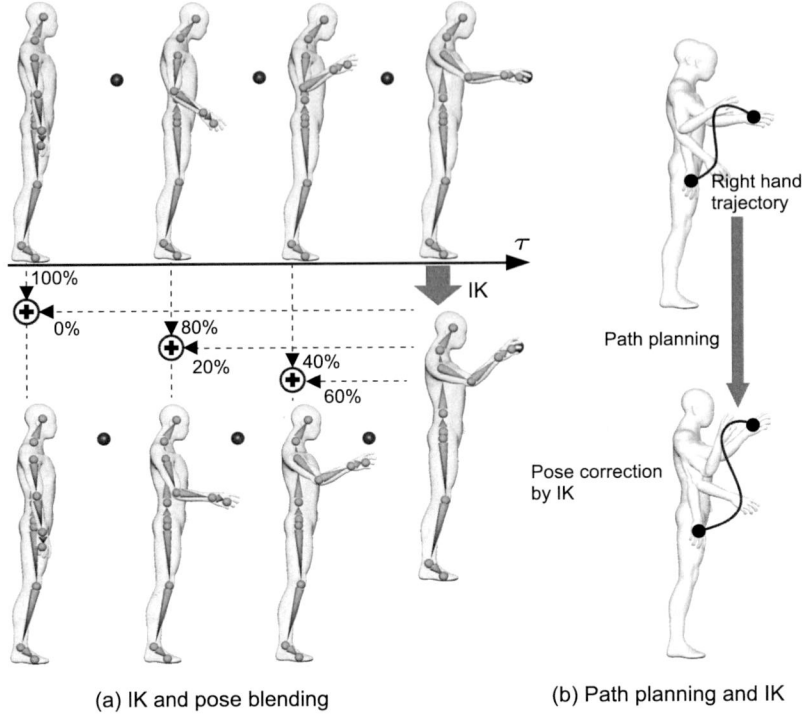

(a) IK and pose blending   (b) Path planning and IK

Fig. 3.12 Motion deformation using inverse kinematics

As a simple solution, a transition interval of a certain length is set before and after the interval where IK is applied, and the deformed pose is blended with the source motion. Within the transition interval, the source motion and the edited pose are blended while changing the blending ratio over time so that it smoothly transitions to the IK correction interval, as shown in Fig. 3.12a. This method can be realized efficiently by simple pose blending, but the time width of the transition interval and the blending ratio must be controlled appropriately.

Alternatively, the constraints of IK can be changed over time. In this method, the motion trajectory of the right hand is generated using a path planning algorithm, as shown in Fig. 3.12b. Then, based on the obtained right-hand trajectory, the entire motion is generated by performing IK at each frame. However, even if the effector's trajectory changes continuously, the pose does not necessarily change smoothly after IK because an infinite number of poses satisfy the trajectory constraints. In the iterative computation used by many IK algorithms, the convergence result varies greatly depending on the initial pose, and problems such as the wrist bending sharply in the opposite direction at any frame may occur. Moreover, it is difficult to predict such problems before performing IK. Therefore, in techniques that use trajectory planning and IK, it is necessary to find a way to ensure continuous pose change [23].

3.4.3 Spacetime Optimization Method

The spacetime optimization method is used to edit the entire motion sequence under arbitrary geometric and temporal constraints. This technique finds the optimal motion Θ that satisfies the constraints specified on multiple joints or frames while minimizing the deformation from the source motion using numerical optimization methods. The spacetime optimization problems are represented by Eq. 3.43.

$$\min_{\Theta} E(\Theta, \overline{\Theta})$$
$$\text{subject to } \forall b, \ C_b(\Theta) = 0 , \tag{3.43}$$

where $E(\Theta, \overline{\Theta})$ is a function that evaluates the amount of change from the source motion $\overline{\Theta}$. By minimizing this objective function, we aim to preserve the features of the source motion. $C_b(\Theta)$ is a constraint function that evaluates the error from the given constraints. Note that inequality constraints can also be given instead of equality constraints, as shown in Eq. 3.44.

$$\min_{\Theta} E(\Theta, \overline{\Theta})$$
$$\text{subject to } \forall b, \ \mathbf{c}_b^l \leq C_b(\Theta) \leq \mathbf{c}_b^u . \tag{3.44}$$

Based on this general formulation, a problem-specific formulation is made according to the purpose of the motion deformation, and a numerical optimization algorithm is suitable for each problem. In particular, it is often possible to apply analytical algorithms by making it a least squares problem that evaluates the amount of change from the deformed source motion by the squared error $E(\Theta, \overline{\Theta}) = \|\Theta - \overline{\Theta}\|^2$. In this case, the motion vector Θ whose partial derivative is $\frac{\partial E}{\partial \Theta} = \mathbf{0}$ is the optimal solution if no constraints are given since this objective function E is convex quadratic. The optimal solution can be found by simply solving a linear equation since $\frac{\partial E}{\partial \Theta}$ is linear. Moreover, it becomes a least squares problem with linear constraints if all constraint functions C_b in Eq. 3.43 are linear equalities, which can be solved using the Lagrange multiplier method. Furthermore, if all constraints C_b in Eq. 3.44 are linear equalities or inequalities, it becomes a quadratic programming problem, which can be solved using numerical methods such as the interior point method.

On the other hand, if it is not necessary to strictly satisfy the constraints and some error is allowed, it can be incorporated as an objective function of the minimization problem, as shown in Eq. 3.45.

$$\min_{\Theta} \left\{ E(\Theta, \overline{\Theta}) + \sum_b w_b C_b(\Theta) \right\} , \tag{3.45}$$

where w_b is a coefficient representing the importance of each constraint, and the larger its value, the more error reduction is expected. When the constraints expressed by linear equalities are relaxed into quadratic forms, such as $C_b(\Theta) = \|C_b\Theta - c_b\|^2$, Eq. 3.45 can be reduced to an unconstrained least squares problem, and several efficient algorithms can be applied. In the following, we will explain specific objective functions, constraint functions, and the procedure for computing solutions.

Similarity to the Source Motion

To preserve the original content of the source motion, the difference from the source motion $\overline{\Theta}$ is evaluated as the objective function. The simplest method is to use the sum of the squares of the differences in each joint rotation angle, as shown by E^s in Eq. 3.46.

$$
\begin{aligned}
E^s &= \frac{1}{2} \sum_f \sum_j \left(\overline{\theta}_{f,j} - \theta_{f,j} \right)^2 \\
&= \frac{1}{2} \left(\Theta - \overline{\Theta} \right)^T \left(\Theta - \overline{\Theta} \right) .
\end{aligned}
\tag{3.46}
$$

This evaluation function E^s is convex quadratic, and its minimum value is given by the solution that satisfies the partial derivative $\frac{\partial E^s}{\partial \Theta} = \Theta - \overline{\Theta}$ equal to $\mathbf{0}$, that is, $\Theta = \overline{\Theta}$.

Angular Velocity Similarity

The angular displacement between adjacent frames, i.e., the similarity of the rotation speed, can be used as an evaluation criterion. This method is used, for example, to inherit the trend of pose changes while significantly modifying the pose at the start and end times of the motion. Specifically, as shown in Eq. 3.47, the objective function is defined by the sum of the squared velocity errors for each animation curve as

$$
\begin{aligned}
E^v &= \frac{1}{2} \sum_{f=1}^{F-1} \sum_j \left\{ \left(\theta_{f,j+1} - \theta_{f,j} \right) - \left(\overline{\theta}_{f,j+1} - \overline{\theta}_{f,j} \right) \right\}^2 \\
&= \frac{1}{2} \sum_{f=1}^{F-1} \left\| \left(\boldsymbol{\theta}_{f+1} - \boldsymbol{\theta}_f \right) - \left(\overline{\boldsymbol{\theta}}_{f+1} - \overline{\boldsymbol{\theta}}_f \right) \right\|^2 \\
&= \frac{1}{2} \left(\mathbf{D}\Theta - \mathbf{D}\overline{\Theta} \right)^T \left(\mathbf{D}\Theta - \mathbf{D}\overline{\Theta} \right) ,
\end{aligned}
\tag{3.47}
$$

where $\mathbf{D}$ is a matrix where each row appears as -1 and 1 in F column increments to calculate the angular difference between adjacent frames for the same joint, as shown in Eq. 3.48.

$$\mathbf{D} = \begin{bmatrix} -1 & 0 & \cdots & 0 & 1 & 0 & \cdots 0 \\ 0 & -1 & 0 & \cdots & 0 & 1 & 0 & \vdots \\ \vdots & \ddots & \ddots & \ddots & \ddots & \ddots & \ddots & \vdots \\ 0 & \cdots & 0 & -1 & 0 & \cdots & 0 & 1 \end{bmatrix} \in \Re^{3J(F-1)\times 3JF} \qquad (3.48)$$

The evaluation function E^{v} is a convex quadratic equation like E^{s}, so it gives a minimum value at the solution where $\frac{\partial E^{\mathrm{v}}}{\partial \theta} = \mathbf{D}^T \mathbf{D} \Theta - \mathbf{D}^T \mathbf{D}\overline{\Theta} = 0$, that is, $\Theta = \overline{\Theta}$.

Angle Constraints

The constraint function $C^{\mathrm{a}} = \theta_{f,j} - \theta^*_{f,j}$, which evaluates the difference between the joint angle $\theta_{f,j}$ and the target angle $\theta^*_{f,j}$ at each frame f. This is also expressed using the motion vector Θ as shown in Eq. 3.49.

$$C^{\mathrm{a}} = \frac{1}{2} \left\| \mathbf{a}_{f,j}\Theta - \theta^*_{f,j} \right\|^2$$
$$= \frac{1}{2} \left(\mathbf{a}_{f,j}\Theta - \theta^*_{f,j} \right)^T \left(\mathbf{a}_{f,j}\Theta - \theta^*_{f,j} \right) , \qquad (3.49)$$

$$\mathbf{a}_{f,j} = [0 \; \cdots \; 1 \; \cdots \; 0] \in \Re^{1\times 3JF} , \qquad (3.50)$$

where $\mathbf{a}_{f,j}$ is a matrix that takes one only for the component corresponding to $\theta_{f,j}$ as shown in Eq. 3.50, and zero for all other components. The partial derivative of Θ in Eq. 3.49 is derived as shown in Eq. 3.51.

$$\frac{\partial C^{\mathrm{a}}}{\partial \Theta} = \mathbf{a}^T_{f,j}\mathbf{a}_{f,j}\Theta - \theta^*_{f,j}\mathbf{a}_{f,j} . \qquad (3.51)$$

Constraints on Joint Displacement

As mentioned in the explanation of the Jacobi IK method, the joint position constraint is satisfied by iteratively solving a spacetime optimization problem with a small displacement toward the target position. When the index of the joint to be operated is i and the target displacement in frame f is $\delta\mathbf{p}_{f,i}$, the constraint function C^{d} is derived using the Jacobian matrix $\mathbf{P}'_i$ as shown in Eq. 3.52, and its partial derivative with respect to Θ is derived as shown in Eq. 3.53.

$$C^{\mathrm{d}} = \frac{1}{2} \left\| [\cdots \; \mathbf{0} \; \mathbf{P}'_{f,i} \; \mathbf{0} \; \cdots] \Theta - \delta\mathbf{p}_{f,i} \right\|^2 , \qquad (3.52)$$

$$\frac{\partial C^{\mathrm{d}}}{\partial \Theta} = [\cdots \; \mathbf{0} \; \mathbf{P}'_{f,i} \; \mathbf{0} \; \cdots]^T [\cdots \; \mathbf{0} \; \mathbf{P}'_{f,i} \; \mathbf{0} \; \cdots] \Theta$$
$$-[\cdots \; \mathbf{0} \; \mathbf{P}'_{f,i} \; \mathbf{0} \; \cdots]^T \delta\mathbf{p}_{f,i} , \qquad (3.53)$$

where $[\cdots \; \mathbf{0} \; \mathbf{P}'_{f,i} \; \mathbf{0} \; \cdots]$ is a matrix in which all columns corresponding to frames other than f are 0, and the submatrix corresponding to frame f is $\mathbf{P}'_{f,i}$.

Optimization

As an example using the objective function and constraints above, consider finding the motion vector Θ that minimizes the objective function $E = E^{\mathrm{v}} + w^{\mathrm{a}}C^{\mathrm{a}}$. That is, consider the problem of minimizing the amount of change from the source motion while bringing the arbitrary joint rotation at the specified frame closer to the target angle. Since both E^{v} and C^{a} are convex quadratic, E is also a convex quadratic. Furthermore, since there are no constraints, the optimal Θ makes the partial derivative of E a zero vector. Therefore, the simultaneous linear equations shown in Eq. 3.54 are derived.

$$\frac{\partial E^{\mathrm{v}}}{\partial \Theta} + w^{\mathrm{a}} \frac{\partial C^{\mathrm{a}}}{\partial \Theta} = \mathbf{0}$$

$$\mathbf{D}^T \mathbf{D} \left(\Theta - \overline{\Theta}\right) + w^{\mathrm{a}} \left(\mathbf{a}_{f,j}^T \mathbf{a}_{f,j} \Theta - \theta_{f,j}^* \mathbf{a}_{f,j}\right) = \mathbf{0}$$

$$\left(\mathbf{D}^T \mathbf{D} + w^{\mathrm{a}} \mathbf{a}_{f,j}^T \mathbf{a}_{f,j}\right) \Theta = \mathbf{D}^T \mathbf{D} \overline{\Theta} + w^{\mathrm{a}} \theta_{f,j}^* \mathbf{a}_{f,j} \ . \quad (3.54)$$

An example of applying this motion deformation method by spacetime optimization to a single animation curve given as a simple sine wave is shown in Fig. 3.13. The motion vector Θ is a single time-series data, so its dimension number equals the number of frames F. The constraints are given to the frames corresponding to the two ends of the animation curve, the second maximum value and the third minimum value, as indicated by the four white circles. At this point, the objective function composed of the angular velocity similarity and the four angle constraints is represented as $E^{\mathrm{v}} + w^{\mathrm{a}} \sum_b C_b^{\mathrm{a}}$, and the simultaneous equations shown in Eq. 3.55 are derived from its partial derivative.

$$\left(\mathbf{D}^T \mathbf{D} + \sum_b w_b^{\mathrm{a}} \mathbf{a}_{f_b}^T \mathbf{a}_{f_b}\right) \Theta = \mathbf{D}^T \mathbf{D} \overline{\Theta} + \sum_b w_b^{\mathrm{a}} \theta_{f_b}^* \mathbf{a}_{f_b} \ . \quad (3.55)$$

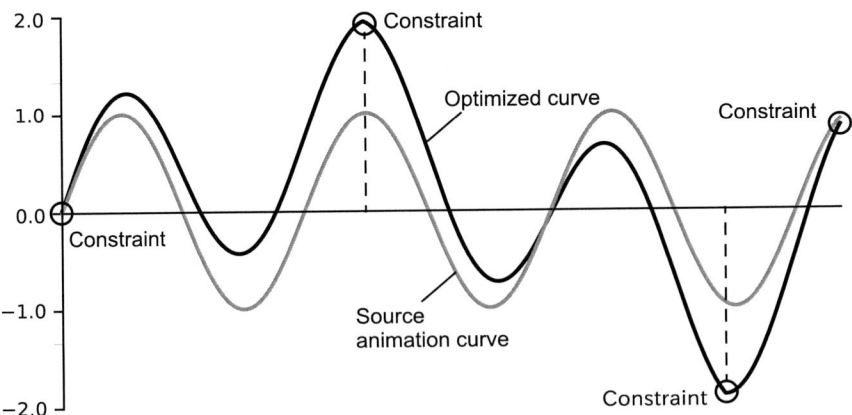

Fig. 3.13 Animation curve deformation by spacetime optimization

Solving this equation gives the result shown in Fig. 3.13. In this way, a deformation result is obtained that satisfies all constraints and preserves the shape of the source animation curve.

The dimensionality of these spacetime optimization problems increases with the number of joints J and the number of frames F, and even an animation of about 100 frames can become a problem of several thousand dimensions. However, since $\mathbf{D}^T \mathbf{D}$ and $\mathbf{a}_{f,j}^T \mathbf{a}_{f,j}$ are sparse matrices with few non-zero elements, they can be computed efficiently using a sparse matrix solver. In addition, the number of frames to be computed can be reduced to speed up the computation further. For example, the source motion curve is first approximated by a B-spline curve, and the optimization is applied only to the control points of the spline curve [24, 25].

Consideration of Spatial Proximity

Among the attempts to extend the spacetime optimization method, we explain here two techniques. First, the spatial proximity between body parts and surrounding objects is considered in the motion deformation problem [26, 27]. In these techniques, instead of the difference in joint angles E^s and angular velocity E^v from the source motion, a pose transformation is performed to preserve the spatial relative distance between joints. For example, the spatial relationship preserving motion deformation [26] first constructs a tetrahedral mesh with the skeleton joint positions as vertices. Then, when a target position is specified for any joint, the tetrahedral mesh is deformed to satisfy the target position. The method minimizes the change in the discrete Laplacian differential coordinates of the tetrahedral mesh while maintaining the edge length corresponding to each bone as a hard constraint. As a result, the deformation result preserves the positional relationship between joints as much as possible. Finally, a skeleton pose is determined to match the shape of the deformed tetrahedral mesh.

Furthermore, the relative position between the external object and the skeleton can be preserved by generating a tetrahedral mesh that targets not only the joints of a single character but also the vertices of external objects and the joints of multiple characters. It is also possible to preserve the positional relationship, such as contacts between characters. However, the valid pose cannot always be reconstructed by fitting the skeleton to the deformed tetrahedral mesh. Although the reconstructed pose must satisfy several structural constraints, such as bone length and the range of joint rotation, these are not considered at the time of tetrahedral mesh deformation.

Therefore, an extension method is proposed that optimizes joint angles instead of directly deforming the tetrahedral mesh vertex coordinates [27]. This method allows for considerations such as the range of joint rotation, but there remain issues with computational stability and convergence due to iterative computations through the Jacobian matrix for small angular displacements.

Introduction of Inequality Constraints

In the spacetime optimization problem explained above, all constraints were included in the objective function to tolerate a certain amount of error, but there are cases where some constraints must be strictly satisfied. For example, the range of rotation

Fig. 3.14 Examples of
spatiotemporal inequality
constraints for a single frame

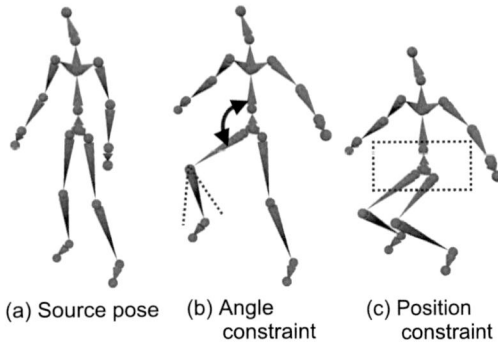

(a) Source pose   (b) Angle   (c) Position
                          constraint   constraint

angles should be treated as linear inequality constraints. Therefore, a motion deformation method using spacetime optimization with inequality constraints has been
proposed [28]. This technique deals with a quadratic programming problem shown
in Eq. 3.57.

$$\min \|\mathbf{D}(\mathbf{\Theta} - \overline{\mathbf{\Theta}})\| \tag{3.56}$$

$$\text{subject to} \quad \forall b, \mathbf{c}_b^l \leq \mathbf{C}_b \mathbf{\Theta} \leq \mathbf{c}_b^u , \tag{3.57}$$

where equality constraints can also be handled by setting $\mathbf{c}_b^l = \mathbf{c}_b^u$.

This formulation can handle different geometric constraints, as shown in
Figs. 3.14 and 3.15. Figure 3.14b shows equality constraints to restrict the joint angle
to a specific value in a single frame and inequality constraints to keep the joint
angle within the valid range. Figure 3.14c shows the constraints to locate the joint
coordinate to a specific position or within a specified range.

Moreover, Fig. 3.15 shows constraints between arbitrary frames and joints. In particular, Fig. 3.15(b) shows how to constrain the spatial distance between any joint in
any frame and another joint in another frame. Figure 3.15(c) constrains the difference in rotation angles of different joints between different frames, and Fig. 3.15(d)
constrains the displacement between the same joints between different frames. Such
a variety of motion deformations satisfying these constraints can be obtained using
the same framework shown in Eq. 3.57. However, a high-dimensional quadratic programming problem becomes complex in proportion to the product of the number
of frames and joints, which tends to increase the computational cost. Computations
also become unstable when dealing with complex constraints.

Fig. 3.15 Examples of spatiotemporal inequality constraints between different frames

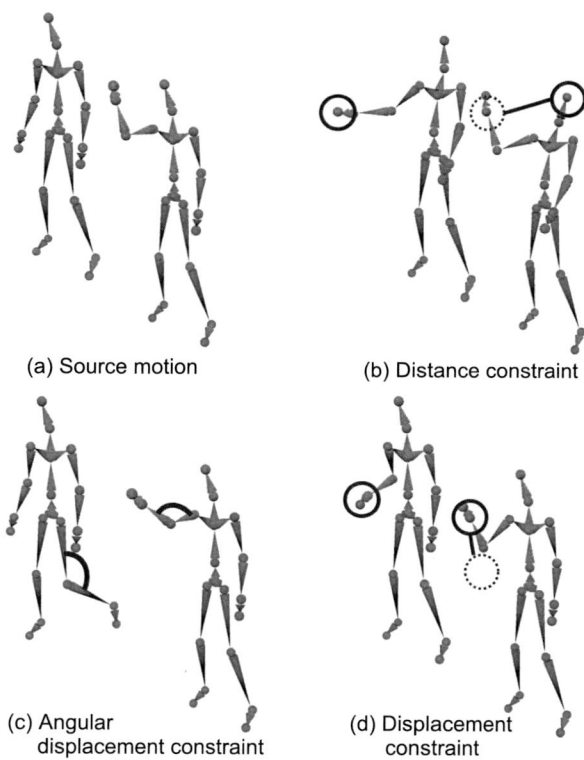

(a) Source motion

(b) Distance constraint

(c) Angular
displacement constraint

(d) Displacement
constraint

3.5 Data-Driven Motion Synthesis

The motion deformation techniques discussed in the last section generate new poses or motions by geometric deformation or time-series processing of a single pose or motion. These algorithms aim to edit poses or motions using simple rules and numerical algorithms, with only a few parameters. Such efforts are also called *procedural animation* and technically aim to reduce the data and control parameters required to generate animation. However, improving animation quality using only numerical or script control requires careful parameter tuning to achieve natural results.

On the other hand, many techniques actively use more data to improve animation quality. In particular, some techniques synthesize new motions by applying statistical analysis or machine learning techniques to large numbers of motion samples. These are called nonparametric approaches because they also handle a large amount of data as input parameters. Because they adjust the output depending on the input data, they are also called *data-driven motion synthesis* methods and have been put into practical use in commercial production. This section explains representative methods of data-driven pose editing and motion synthesis methods.

3.5.1 Application of Nonparametric Regression to IK

As an example that succinctly demonstrates the characteristics of data-driven pose editing techniques, consider the IK problem of matching the 3D position $\mathbf{e}$ of a single effector to the target position $\mathbf{g}$. In this case, computing FK is a problem of finding the world coordinates $\mathbf{e}$ of the effector based on the pose $\boldsymbol{\theta}$, and can be written as $f_{FK}(\boldsymbol{\theta}) = \mathbf{e}$. This IK problem is also expressed as the inverse problem of FK, $f_{IK}(\mathbf{g}) = f_{FK}^{-1}(\mathbf{g}) = \boldsymbol{\theta}$. As mentioned earlier, since f_{IK} is not uniquely determined, both numerical methods and heuristics use an iterative approach to converge to an approximate solution.

In data-driven methods, a new pose that satisfies the target position is synthesized using multiple sample poses. First, given N sample poses $\{\boldsymbol{\theta}_n | n \in \{1, \ldots, N\}\}$, the effector positions $\{\mathbf{e}_n = f_{FK}(\boldsymbol{\theta}_n)\}$ corresponding to each sample are computed using FK. Then, these sample data are also considered as parameters to estimate the inverse function $f_{IK}(\mathbf{g}; \{\boldsymbol{\theta}_n\}, \{\mathbf{e}_n\})$.

One of the representative methods is the radial basis function interpolation method, also known as the *RBF interpolation method* [29]. In this method, the output pose is determined by blending the N pairs of sample poses $\{(\mathbf{e}_n, \boldsymbol{\theta}_n) | n \in \{1, \ldots, N\}\}$. This estimates the optimal blend coefficients so that the output pose matches the target position.

Consider a skeleton with two rotational joints and an effector connected in series. The pose blending is performed by linearly interpolating quaternions for each of the two joints, as shown in Eq. 3.58.

$$\mathbf{q}_1 = \frac{\sum_n w_n \mathbf{q}_{1,n}}{\| \sum_n w_n \mathbf{q}_{1,n} \|} \ , \quad \mathbf{q}_2 = \frac{\sum_n w_n \mathbf{q}_{2,n}}{\| \sum_n w_n \mathbf{q}_{2,n} \|} \ , \tag{3.58}$$

where $\mathbf{q}_1$ and $\mathbf{q}_2$ are unit quaternions representing the rotation of the two joints, and w_n is the blending coefficient for the n-th sample. The RBF interpolation method determines the optimal blend coefficient w_n by solving a system of equations using a kernel function ϕ related to the effector positions $\{\mathbf{e}_n\}$ and the target position $\mathbf{g}$, as shown in Eq. 3.59.

$$\begin{bmatrix} \phi(\mathbf{e}_1, \mathbf{e}_1) & \phi(\mathbf{e}_1, \mathbf{e}_2) & \cdots & \phi(\mathbf{e}_1, \mathbf{e}_N) \\ \phi(\mathbf{e}_2, \mathbf{e}_1) & \ddots & \ddots & \vdots \\ \vdots & \ddots & \ddots & \vdots \\ \phi(\mathbf{e}_N, \mathbf{e}_1) & \cdots & \cdots & \phi(\mathbf{e}_N, \mathbf{e}_N) \end{bmatrix} \begin{bmatrix} w_1 \\ w_2 \\ \vdots \\ w_N \end{bmatrix} = \begin{bmatrix} \phi(\mathbf{g}, \mathbf{e}_1) \\ \phi(\mathbf{g}, \mathbf{e}_2) \\ \vdots \\ \phi(\mathbf{g}, \mathbf{e}_N) \end{bmatrix} , \tag{3.59}$$

where the kernel function $\phi(\mathbf{e}_n, \mathbf{e}_m)$ is a function that evaluates the dissimilarity between $\mathbf{e}_n$ and $\mathbf{e}_m$. For example, the inverse square kernel calculates the inverse square of the Euclidean distance between two points as $\phi(\mathbf{e}_n, \mathbf{e}_m) = \left(1 + \sigma \|\mathbf{e}_n - \mathbf{e}_m\|^2\right)^{-1}$. In the Gaussian kernel, the exponent of the square of the

Euclidean distance is used as $\phi(\mathbf{e}_n, \mathbf{e}_m) = \exp\left(-\sigma \|\mathbf{e}_n - \mathbf{e}_m\|^2\right)$. Note that σ is a manual parameter that determines the spread and distribution of the kernel function.

The RBF interpolation method always results in an intermediate pose similar to the sample data and can be computed in constant time without the need for iterative computations. However, the more sample data there is, the more computational and memory resources are consumed.

3.5.2 Application of Latent Space Model to IK

The optimization target of IK is the pose vector $\boldsymbol{\theta}$, and its dimension increases linearly with the number of joints. The degrees of freedom of a typical humanoid skeleton extend to several tens of dimensions, which reduces the convergence of optimization and search computations in such high-dimensional spaces. Therefore, methods have been proposed to search for poses that satisfy the constraints of IK in a lower dimensional space or *latent space*, that preserve the amount of information in the pose vector. In particular, several methods have been studied for constructing a latent space where similar poses are placed close together [30, 31]. Many of them perform computations to reduce the dimensionality of the latent space by exploiting various correlations inherent in the data, such as the interrelation between multiple joints. At this point, transforming a given pose to satisfy the constraints by IK becomes a problem of finding coordinates in the latent space corresponding to the pose that satisfies the constraints.

The *multidimensional scaling* (MDS) is known as one of the classical methods for constructing a latent space. In a typical method called classical MDS (CMDS), the coordinate values of each sample in the latent space are determined based on the distance information between samples. First, for the given N sample poses $\{\boldsymbol{\theta}_n | n = \{1, \ldots, N\}\}$, a distance matrix $\boldsymbol{\Psi}$ is computed using an evaluation function ψ that calculates the dissimilarity between two poses.

$$\boldsymbol{\Psi} = \begin{bmatrix} \psi(\boldsymbol{\theta}_1, \boldsymbol{\theta}_1) & \psi(\boldsymbol{\theta}_1, \boldsymbol{\theta}_2) & \cdots & \psi(\boldsymbol{\theta}_1, \boldsymbol{\theta}_N) \\ \psi(\boldsymbol{\theta}_2, \boldsymbol{\theta}_1) & \psi(\boldsymbol{\theta}_2, \boldsymbol{\theta}_2) & \ddots & \vdots \\ \vdots & \ddots & \ddots & \vdots \\ \psi(\boldsymbol{\theta}_N, \boldsymbol{\theta}_1) & \cdots & \cdots & \psi(\boldsymbol{\theta}_N, \boldsymbol{\theta}_N) \end{bmatrix} \in \mathfrak{R}^{N \times N}, \tag{3.60}$$

where the m-th row and n-th column of the distance matrix $\boldsymbol{\Psi}$ is a distance function $\psi(\boldsymbol{\theta}_m, \boldsymbol{\theta}_n)$ that evaluates the dissimilarity of the m-th and n-th poses. As a distance function ψ, the Euclidean distance between pose vectors $\psi(\boldsymbol{\theta}_m, \boldsymbol{\theta}_n) = (\sum_j (\boldsymbol{\theta}_{m,j} - \boldsymbol{\theta}_{n,j})^2)^{1/2}$, or a weighted distance $\psi(\boldsymbol{\theta}_m, \boldsymbol{\theta}_n) = (\sum_j w_j (\boldsymbol{\theta}_{m,j} - \boldsymbol{\theta}_{n,j})^2)^{1/2}$ is used. We can also use the difference in joint coordinates obtained by FK, $\psi(\boldsymbol{\theta}_m, \boldsymbol{\theta}_n) = (\sum_j \|\text{pos}(\mathbf{M}_{m,j}) - \text{pos}(\mathbf{M}_{n,j})\|^2)^{1/2}$.

Next, a *singular value decomposition* (SVD) is applied to the distance matrix as
shown in Eq. 3.61.

$$\mathbf{U}\boldsymbol{\Sigma}\mathbf{V}^T = \text{SVD}\left(-\frac{1}{2}(\mathbf{I} - \boldsymbol{\Lambda})\boldsymbol{\Psi}(\mathbf{I} - \boldsymbol{\Lambda})^T\right), \qquad (3.61)$$

where $\boldsymbol{\Lambda} \in \mathfrak{R}^{N \times N}$ is a matrix where all elements are $1/N$. As a result, the coordinate values of each sample in the multidimensional latent space are obtained as the
row vectors $\{\mathbf{u}_n | n = \{1, \ldots, N\}\}$ of the left singular matrix $\mathbf{U}$. In the constructed
N-dimensional latent space, the Euclidean distance between two coordinate val-
ues $\|\mathbf{u}_m - \mathbf{u}_n\|$ approximates the dissimilarity $\psi(\boldsymbol{\theta}_m, \boldsymbol{\theta}_n)$ between the corresponding
poses.

In the latent space constructed by CMDS, the first dimension is the most important in approximating the dissimilarity, while the importance of the second to N-th
dimensions is relatively small. Their contributions are represented by $\sqrt{\text{diag}(\boldsymbol{\Sigma})}$,
which decreases monotonically from the first to the N-th component. Therefore, the
original dissimilarity can be accurately approximated even in a reduced latent space
without higher order components.

For example, the CMDS-based method [32] is applied to landing and jumping
motions as samples, and a two-dimensional latent space is constructed using only
the first and second dimensions, as shown in Fig. 3.16. The poses change smoothly
over time for both motions so that continuous curves are drawn in the latent space.
For example, poses a1 and b4 are similar in that they raise both arms and bend the
legs, so they are relatively close together in latent space. On the other hand, b1 and
b3 have opposite arm swings and different leg extensions, so they are far apart in
latent space.

IK in the latent space is achieved by finding the optimal coordinate $\mathbf{u}$ that satisfies
the given constraints $C(\boldsymbol{\theta}(\mathbf{u})) = 0$, where the pose corresponding to $\mathbf{u}$ is expressed as
$\boldsymbol{\theta}(\mathbf{u})$. At this point, assuming that the constraint function $C(\boldsymbol{\theta}(\mathbf{u}))$ changes smoothly
in response to a slight change in $\mathbf{u}$, we search for a locally optimal solution using the

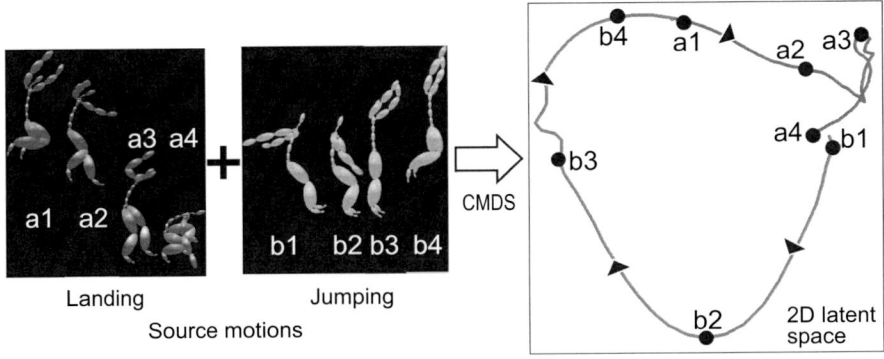

Fig. 3.16 Example of constructing a two-dimensional latent space

gradient descent method. First, we find the coordinate $\mathbf{u}$ in latent space that corresponds to the source pose $\overline{\boldsymbol{\theta}}$. Next, we compute the constraint function $C(\boldsymbol{\theta}(\mathbf{u}))$, as well as the gradient $\frac{\partial C}{\partial \mathbf{u}}$ in latent space. Then we update $\mathbf{u}$ in the direction that reduces the value of the constraint function, as in $\mathbf{u} \leftarrow \mathbf{u} - \alpha \frac{\partial C}{\partial \mathbf{u}} \mathbf{u}$. After repeating this process until $C(\boldsymbol{\theta}(\mathbf{u}))$ becomes sufficiently small, we find the pose $\boldsymbol{\theta}(\mathbf{u})$ corresponding to coordinate $\mathbf{u}$ after convergence. Note that there is an overhead in computing the joint pose by FK after finding the corresponding pose $\boldsymbol{\theta}(\mathbf{u})$ when evaluating the constraint function. Although this computational cost issue remains, a natural pose similar to the sample pose is expected to be obtained.

In addition to the MDS-based method, the *Gaussian process latent variable model* [33] and the *Gaussian process dynamical model* [34], are also used. These latent space models are used not only for motion generation and deformation but also for various methods in the field of computer vision, such as motion recognition and identification.

3.5.3 Application of Neural Networks

The regression methods and latent space models discussed in Sects. 3.5.1 and 3.5.2 are well-established machine learning techniques with ongoing research and practical applications. At the time of writing, technologies using *neural networks*, especially *deep learning* technologies, are being actively researched, and new computational methods are being actively reported. In this section, we explain some of these neural network-based technologies.

First, in Sect. 3.5.1, we introduced a regression-based IK technique that blends many sample poses using RBF interpolation. Such regression models are used for *motion interpolation*, which uses several parameters to control motion blending intuitively [35]. However, dealing with complex problems that introduce many motion samples and achieve flexible motion control with high-dimensional control parameters is difficult.

Therefore, recent approaches use deep learning techniques to overcome those problems. One of these methods is to construct a neural network that uses supervised learning to take motion samples and control parameters as the training dataset. For example, in the walking motion generation method [36], a fully connected network predicts the pose at the next time step based on the pose at a current time and terrain information on the target future trajectory. By learning the network parameters according to the gait phase information, pose prediction suitable for any time in the walking cycle can be achieved. In addition, there have been many attempts to acquire latent space through deep learning. For example, a *convolutional autoencoder* is used to construct a latent space of character poses [37]. Specifically, neurons corresponding to the dimension of the pose vector are first prepared on the input and output layers, and an intermediate layer consisting of fewer neurons is built. Then, the same sample pose is given to the input and output layers, and the parameters

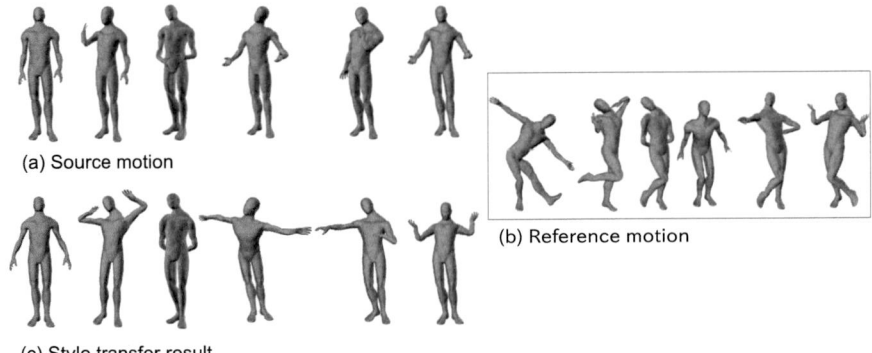

(a) Source motion

(b) Reference motion

(c) Style transfer result

Fig. 3.17 Motion style transfer using neural networks

of the intermediate layer are learned so that the network outputs approximate the inputs. As a result, the network from the input layer to the intermediate layer, called the encoder, learns a mapping from the pose vector to the low-dimensional latent space. On the other hand, the network from the intermediate layer to the output layer, called the decoder, learns to reverse mapping from the latent space to the pose.

Furthermore, several state-of-the-art network models are applied to the motion synthesis problems. For example, a *motion style transfer* method for gesture motion uses a *transformer*-based architecture [38]. This method learns a network to transfer the motion style of general gesture motion during the conversation between different motions, as shown in Fig. 3.17a, b. This network model synthesizes a motion that performs different gesture styles while corresponding to the conversation content of Fig. 3.17a, as shown in Fig. 3.17c.

3.6   Conclusion

We have introduced techniques for editing the poses and motions of 3DCG characters. We explained that character poses are expressed based on 3D coordinate transformations and edited by various numerical optimization techniques, such as least squares methods, time-series analysis techniques, including signal processing, and machine learning techniques, such as nonparametric regression and latent space models. There are widespread attempts to improve these techniques by applying deep learning techniques, and the technical basis for easily creating more natural animations is expected to be further developed in future research.

Although we have not discussed in this chapter, physics-based motion generation techniques are also considered promising. Traditional dynamics-based methods have a major problem in that they are difficult for animators to control, but solutions are beginning to be sought using cutting-edge theories proposed in the fields of control engineering and neural networks, such as deep reinforcement learning. Attempting to manipulate dynamically controlled characters freely is challenging because physical validity and animation production do not necessarily coincide. We look forward to the development of future research.

References

1. Magnenat-Thalmann, N., Laperrière, R. & Thalmann, D. Joint-Dependent Local Deformations for Hand Animation and Object Grasping. *Proceedings On Graphics Interface '88*. pp. 26-33 (1988)
2. Kavan, L., Collins, S., Zara, J. & O'Sullivan, C. Skinning with Dual Quaternions. *Proceedings Of ACM SIGGRAPH Symposium On Interactive 3D Graphics 2007*. pp. 39-46 (2007)
3. Kavan, L. & Sorkine, O. Elasticity-Inspired Deformers for Character Articulation. *ACM Transactions On Graphics*. **31**, 196:1-196:8 (2012)
4. Le, B. & Lewis, J. Direct Delta Mush Skinning and Variants. *ACM Transactions On Graphics*. **38**, 113:1-113:13 (2019)
5. Le, B., Villeneuve, K. & Gonzalez-Ochoa, C. Direct Delta Mush Skinning Compression with Continuous Examples. *ACM Transactions On Graphics*. **40**, 72:1-72:13 (2021)
6. Tolani, D., Goswami, A. & Badler, N. Real-Time Inverse Kinematics Techniques for Anthropomorphic Limbs. *Graphical Models*. **62**, 353-388 (2000)
7. Kanoun, O., Lamiraux, F. & Wieber, P. Kinematic Control of Redundant Manipulators: Generalizing the Task-Priority Framework to Inequality Task. *IEEE Transactions On Robotics*. **27**, pp. 785 - 792 (2011)
8. Stellato, B., Banjac, G., Goulart, P., Bemporad, A. & Boyd, S. OSQP: an operator splitting solver for quadratic programs. *Mathematical Programming Computation*. **12**, 637-672 (2020)
9. Wang, L. & Chih Cheng Chen A Combined Optimization Method for Solving the Inverse Kinematics Problems of Mechanical Manipulators. *IEEE Transactions On Robotics And Automation*. **7**, 489-499 (1991)
10. Welman, C. Inverse Kinematics and Geometric Constraints for Articulated Figure Manipulation. (1993)
11. Hecker, C., Raabe, B., Enslow, R., DeWeese, J., Maynard, J. & Prooijen, K. Real-time Motion Retargeting to Highly Varied User-Created Morphologies. *ACM Transactions On Graphics*. **27**, 27:1-27:11 (2008)
12. Aristidou, A. & Lasenby, J. FABRIK: A fast, iterative solver for the Inverse Kinematics problem. *Graphical Models*. **73**, 243-260 (2011)
13. Aristidou, A., Chrysanthou, Y. & Lasenby, J. Extending FABRIK with Model Constraints. *Computer Animation And Virtual Worlds*. **27**, 35-57 (2016)
14. Bruderlin, A. & Williams, L. Motion Signal Processing. *SIGGRAPH '95*. pp. 97-104 (1995)
15. Lee, J. & Shin, S. A Hierarchical Approach to Interactive Motion Editing for Human-like Figures. *SIGGRAPH '99*. pp. 39-48 (1999)
16. Choi, B., Ribera, R., Lewis, J., Seol, Y., Hong, S., Ein, H., Jung, S. & Noh, J. SketchiMo: Sketch-Based Motion Editing for Articulated Characters. *ACM Transactions On Graphics*. **35**, 146:1-146:12 (2016)
17. Wang, J., Drucker, S., Agrawala, M. & Cohen, M. The Cartoon Animation Filter. *ACM Transactions On Graphics*. **25**, 1169-1173 (2006)
18. Lee, J. & Shin, S. General Construction of Time-domain Filters for Orientation Data. *IEEE Transactions On Visualization And Computer Graphics*.
19. Kovar, L. & Gleicher, M. Flexible Automatic Motion Blending with Registration Curves. *Proceedings Of ACM SIGGRAPH/Eurographics Symposium On Computer Animation*. pp. 214-224 (2003)

20. Hsu, E., Silva, M. & Popović, J. Guided TimeWarping for Motion Editing. *Proceedings Of ACM SIGGRAPH/Eurographics Symposium On Computer Animation*. pp. 45-52 (2007)

21. Unuma, M., Anjyo, K. & Takeuchi, R. Fourier Principles for Emotion-Based Human Figure Animation. *SIGGRAPH '95*. pp. 91-96 (1995)

22. Ersin, M. & Mitra, N. Spectral Style Transfer for Human Motion between Independent Actions. *ACM Transactions On Graphics*. **35**, 137.1-137.8 (2016)

23. Yamane, K., Kuffner, J. & Hodgins, J. Synthesizing Animations of Human Manipulation Tasks. *ACM Transactions On Graphics*. **23**, 532-539 (2004)

24. Popović, Z. & Witkin, A. Physically Based Motion Transformation. *SIGGRAPH '99*. pp. 11-20 (1999)

25. Abe, Y., Liu, K. & Popović, Z. Momentum-Based Parameterization of Dynamic Character Motion. *Proceedings Of ACM SIGGRAPH/Eurographics Symposium On Computer Animation*. pp. 173-182 (2004)

26. Ho, E., Komura, T. & Tai, C. Spatial Relationship Preserving Character Motion Adaptation. *ACM Transactions On Graphics*. **29**, 33:1-33:8 (2010)

27. Ho, E. & Shum, H. Motion Adaptation for Humanoid Robots in Constrained Environments. *IEEE International Conference On Robotics And Automation*. pp. 1-6 (2013)

28. Mukai, T., Kuriyama, S. & Oshita, M. Motion Adaptation with Cascaded Inequality Tasks. *ACM SIGGRAPH Conference On Motion, Interaction And Games 2019*. pp. 30:1-30:10 (2019)

29. Rose, C., Sloan, P. & Cohen, M. Artist-Directed Inverse-Kinematics Using Radial Basis Function Interpolation. *Compuer Graphics Forum*. **20**, 239-250 (2001)

30. Shin, H. & Lee, J. Motion Synthesis and Editing in Low-Dimensional Spaces. *Computer Animation And Virtual Worlds*. **17**, 219-227 (2006)

31. Tournier, M., Wu, X., Courty, N., Arnaud, E. & Reveret, L. Motion Compression using Principal Geodesics Analysis. *Computer Graphics Forum*. **28**, 337-346 (2009) 8, 119-128 (2002)

32. Mukai, T. Spline Motion Transitions in Linear Subspaces. *Proc. Of SIGGRAPH Asia 2011 Sketches*. pp. 11 (2011)

33. Grochow, K., Martin, S., Hertzmann, A. & Popović, Z. Style-Based Inverse Kinematics. *ACM Transactions On Graphics*. **23**, 522-531 (2004)

34. Wang, J., Fleet, D. & Hertzmann, A. Gaussian Process Dynamical Models for Human Motion. *IEEE Transactions On Pattern Analysis And Machine Intelligence*. **30**, 283-298 (2008)

35. Mukai, T. & Kuriyama, S. Geostatistical Motion Interpolation. *ACM Transactions On Graphics*. **24**, 1062-1070 (2005)

36. Holden, D., Komura, T. & Saito, J. Phase-Functioned Neural Networks for Character Control. *ACM Transactions On Graphics*. **36**, 42:1-42:13 (2017)

37. Holden, D., Saito, J., Komura, T. & Joyce, T. Learning Motion Manifolds with Convolutional Autoencoders. *ACM SIGGRAPH Asia 2015 Technical Briefs*. (2015)

38. Kuriyama, S., Mukai, T., Taketomi, T. & Mukasa, T. Context-based Style Transfer of Tokenized Gestures. *Computer Graphics Forum*. **41** (2022)

Chapter 4
Physics Simulation

Makoto Fujisawa🄳

Abstract For computer graphics (CG) animation, not only the shapes and character motions created by CG creators are important, but also the movement of hair
and clothing associated with the character's movement, or the surrounding environment, such as the flow of rivers and waves of the sea, clouds flowing in the wind,
swinging trees, and various other natural phenomena are also important for realistic
CG. However, such natural phenomena are very complex and difficult to manually
reproduce. The attempt to calculate these complex phenomena automatically using
a computer is the subject of this chapter, physics simulation. This chapter explains
what physics simulation is, from the basics, to how to actually reproduce objects
such as rigid/elastic bodies, water, and air in CG.

4.1 Introduction

One of the purposes of CG animation is to reproduce the real world. Although CG can
generate phenomena that are not realistically possible, in many cases, it is necessary
to reproduce natural phenomena and the movements of humans and animals that
exist in reality. The movements of characters such as humans and animals have been
discussed in previous chapters, but here we will consider the generation of movements
that are not intentional, but follow the laws of the real world. For example, let's
consider what happens to the movement of a ball in a scene where you throw the
ball. To throw the ball far, a person applies force to the ball. The ball applied the
force will move in the direction in which the force was applied according to the law
of inertia, but its trajectory is not a straight line, but draws a curve called a parabola.
This is because a downward force due to gravity and a resistance due to air. If it is
possible to express the force acting on the ball in motion as a formula, the computer
will be able to calculate the parabola drawn by the ball. This is the basic idea of
physics simulation.

Even if it is a simple trajectory calculation like a parabola, the laws are mostly
composed of simple arithmetic operations, so it is easy to implement as a program.
However, what if you deal with an object of a more complex shape than a ball? If it is
a spherical ball, the projection area against the air is the same no matter which surface

it faces, so the calculation of air resistance is relatively easy, but it is not so easy if the shape is complex. Furthermore, if it is a shape like a wing, not only the force due to air resistance but also the lift force acting upward must be calculated, and if we want to accurately calculate these resistance/lift forces, the flow of the surrounding air must also be calculated. Furthermore, if there is more than one object, a motion change due to the collision between objects and the shape deformation if the object deforms must be considered. Many phenomena are involved in simply throwing an object. If there is a unified law that solves all of these, it will be possible to calculate everything, but in reality, physical laws have been found for each phenomenon. In this chapter, from Sect. 4.2, we will explain what laws exist for each phenomenon and how to calculate them in a computer.

The explanation for each phenomenon will be given from the next section, but here we will explain *discretization*, which is a necessary element for physics simulation. Discretization has been mentioned in the chapters so far in order to calculate objects and laws on a computer, but in most physics simulations, we must discretize *spatial gradient* and *time integration*. The reality we live in is a three-dimensional space, and objects exist in this space in an "inhomogeneous" state. This inhomogeneity gives rise to various phenomena. For example, differences in air pressure and temperature cause wind, and uneven terrain creates the flow of rivers. The important thing is that objects move in order to make these inhomogeneous states homogeneous or to stabilize unstable states. To make this a formula, let's try to express the degree of inhomogeneity in a mathematical formula. Let the physical quantities at two points in three-dimensional space be $f(x_1)$, $f(x_2)$. If we want to express the degree of inhomogeneity as how much the physical quantity has changed in space, we can divide the difference by the distance between the two points,

$$\frac{f(x_1) - f(x_2)}{||x_1 - x_2||} . \tag{4.1}$$

This is called the *gradient*, and if you want to find the gradient at a certain point, you should take the limit that makes the distance between the two points zero. Taking the limit $||x_1 - x_2|| \to 0$ in the above equation is equivalent to calculating the derivative df/dx of the function $f(x)$, which is called the spatial gradient, and is denoted by ∇f including the case of multiple dimensions. This spatial gradient is used in almost all phenomena, especially in laws describing fluids and other substances where spatial changes easily affect behavior. Therefore, when trying to calculate physical laws on a computer, in many cases, we must consider how to discretize and calculate the spatial gradient. Of course, as in Eq. 4.1, we can consider not a single point but a range with a certain width, and in many actual methods, discretization is done in this way, but what must be considered in this case is the error caused by not taking the limit $||x_1 - x_2|| \to 0$. In CG animation for visualization purposes, a certain degree of error can be tolerated, but in the CG field, complex shapes are often dealt with, and methods with poor accuracy can result in a lack of realism. A major goal of physics simulation in CG is to be able to handle complex boundary shapes while allowing for efficient computation and without affecting visualization.

The movement of objects is not determined only by the spatial gradient. Although the real world is a three-dimensional space, when expressing "movement", we must also consider another axis, the time axis. In the real world, the time axis is one-directional, and unlike space, it does not move in the opposite direction. If the state of an object at a certain time t_1 is determined by the state change from a past time t_0, then the current state is expressed by the integration in the time direction:

$$\int_{t_0}^{t_1} g(t)dt \ .$$

The function $g(t)$ here represents the state change at time t, which is determined for each phenomenon using the aforementioned spatial gradient, etc., and this is called the *governing equation*. What we have to consider in physics simulation is to "discretize the spatial gradient" for calculating the governing equation, and to "discretize the time integration" for calculating the change over time. Of course, there are not only that, but also devising for efficient calculation, adding random elements to make it more realistic, generating surfaces for visualization, etc., but the aforementioned two occupy a large area. Therefore, in the following sections, we will mainly describe the laws used for various objects including spatial gradients and the methods of time integration calculation of those laws.

4.2 Rigid Body Simulation

4.2.1 What Is a Rigid Body

If many physical laws are made based on the idea of the inhomogeneous state inside the object, the simplest way to simplify it is to assume that the state inside the object is uniform and does not change over time. Since the state inside the object does not change, its shape does not change, and it is sufficient to define one movement for one object (from the next sections, we have to consider multiple movements within one object for elastic bodies and fluids). An object with such an assumption is called a *rigid body*.

Let's express one movement in a formula. Assuming a rigid body moving in three-dimensional space, its movement can be represented by three-dimensional coordinates (x, y, z). However, only the position of the rigid body can be represented in three-dimensional coordinates, so in addition to that, information on the posture of the rigid body is also required. The posture in three-dimensional space is represented by the rotation angles (α, β, γ) around the three axes (x axis, y axis, z axis) relative to the initial posture (this is called *Euler angles*). The position and posture of the rigid body can be represented by six degrees of freedom: the three-dimensional coordinates representing the position and the Euler angles representing the rotation. When drawing the rotating rigid body, the transformation is performed by the transformation matrix R obtained from the Euler angles. The conversion from Euler angles to matrix is

$$R = \begin{pmatrix} 1 & 0 & 0 \\ 0 & \cos\alpha & -\sin\alpha \\ 0 & \sin\alpha & \cos\alpha \end{pmatrix} \begin{pmatrix} \cos\beta & 0 & \sin\beta \\ 0 & 1 & 0 \\ -\sin\beta & 0 & \cos\beta \end{pmatrix} \begin{pmatrix} \cos\gamma & -\sin\gamma & 0 \\ \sin\gamma & \cos\gamma & 0 \\ 0 & 0 & 1 \end{pmatrix}. \tag{4.2}$$

For computer graphics rendering, a 4×4 homogeneous matrix including parallel translation is used to represent the transformation, but in *rigid body simulation*, different motion equations are used for rotation and translation, so they are often treated separately. Also, the representation of rotation using Euler angles and matrices has problems due to a large number of data and gimbal lock caused by overlapping rotation axes, so a quaternion is often used instead. When using quaternion q to represent rotation, it is determined by the rotation axis $\boldsymbol{a} = (a_x, a_y, a_z)$ and the rotation angle θ,

$$q(\boldsymbol{a}, \theta) = \left(a_x \sin\frac{\theta}{2}, a_y \sin\frac{\theta}{2}, a_z \sin\frac{\theta}{2}, \cos\frac{\theta}{2} \right). \tag{4.3}$$

Now that we can represent the position and posture of a rigid body, let's calculate the movement of the rigid body next. As shown in Fig. 4.1, when a rigid body is moving with a velocity vector $\boldsymbol{v}(t)$ that changes over time, the relationship with the position vector $\boldsymbol{x}$ is expressed using time differentiation as,

$$\boldsymbol{v}(t) = \frac{d\boldsymbol{x}}{dt} = \left(\frac{dx}{dt}, \frac{dy}{dt}, \frac{dz}{dt} \right). \tag{4.4}$$

If a rigid body moves at a velocity $\boldsymbol{v}(t)$ from a certain time t to $t + \Delta t$, the amount of movement $\Delta \boldsymbol{x}$ is expressed by the following formula using time integration.

Fig. 4.1 Movement trajectory and velocity vector of a rigid body

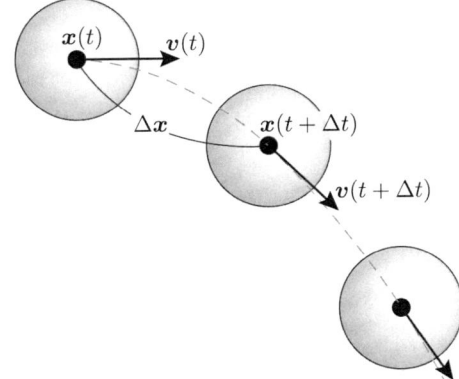

$$\Delta x = \int_t^{t+\Delta t} v(t)dt \ . \tag{4.5}$$

If the velocity is constant during the time step width Δt, the above equation simply becomes $\Delta x = v(t)\Delta t$, and the position at the next step can be calculated from the current step position $x(t)$ using the following formula.

$$x(t + \Delta t) = x(t) + \Delta x = x(t) + v(t)\Delta t \ . \tag{4.6}$$

By repeating this process of calculating the position at the next step from the current position and velocity, an animation can be created. In Eq. 4.6, the time integral is approximately calculated using the initial velocity of the time step, and this approximation method is called the *forward Euler method*. Note that we are assuming that the state does not change within the object as a definition of a rigid body, so we are not considering spatial gradients here.

If $v(t)$ changes during the time step width Δt, there is a possibility of a large error in the assumption that the velocity is constant. Therefore, if the change of the velocity $v(t)$ is known and the velocity $v(t + \Delta t)$ at $t + \Delta t$ can also be obtained (in fact, $v(t)$ is calculated in the same way as $x(t)$, but that will be described later), the accuracy can be improved by taking the average of both as in the following formula.

$$x(t + \Delta t) = x(t) + \frac{v(t) + v(t + \Delta t)}{2}\Delta t \ . \tag{4.7}$$

This is a method called the *improved Euler method*. There are other discretization methods for time integration, such as a Runge-Kutta method and an implicit method.

We can now calculate the position of a rigid body from time integration, but for this, the velocity v at each step $(t, t + \Delta t, t + 2\Delta t, ...)$ is required. The velocity of rigid body motion can be calculated from time integration in the same way as the position, based on the equation of motion. The equation of motion without considering elasticity or damping is

$$f = \frac{d}{dt}(mv) = ma \ , \tag{4.8}$$

where f is the external force acting on the rigid body, and m, a are the mass and acceleration of the rigid body, respectively. Equation 4.8 assumes that the mass m does not change over time. The acceleration $a = f/m$ can be obtained from Eq. 4.8. As the relationship between position and velocity was expressed by time differentiation in Eq. 4.4, velocity and acceleration are also related by time differentiation ($a(t) = dv/dt$). Let's discretize this with the forward Euler method in the same way as Eq. 4.6.

$$v(t + \Delta t) = v(t) + \frac{f}{m}\Delta t \ . \tag{4.9}$$

At a certain time t, when an external force f acts on a rigid body, the change in velocity caused by it is calculated by Eq. 4.9, and the updated velocity v is used to update the position using equations such as Eq. 4.6. This allows the trajectory (change in position) of the rigid body to be calculated, and then the rigid body can be drawn as a CG with the calculated position as the center. This is the basic flow of rigid body simulation.

The velocity update by Eq. 4.9 does not consider the rotation of the rigid body. The velocity v used in the equations so far describes the movement of the center of gravity (translation of the rigid body), so to describe rotation, we first define the rotational version of velocity, angular velocity ω. If the velocity v is the distance moved per unit time, the angular velocity ω represents the change in angle of posture per unit time. In a two-dimensional plane, the change in angle can be represented by one rotation angle centered on an axis perpendicular to the plane, but in three-dimensional space, the rotation axis can take any direction. Therefore, the angular velocity is defined as a three-dimensional vector ω, with the direction of the vector representing the direction of the rotation axis and the magnitude of the vector $|\omega|$ representing the rotation angle (see Fig. 4.2). Next, we explain the relationship between Euler angles and angular velocity. It would be simple if the time derivative $\dot{R}$ of the rotation matrix R obtained from the Euler angles corresponds to the three-dimensional angular velocity ω, but ω is a vector and R is a matrix, so they cannot be directly equated. From the fact that the rotated coordinates can be obtained by multiplying the rotation matrix R by any coordinate r in the rigid body ($r' = Rr$), we can know that each column of R represents the transformation of the x, y, z coordinates. In other words, each column of $\dot{R}$, which is the time derivative of R, represents the transformation speed of the x, y, z coordinates. On the other hand, the relationship between the time changes $\dot{r}$ of any point r in the rigid body and the angular velocity vector ω is $\dot{r} = \omega \times r$. From this, $\omega \times$ (Each column of the rotation matrix R) represents the time change of the rotation matrix $\dot{R}$. By using a matrix representation of the cross product, we define ω^*.

$$\omega^* = \begin{pmatrix} 0 & -\omega_z & \omega_y \\ \omega_z & 0 & -\omega_x \\ -\omega_y & \omega_x & 0 \end{pmatrix} ,$$

Fig. 4.2 Definition of angular velocity in rigid body rotation

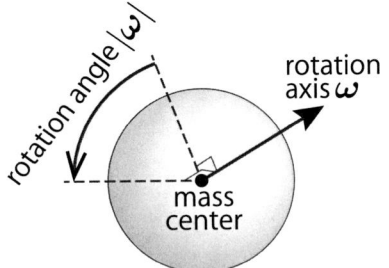

where $\boldsymbol{\omega} = (\omega_x, \omega_y, \omega_z)^T$, and the relationship between angular velocity and rotation matrix can be described as

$$\dot{R} = \omega^* R .\tag{4.10}$$

In the case of quaternions, it can be expressed more simply,

$$\dot{q} = \frac{1}{2}[0, \boldsymbol{\omega}]q ,\tag{4.11}$$

where $[0, \boldsymbol{\omega}]$ is a quaternion with a scalar part of 0 and a vector part of $\boldsymbol{\omega}$.

Next, consider the rotational version of the equation of motion. Unlike translation, the rotational force in a rigid body changes depending on the relative position from the center of gravity. This can be expressed in the equation as torque $\boldsymbol{\tau}_i = \boldsymbol{r}_i \times \boldsymbol{f}_i$, where $\boldsymbol{r}_i, \boldsymbol{f}_i$ are the relative position coordinates of a certain point i in the rigid body and the force applied to that point. The torque, angular velocity, and the moment of inertia I, which is the mass for rotation, can be used to define the equation of motion for rotation.

$$\boldsymbol{\tau} = \frac{d}{dt}(I\boldsymbol{\omega}) = I\dot{\boldsymbol{\omega}} + \boldsymbol{\omega} \times I\boldsymbol{\omega} .\tag{4.12}$$

If we set $L = I\boldsymbol{\omega}$, then $\boldsymbol{\tau} = \dot{L}$ updates L, and $\boldsymbol{\omega} = I^{-1}L$ updates $\boldsymbol{\omega}$. Then, by updating the rotation matrix or quaternion with $\boldsymbol{\omega}$, we can calculate the change in posture.

4.2.2 Collision Detection and Response

If there is only one rigid body in the scene, its motion can be calculated with the aforementioned equations of motion. However, in actual CG scenes, many rigid bodies exist in the same space, and it is necessary to handle collisions between them. It can be said that the most computationally expensive part of rigid body simulation is this collision processing.

Collision processing consists of two major phases. The first is *collision detection*, which determines whether or not rigid bodies have collided. Collision detection between rigid bodies can be considered a problem of determining the distance between shapes. For example, consider the case of a collision between spheres as shown in Fig. 4.3. If the center coordinates of the two spheres are c_1, c_2 and the radii are r_1, r_2, the distance between the two rigid bodies is calculated by $d = |c_1 - c_2| - (r_1 + r_2)$ and when $d \leq 0$, a collision is detected. This process is called collision detection. In simple examples like spheres, the computational cost is not so high, but collision detection between complex shapes requires a lot of computational cost, and as the number of rigid bodies increases, the number of combinations that must be judged also increases at $O(N^2)$. Therefore, how to speed up collision detection processing becomes important. This acceleration will be explained in Sect. 4.2.3.

Fig. 4.3 Collision detection between spheres

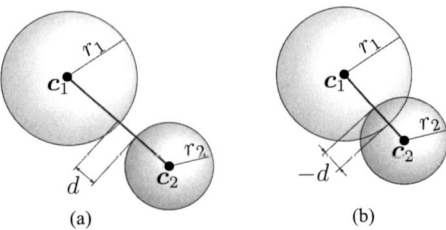

The second phase of collision processing is *collision response*. When rigid bodies collide, their motion changes due to the impact at that time. Calculating this motion change is the collision response. What is important in collision response is that the calculation of the applied force is not performed at any time, but at discrete times in rigid body simulation. For example, after being calculated at a certain time t, the next time the force is calculated is a finite time Δt later, which is $t + \Delta t$. So that, it is not always possible to respond to the collision at the moment of collision, and the phenomenon of rigid bodies penetrating each other occurs. This penetration must be resolved while calculating the response after the collision.

To resolve the penetration, we will start by explaining the *constraint-based method*. Consider the state where two rigid bodies have collided and penetration has occurred, as shown in Fig. 4.4a. If the collision is judged by the distance d between the rigid bodies as mentioned above, the state where penetration has occurred means that the distance d has become a negative value ($d < 0$). If we capture this distance between the rigid bodies as the constraint condition $C(x) = d$ that should be satisfied at the time of collision, the condition for no penetration can be written as

$$C(x) \geq 0 . \tag{4.13}$$

From the state where penetration between rigid bodies has occurred ($C(x) < 0$), to the state where they are in contact without penetration, that is, $C(x) = 0$, we need to find out what kind of force f_c should be applied. First, consider the state where the constraint condition is satisfied. If $C(x) = 0$ continues to be satisfied, the time derivative of the constraint condition also becomes zero ($\dot{C} = 0$). If we rewrite the

Fig. 4.4 Penetration and joints

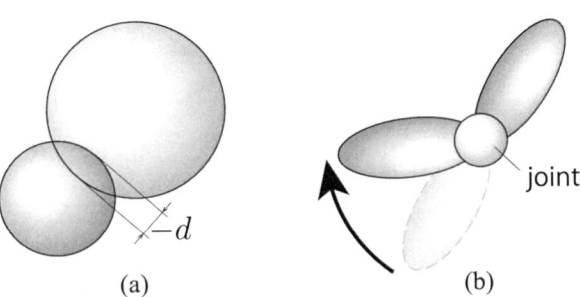

time derivative of the constraint condition using the chain rule of differentiation, it becomes:

$$\dot{C} = \frac{\partial C}{\partial x}\frac{\partial x}{\partial t} = J\dot{x} = 0 \, , \tag{4.14}$$

where $\partial C/\partial x$ is the Jacobian of C, so it is represented as J.

Similarly, the second time derivative is

$$\ddot{C} = \dot{J}\dot{x} + J\ddot{x} \, . \tag{4.15}$$

If the rigid body is moving while the constraint condition continues to be satisfied, it should be $\ddot{C} = 0$, but if penetration is occurring, it becomes $\ddot{C} \neq 0$. At this time, consider that $\ddot{C} = 0$ by adding a force f_c to satisfy the constraint condition. If you add f_c to the external force of the equation of motion (Eq. 4.8), it becomes $\ddot{x} = (f + f_c)/m$, substitute this into Eq. 4.15, and solve for f_c.

$$f_c = J^T\lambda \, , \tag{4.16}$$

where λ is a scalar coefficient, and can be considered as a Lagrange multiplier. f_c is the force that should be applied to the rigid body to satisfy the constraint condition, and by applying a force multiplied by the scalar value λ in the direction of the spatial differentiation of the constraint condition, the behavior after collision can be calculated, that is, the constraint condition is satisfied. In practice, it is necessary to consider the coefficient of restitution, but this is a collision response processing method based on the constraint condition. This method is not only used for collision processing but also used to connect rigid bodies with joints as shown in Fig. 4.4b.

For the coefficient λ, from the process of making Eq. 4.16, the relationship $JM^{-1}J^T\lambda = -JM^{-1}f - \dot{J}\dot{x}$ can be derived. If this is solved as a linear system $A\lambda = b$, even when many objects collide at the same time, λ can be determined (M is a diagonal matrix with mass m as its diagonal components). In actual processing, errors due to other than collisions (numerical errors, etc.) occur, so strictly speaking, $\ddot{C} \neq 0$, resulting in unstable collision processing. To make it a stable simulation, instead of $\ddot{C} = 0$, it is proposed to stabilize with two coefficients α, β by setting $\ddot{C} = \alpha\dot{C} + \beta C$ [1].

In addition to the constraint-based method for performing collision responses, there are the *penalty-based method* and the *impulse-based method*. The former penalty-based method, as shown in Fig. 4.5, assumes a spring with a repulsive force in the penetrating area and realizes a collision response by applying a force equivalent to the spring's repulsive force to the rigid body. Unlike the constraint-based method, instead of solving the linear system at once for all rigid bodies where a collision occurs, it calculates the force applied to each individual rigid body. In a scene where many rigid bodies overlap, it becomes difficult to achieve stable calculations by vibrating when trying to eliminate the penetration of an object surrounded by

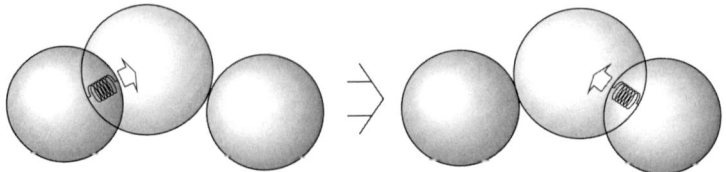

Fig. 4.5 Collision response by a spring according to the amount of penetration

other rigid bodies, but the penalty-based method improves the stability of calculations by returning a force according to the amount of penetration while allowing a
certain amount of penetration.

The impulse-based method is similar to the constraint-based method, but it differs
in that it seeks a force (the integrated force that works during the time step Δt) with a
direction and magnitude such that the contact points of the two rigid bodies coincide
after the time step Δt in order to satisfy the constraint conditions. As a method to
find the impulse, there are methods such as finding a nonlinear form to satisfy the
above conditions by Newton's iteration method [2] or finding it by solving a linear
system about the impulse in the same way as the constraint-based method [3]. A
characteristic of the impulse-based method is that it can be stabilized without using
user-defined coefficients α, β like the constraint-based method.

4.2.3 Acceleration of Collision Detection

The collision detection between spheres, which was shown as an example in
Sect. 4.2.2 (Fig. 4.3), was simple, but it is also possible to detect collisions between
triangular polygons, which are often used in CG for shape representation, by mathematically calculating distances such as between a point and a surface, or a point and
a line. However, the number of polygons that make up a 3D model is generally in
the hundreds to tens of thousands. For example, if collision detection is performed
between models with a polygon count of N, the order of the number of combinations
of polygons that must be collision detected is $O(N^2)$. This may not be a problem if
there is only one pair of polygon models, but real-time calculation becomes difficult
if there are hundreds of models in the scene. Therefore, a method is used to speed up
the process by dividing it into two stages: the *broad phase*, which reduces the number
of combinations that must actually calculate distances, and the *narrow phase*, which
performs collision detection by distance calculation.

In the broad phase, a simple shape that completely covers one rigid body shape
is found, and collision detection is performed with this shape to search for pairs that
may collide. The shape at this time is called a *boundary volume*. The purpose of
the broad phase is to reduce the amount of computation in the narrow phase by first
performing collisions between boundary volumes, thereby eliminating combinations
that have no possibility of collision.

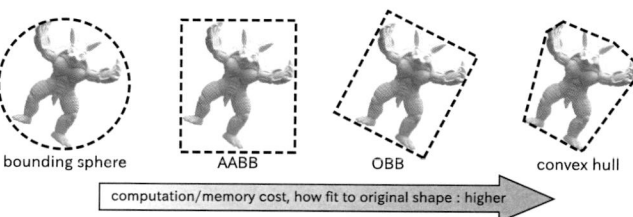

Fig. 4.6 Example of a boundary volume

The first thing to consider in the broad phase is what shape to use as the boundary volume. Figure 4.6 shows the boundary volume shapes often used in rigid body simulation. The purpose of using a boundary volume is to improve the efficiency of collision detection, so it is better to have a shape that is easy to intersect, and also has a low cost of volume creation and requires a small amount of memory. Also, the closer the fit to the original shape, the less unnecessary calculation is needed in the narrow phase. As you move from left to right in Fig. 4.6, the intersection determination cost and required memory amount increase, but on the other hand, the fit to the original shape becomes higher.

For example, the *bounding sphere* shown in Fig. 4.6 is a method of using a sphere that encloses a rigid body shape as a boundary volume. The bounding sphere can be defined by only the center coordinates and radius, so it requires a small amount of memory, and intersection determination is possible with just the distance calculation between the center coordinates. On the other hand, the fit to the shape is low, and the computational cost for determining the circumscribed sphere for a rigid body shape represented by polygons also becomes large. On the other hand, the *OBB* (Oriented Bounding Box) and the *convex hull* that surrounds objects with a box or concave shape requires a high amount of memory and intersection determination cost, but it can reduce the amount of computation in the narrow phase due to its high degree of fit. Among these bounding volume shapes, the most commonly used is the *AABB* (Axis Aligned Bounding Box). The AABB is rectangular each side is parallel to the x, y, z axes, and not only its construction cost (the cost of finding the AABB that covers the rigid body shape) is low, but also its collision detection is easy, only requiring the comparison of maximum and minimum coordinate values. Although the collision detection of AABB is low cost, it still cannot handle the increased number of combinations when the number of rigid bodies is large. Therefore, there are several methods to further improve efficiency. Here, we will explain about the 3D sweep & prune, AABB tree, and grid structure.

The *3D sweep and prune* method, as shown in Fig. 4.7, uses the positional relationship when the endpoints of the maximum and minimum coordinate values of the AABB are sorted by the values on the axis when projected onto the x, y, z axes. For example, if you look at the endpoints projected onto the x axis in Fig. 4.7, if they do not intersect on that axis, the minimum and maximum endpoints of the same object are adjacent, like ①①②②. But if they overlap, another object number is

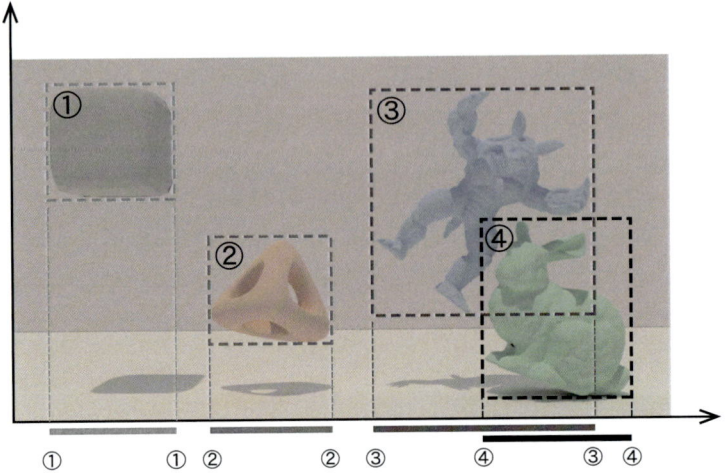

Fig. 4.7 3D sweep & prune

sandwiched between them, like ③④③④. This is determined for all three axes, and if they overlap on all axes, it is considered that the AABBs overlap each other. The advantage of this method is that it requires a one-dimensional search instead of a three-dimensional search, and if the rigid bodies move continuously, it is considered that the sort results of the previous step are mostly in the correct order in the next step. Using a fast sorting algorithm when most of the initial values are sorted, such as insertion sort, makes it possible to efficiently detect collisions.

The *AABB tree*, as shown in Fig. 4.8, is a method of searching for colliding objects by creating a tree structure by finding AABBs that further cover the AABB. In the construction of the AABB tree, first, an AABB that encompasses all objects is found and set as the root node, and then the process of dividing the objects contained in the root node spatially into two and finding the AABB that covers each to make them child nodes is repeated until there is only one object in the node. When detecting collisions,

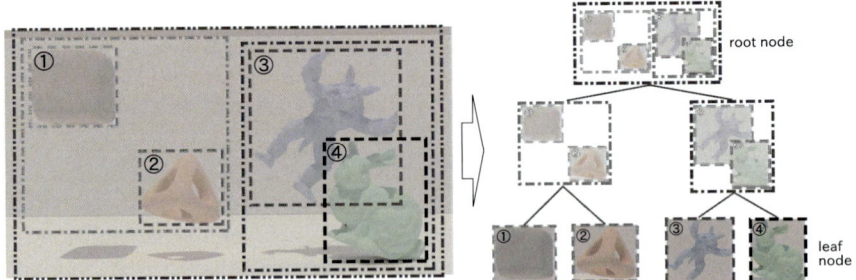

Fig. 4.8 AABB tree

first collide with the root node and then collide with the child nodes contained in that node, repeating this process until the leaf node. The number of combinations, that was $O(N^2)$ in a full search, can be reduced to $O(N \log N)$. However, it is necessary to be aware that the cost of constructing the tree structure is necessary, so if most of the rigid bodies in the scene are always moving, the construction is necessary at every step.

The *grid structure* is, A method that uses spatially divided areas like the AABB tree. The difference from the AABB tree is that instead of using a tree structure, the space is divided into equal interval cells. By making all grid cell widths the same, only a simple division is needed to determine which grid a given coordinate belongs to. For example, if the grid cell width is h, the grid cell number to which the coordinate x belongs can be determined by $floor(x/h)$ ($floor()$ represents rounding down after decimal point). Although AABB has a volume, from its shape, all the grid cells to which it belongs can be found just by performing the above calculation for the maximum/minimum coordinate values. For collision detection, only the AABBs in the grid cell to which the target AABB belongs need to be included in the calculation. One thing to note is that depending on the setting of the grid cell width h, the number of grid cells to be searched may increase, so this parameter must be set considering the size of the objects contained in the space. Unlike the AABB tree, the cost of constructing the structure is low, so it is more efficient when many rigid bodies are always moving, and it is easy to parallelize. Because of this feature, it is often used not only for rigid body simulation but also for searching for neighboring particles in the particle method explained in Sect. 4.4.

4.3 Elastic Body Simulation

4.3.1 Elastic and Plastic Bodies

In Sect. 4.2, we assumed rigid bodies as objects that do not deform, defining the movement of objects with one position vector and one matrix/quaternion of posture information. However, actual objects can change their shape. If we can simulate not only rigid bodies but also such *deformable body*, we can greatly expand the range of representations for CG animation.

Among deforming objects, those that have a property to return to their original shape are called a *elastic body* (the top row of Fig. 4.9), and their deformation is called *elastic deformation*. In the case of a perfect elastic body, after deforming due to external force, if the external force is removed, it will rotate and move overall but return completely to its original shape. In reality, there are almost no perfect elastic bodies, just like rigid bodies, but in the CG field, many objects such as hair, clothes, character animations including deformations due to muscles and fat, trees and grass swaying in the wind, etc. are simulated as elastic bodies. This section mainly explains the methods for simulating these elastic bodies.

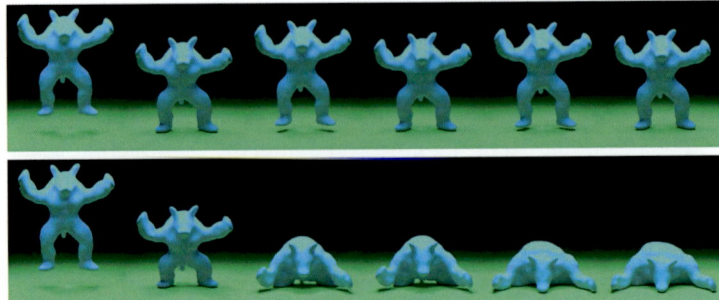

Fig. 4.9 Examples of elastic body simulation (top) and elastoplastic body simulation (bottom)[4]

On the other hand, objects that maintain their deformed shape, even when the external force is removed, are called a *plastic body* (the bottom row of Fig. 4.9), and such deformation is called *plastic deformation*. Fluids, which will be explained in Sect. 4.4, can be considered as perfect plastic bodies, but for example, even elastic bodies like rubber, if subjected to a very large force, will not completely return to their original shape, and some deformation will remain. Such objects are called a *elastoplastic body*. Many solids in the real world are these elastoplastic bodies, and in CG animation, when you want to represent clay, cream, snow, etc., the object is simulated as an elastoplastic body.

When calculating the behavior of these deformable bodies in CG with physics simulation, the position vector is not fixed to a single position vector within an object, resulting in different movements at different locations. To calculate this on a computer, the object itself must be discretized in some way. It becomes necessary to place multiple calculation points inside the object or to represent the deformation and force distribution inside the object by some function. In the remainder of this section, we will introduce the physical equations that is the basis for deformation calculations, and introduce these discretization methods.

4.3.2 Mechanical Simulation Methods

Before explaining how to simulate the deformation of the elastic body, we will explain the basic equations of motion that describe object deformation. The following *Lagrangian equation of motion* is an equation that represents the balance of energy in the motion of an object.

$$\frac{d}{dt}\left(\frac{\partial L}{\partial \dot{q}}\right) - \frac{\partial L}{\partial q} = f_{ext} \, , \tag{4.17}$$

where q is a generalized coordinate that includes positions such as x (if q is position, then $\dot{q}$ is velocity). f_{ext} is an external force, and $L = T - U$ is the Lagrangian, which represents the difference between kinetic energy T and potential energy U. For example, consider a situation where an object with mass m is falling freely under gravity with gravitational acceleration g. If the height of the object is y, the Lagrangian at height y can be expressed as $L = \frac{1}{2}m\dot{y}^2 - mgy$, which is the difference between the kinetic energy of the object with velocity $\dot{y}$ and the potential energy at height y. Substituting this into Eq. 4.17 gives $\ddot{y} = g$. This represents that the acceleration of a freely falling object is independent of its mass m and is equal to the gravitational acceleration g.

To apply the Lagrangian equation of motion to the elastic body, we make two assumptions. The first is that the kinetic energy T is proportional to the square of the velocity. As shown in the example of free fall, the kinetic energy is expressed as $T = \frac{1}{2}m\dot{q}^2$, and if q is a vector, it is expressed as $T = \frac{1}{2}\dot{q}^T M \dot{q}$ using the mass matrix M which has mass m as its diagonal elements. The second assumption is that the potential energy U is independent of velocity. In this case, $\frac{\partial U}{\partial \dot{q}} = 0$. Using these two assumptions, and assuming that the generalized coordinates are vectors, the Lagrangian equation of motion can be rewritten as follows.

$$M\ddot{q} + f(q) = f_{ext} , \tag{4.18}$$

where $f(q) = \frac{\partial U}{\partial q}$. Equation 4.18 is called *Newton's equation of motion*, If the force $f(q)$ due to the potential energy inside the object does not act, it takes the same form as Eq. 4.8.

In the case of *elastic body simulation*, the force $f(q)$ due to the potential energy inside the object in Eq. 4.18 is considered to work to restore the shape of the object to its original form. Let's consider the internal region of the elastic body as Ω as shown in Fig. 4.10, and consider the case where it became Ω' due to deformation. p denote the point inside the elastic body before deformation, and the corresponding point after deformation as x. The potential energy acting inside the elastic body can be expressed as

$$U = \int_{\Omega} W_e(x, p) dp , \tag{4.19}$$

Fig. 4.10 Displacement of an internal point in elastic deformation

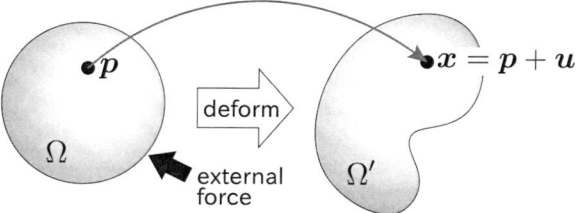

where $W_e(x, p)$ is the elastic potential energy density at point p. If W_e is considered as the energy density that works to return to the original shape, it can be described by the gradient $\nabla x(p)$ indicating how much it has deformed from the original shape,

$$U = \int_\Omega W_e(\nabla x)d p \ . \tag{4.20}$$

If the displacement from point p to point x is u ($x = p + u$), then $\nabla x = \nabla p + \nabla u$, the elastic potential energy is determined by the gradient value of the displacement ∇u, if the original point p is a fixed value. This ∇u is called the *deformation gradient*.

If the displacement in three-dimensional space is $u = (u, v, w)^T$, the deformation gradient is described as a 3×3 matrix (a second-order tensor).

$$\nabla u = \begin{pmatrix} \frac{\partial u}{\partial x} & \frac{\partial u}{\partial y} & \frac{\partial u}{\partial z} \\ \frac{\partial v}{\partial x} & \frac{\partial v}{\partial y} & \frac{\partial v}{\partial z} \\ \frac{\partial w}{\partial x} & \frac{\partial w}{\partial y} & \frac{\partial w}{\partial z} \end{pmatrix} \ . \tag{4.21}$$

If each element of Eq. 4.21 can be calculated by the discretization method described later, it will be possible to calculate the elastic potential energy. But what is needed in the calculation of Eq. 4.18 is the "force" acting internally, therefore, an equation representing a relationship between the deformation gradient and the force is needed. To express this relationship, we use *Hooke's law*. Hooke's law is a principle stating that the *stress* σ, which is the force per unit area, and the *strain* ε, which is the amount of deformation per unit length, are proportional. It is expressed by the following equation.

$$\sigma = E\varepsilon \ , \tag{4.22}$$

where E is a proportional constant called Young's modulus. Now what we need is a "force", but if we think of it as a force per unit volume in three dimensions and use density ρ instead of mass m, we can turn Eq. 4.18 into an equation for stress. Therefore, what is needed next is the relationship between strain ε and deformation gradient ∇u.

If the strain ε in a certain region within the elastic body is represented as a matrix as a *strain tensor*, the strain tensor defined by Cauchy is given by the following equation.

$$\varepsilon_C = \frac{1}{2} \left(\nabla u + (\nabla u)^T \right) \ . \tag{4.23}$$

In addition to the strain tensor by Eq. 4.23, there are several relationship formulas proposed, such as Green's strain tensor ($\varepsilon_G = \frac{1}{2} \left(\nabla u + (\nabla u)^T + (\nabla u)^T \nabla u \right)$), depending on the difference in materials, etc. By using these equations, we can calculate strain from the deformation gradient, and stress from Hooke's law, and finally, we can calculate the displacement at each point inside the elastic body based on the equation of motion (for the calculation of displacement at each point, we can use the time integration explained in Sect. 4.2). This is the basic idea for the elastic body simulation using dynamics.

With the method explained so far, we can calculate the displacement of any point inside the elastic body from the external force f_{ext}, but the problem is whether to calculate this for all points inside the object. Considering the computational cost on a computer, it is currently unrealistic. Furthermore, how to calculate ∇u is also a problem. Of course, it would be best if we could solve it analytically, but in the CG field, we often have to deal with objects with complex shapes, and there are many cases where it is difficult to solve analytically. Therefore, we take a method of discretizing the elastic body in some way and calculating the displacement at the discrete points by numerical calculation. There are methods such as spring-mass system, finite difference method, finite element method, and mesh-free methods such as particle method for discretizing the elastic body. In this section, we will briefly introduce the spring-mass system and the finite element method, which are often used in the CG field for elastic body simulation.

Spring-Mass System

The deformation gradient tensor and strain tensor become matrices in 3D and become complex and time-consuming to analyze, but what about a 1D elastic body? In a 1D elastic body, deformation and strain can be represented as scalar values (0th-order tensors), and the calculation becomes simple. Here, we consider a *spring* as a 1D elastic body, as shown in Fig. 4.11.

If we do not consider it per unit length in 1D, the strain ε can simply be the change in length of the spring $\Delta x = l - l_0$, and the force applied to the spring (note that this is not stress) from Hooke's law is,

$$f_{spring} = k\Delta x , \tag{4.24}$$

where k is a proportional constant called the spring constant.

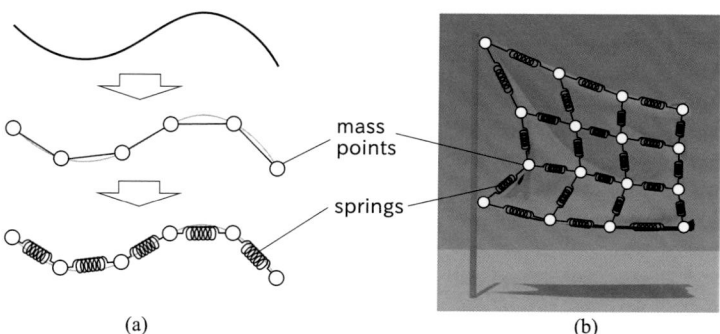

(a)   (b)

Fig. 4.11 Spring-mass system

Consider approximating a real object with this collection of springs. In order to approximate an object with mass, not only the spring but also a mass point with mass m is placed at both ends of the spring. With the mass point with the positions at both ends being x_1, x_2, and when external forces such as damping force and gravity are added to the force by the spring, the force acting on the mass point is expressed as follows.

$$f_1 = k\Delta x + k_d \dot{x}_1 + f_{ext} , \qquad (4.25)$$
$$f_2 = -k\Delta x + k_d \dot{x}_2 + f_{ext} , \qquad (4.26)$$

where $\Delta x = (|x_1 - x_2| - l_0)\frac{x_1-x_2}{|x_1-x_2|}$ from both end coordinates, when the original length of the spring is l_0. k_d is the damping coefficient, and f_{ext} is the external force. The damping term represents energy loss within the object and air resistance, and also plays a role in stabilizing the simulation. If you extract only the force by the spring and set the original length of the spring to 1, the equation can be expressed using a matrix,

$$\begin{pmatrix} f_1 \\ f_2 \end{pmatrix} = \begin{pmatrix} k & -k \\ -k & k \end{pmatrix} \begin{pmatrix} x_1 \\ x_2 \end{pmatrix} , \qquad (4.27)$$

and the matrix in Eq. 4.27 is denoted as K.

In the case of simulating an elastic body with a three-dimensional volume, the shape is approximated by a collection of mass points and springs. In this way, using mass points and springs to determine the behavior of an elastic body is called a *mass-spring system*. Here we define the vector $x = (x_1, x_2, ..., x_n)^T$ that summarizes the coordinate values of the mass points and the diagonal matrix (mass matrix) M with the mass of each point as the diagonal element, and the matrix K defined by Eq. 4.27 calculated from the influence of the spring at all mass points and the matrix C defined in the same way about the damping coefficient. The equation of motion of a mass-spring system with multiple mass points is obtained as follows.

$$M\ddot{x} + C\dot{x} + Kx = f_{ext} . \qquad (4.28)$$

$C\dot{x} + Kx$ in this equation represents the force due to the internal potential energy corresponding to $f(q)$ in Eq. 4.18.

The spring-mass system can approximate various elastic bodies, from one-dimensional objects like strings and hair to thin objects like cloth, by changing the arrangement of the springs. If it is an object like cloth, we can use masses and springs arranged in a grid on a two-dimensional space as shown in Fig. 4.11b. In that case, springs may be set diagonally or springs may be set every other one to express the sagging of the cloth [5]. However, only springs cannot express twisted components like curly hair. Therefore, when simulating such objects, methods such as arranging springs in a grid along the hair can also be taken [6].

While the spring-mass system allows for simple implementation and fast computation, depending on the time integration method, it has the disadvantage of being prone to divergence (oscillation) depending on the time step width Δt. Methods using implicit calculation have been proposed [7], but it is necessary to choose a calculation method that suits the purpose since this will increase the computation time. If it is okay to take computation time and accurate calculation is necessary, the finite element method mentioned later or, if you want to calculate quickly and stably, you should consider methods such as the position-based method described in Sect. 4.3.3.

Finite Element Method

In the spring-mass system, the elastic body is approximated by a set of mass points, which are points in space. However, actual elastic bodies are not such discrete objects, They are spatially continuous bodies with volume. Such bodies will be referred to as *continuum body* (there is a field of study dealing with the deformation of continuum bodies, continuum mechanics). In the spring-mass system, the deformation between mass points was assumed to be a spring that changes linearly and uniformly with displacement, but in reality, it changes nonlinearly and continuously between mass points. This causes problems with accuracy and computational stability because it is simply approximated by a spring. In contrast, the *FEM* (Finite Element Method) captures not the change in "value" at a point in space, but the force and displacement within that element as the change in the "distribution function".

In the finite element method, first, the object shape is approximated as a collection of elements such as triangles in two dimensions and tetrahedra in three dimensions, and how the distribution function changes within each element is calculated. For example, the Poisson equation $\frac{d^2u(x)}{dx^2} = f$, which is used to simulate phenomena such as heat diffusion within an object, is considered to be discretized and solved. In methods that use the values at calculation points, like a spring-mass system, the value of the physical quantity $u(x)$, is stored at the calculation points as u_i, and the governing equation (in this case, the Poisson equation) is discretized using methods such as the difference method, and the values of each u_i are updated. In the finite element method, on the other hand, the left-hand side of the Poisson equation itself is treated as a functional $G(u(x))$ that takes the function $u(x)$ as an argument, and we seek a function that satisfies the functional.

So how do we find such a function? One method is to use a variational method, which is a method for solving the minimization problem of such a functional. Using the variational method, we can mathematically find a solution, but it is difficult to apply it directly to general-purpose calculations using a computer. The problem when applying it to general-purpose calculations is that we do not know what kind of function $u(x)$ is. Therefore, we consider a linear combination of certain basis functions $\Phi(x)$ as an approximation function $\hat{u}(x)$ for the function $u(x)$.

$$u(x) \approx \hat{u}(x) = \sum_i a_i \Phi_i(x) . \tag{4.29}$$

Once the basis functions $\Phi_i(x)$ are determined, what we need to calculate are the values of the coefficients a_i, and we can reduce the problem of finding a function to the problem of finding a value. This method of using a linear combination of basis functions is called the *Galerkin method* in the finite element method. In the finite element method, we also use the principle of virtual work to reduce the order of the problem, but the basic idea is to divide the object into elements and find the coefficients of the approximation function for each element. Here, we only explain the concept of the finite element method, and omit the specific discretization and calculation methods, but if you want to know more, please refer to SIGGRAPH course notes [8], etc.

The finite element method allows for high-precision and stable calculations due to its approximation by distribution functions, and it can handle a wider range of objects and problems than the spring-mass system (not only elastic bodies and fluids explained in the next section, but also problems such as heat conduction), and is widely used in the CG field. On the other hand, the need to solve large linear systems in the calculation process often results in a long computation time. Regarding computation time, there is the Condensed FEM [9] which calculates only on the surface of the object, and the co-rotation FEM, which improves efficiency by extracting rotational components from elements [10], or methods such as the acceleration of calculations using dimension reduction, which requires large pre-calculations (model reduction) [11, 12], have also been proposed in the CG field.

4.3.3 Position-Based Method

When calculating elastic bodies by mechanical methods, such as continuum mechanics, accuracy and calculation time are important factors, but control is also important when used in the CG field. In mechanical simulation methods, forces and accelerations are first calculated, then velocities are derived, and finally, positions are determined to obtain simulation results. With such methods, for example, if you want to move point A of an object to another point B, you have to calculate the force that makes the object at point A move toward point B by reversing the above process. If the calculation process includes nonlinear formulas, you need to use an optimization method or determine the force through trial and error, which can make intuitive control difficult. Furthermore, errors that occur in deriving velocity from acceleration and position from velocity, accumulate over time due to time integration, making the calculation unstable. The latter problem can be somewhat solved by using implicit methods for time integration, but it takes a long time to calculate, and the former problem of control is still not solved. To improve the controllability of the simulation, while maintaining a visually acceptable level of accuracy, stability, and speed of calculation, the method recently used in the CG field is the *position-based method* (PBD: Position-Based Dynamics).

The position-based method uses the constraint conditions explained in Sect. 4.2.2, applies these constraints directly to the position, and calculates the position directly without using forces or accelerations, providing a method that can simulate various objects. If you want to control an object, you only need to change the position directly, so the controllability is very good. Because it does not apply the process of force/acceleration → velocity → position, it excels in calculation stability and speed. On the other hand, since it is not simulating mechanically, and is a "geometric" method that describes the relationship between multiple calculation points with constraint conditions, it has the problem of being difficult to use for analysis of objects where physical correctness is required. However, what is required in the CG field is visual plausibility, so this point is not a major problem.

We will explain the basic concept and theory of the position-based method. Now, suppose that the object/shape you want to deform elastically is approximated as a set of points p_i. Let's denote the constraint that this set $p \in [p_1, ..., p_n]$ should satisfy as $C(p) = 0$. For example, if you want to express the property of an elastic body trying to return to its original shape, you set $C(p)$ to be a condition that the relative position relationship between the points p_i maintains the original shape. Then, if this constraint was satisfied at a step t, it should also be satisfied at the next step $t + \Delta t$. If p changes by Δp between t and Δt, the following condition should also be satisfied.

$$C(p + \Delta p) = 0 , \tag{4.30}$$

where Δp is not considered as a change due to external force etc., but as the displacement of p necessary to satisfy the constraint. By solving the problem of finding Δp that satisfies Eq. 4.30, we can understand how to move the point set p to satisfy the constraint.

Assuming that Δp is small, we expand Eq. 4.30 around p using Taylor's theorem (ignoring terms of second order and higher).

$$C(p + \Delta p) \approx C(p) + \nabla_p C(p) \cdot \Delta p = 0 . \tag{4.31}$$

To solve Eq. 4.31 for Δp, we consider the condition that Δp should satisfy. If the constraint $C(p)$ is a restriction on the internal state of the object, $C(p)$ can be considered independent of the overall translation or rotation of the object. In other words, the direction of change of the constraint $\nabla_p C(p)$, is orthogonal to the motion change of the entire object. If you want to prevent the overall motion of the object from changing due to the internal change represented by Δp, you should change p in the direction of this $\nabla_p C(p)$. If you set the change amount to λ, it can be described as follows.

$$\Delta p = \lambda \nabla_p C(p) . \tag{4.32}$$

By substituting Eq. 4.32 into Eq. 4.31, we can derive λ. Therefore, by substituting the derived λ into Eq. 4.32, we can get the following equation to find the displacement vector Δp that satisfies the constraint.

$$\Delta p = -\frac{C(p)}{||\nabla_p C(p)||^2} \nabla_p C(p) . \tag{4.33}$$

So far, we have used the set $\boldsymbol{p}$ in the equations, but in actual calculations, we will need the displacement amount $\Delta \boldsymbol{p}_i$ at each calculation point i. If we add a weight $w_i = 1/m_i$ that represents the ease of movement for each calculation point, Eq. 4.33 can be rewritten as follows.

$$\Delta \boldsymbol{p}_i = \lambda_i w_i \nabla_{\boldsymbol{p}_i} C_i(\boldsymbol{p}) , \quad \lambda_i = -\frac{C_i(\boldsymbol{p}_1, ..., \boldsymbol{p}_n)}{\sum_j w_j \|\nabla_{\boldsymbol{p}_j} C_i(\boldsymbol{p}_1, ..., \boldsymbol{p}_n)\|^2} , \tag{4.34}$$

where C_i is the constraint for calculation point i. If we let $\boldsymbol{p}_i = (x_i, y_i, z_i)^T$, $\nabla_{\boldsymbol{p}_i} = \left(\frac{\partial}{\partial x_i}, \frac{\partial}{\partial y_i}, \frac{\partial}{\partial z_i} \right)$, and it should be noted that this is not a simple spatial derivative, but a derivative with respect to the coordinates $\boldsymbol{p}_i$.

Let's give an example of the constraint $C(\boldsymbol{p})$. As mentioned earlier, elastic bodies like rubber have the property to return to their original shape. To reproduce this, in the spring-mass system, the object is approximated by a set of one-dimensional springs. If we consider this spring to behave in a way that keeps its original length, we can consider this as a constraint against stretching (*stretching constraint*). As shown in Fig. 4.12b, let's put the constraint to keep the length between the two points $\boldsymbol{p}_1$, $\boldsymbol{p}_2$ to l_0 into an equation. The condition is satisfied if the distance between two points $\|\boldsymbol{p}_1 - \boldsymbol{p}_2\|$ is equal to l_0, and it can be formulated as follows.

$$C_{stretch}(\boldsymbol{p}_1, \boldsymbol{p}_2) = \|\boldsymbol{p}_1 - \boldsymbol{p}_2\| - l_0 = 0 . \tag{4.35}$$

The gradients of $C_{stretch}$ with respect to $\boldsymbol{p}_1$, $\boldsymbol{p}_2$ are $\nabla_{\boldsymbol{p}_1} C_{stretch} = \frac{\boldsymbol{p}_1 - \boldsymbol{p}_2}{\|\boldsymbol{p}_1 - \boldsymbol{p}_2\|}$ and $\nabla_{\boldsymbol{p}_2} C_{stretch} = -\frac{\boldsymbol{p}_1 - \boldsymbol{p}_2}{\|\boldsymbol{p}_1 - \boldsymbol{p}_2\|}$. Therefore, the position corrections $\Delta \boldsymbol{p}_1$, $\Delta \boldsymbol{p}_2$ are given by the following equations.

$$\Delta \boldsymbol{p}_1 = -\frac{w_1}{w_1 + w_2}(\|\boldsymbol{p}_1 - \boldsymbol{p}_2\| - l_0)\frac{\boldsymbol{p}_1 - \boldsymbol{p}_2}{\|\boldsymbol{p}_1 - \boldsymbol{p}_2\|} , \tag{4.36}$$

$$\Delta \boldsymbol{p}_2 = \frac{w_1}{w_1 + w_2}(\|\boldsymbol{p}_1 - \boldsymbol{p}_2\| - l_0)\frac{\boldsymbol{p}_1 - \boldsymbol{p}_2}{\|\boldsymbol{p}_1 - \boldsymbol{p}_2\|} . \tag{4.37}$$

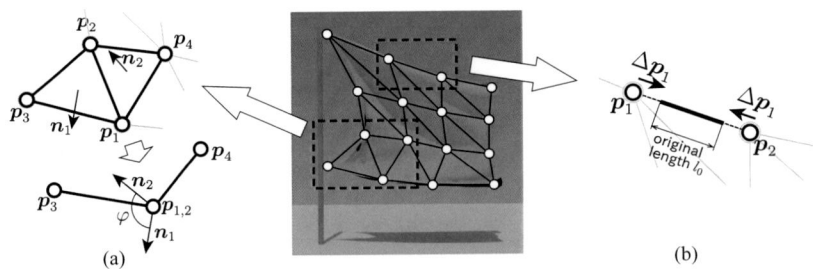

(a)   (b)

Fig. 4.12 Constraints for bending and stretching

By using this constraint for stretching, motion of objects like hair can be reproduced, and by applying this condition between calculation points arranged in 2D/3D like a spring-mass system, thin objects like cloth and voluminous objects like rubber balls can also be represented. However, this constraint only relates to the distance between calculation points, so it cannot reproduce things that resist bending, like stiff cloth. In that case, it is necessary to apply a *bending constraint* as another constraint condition.

Now, assuming that the shape of the object is approximated by a set of triangles(polygons) with vertices as calculation points. As shown in Fig. 4.12a, take one edge and the two triangles connected to it, and let the vertices be p_1, p_2, p_3, p_4 (with p_1, p_2 forming the central edge). Let φ be the angle between the unit normal vectors n_1, n_2 of the two triangles, and if the original angle before deformation is φ_0, the constraint condition is,

$$C_{bend}(p_1, p_2, p_3, p_4) = \varphi - \varphi_0 = 0 , \tag{4.38}$$

where $\varphi = \mathrm{acos}(n_1 \cdot n_2)$. The unit normal vector is calculated from the cross product of the polygon vertices (for example, $n_1 = \frac{(p_2-p_1)\times(p_3-p_1)}{||(p_2-p_1)\times(p_3-p_1)||}$. Equation 4.38 is a constraint that maintains the angle between two polygons across an edge at the initial value φ_0, which allows for the representation of stiff cloth that is difficult to bend. The position correction calculated from Eq. 4.38 is as follows.

$$\Delta p_i = -\frac{4w_i}{\sum_j w_j} \frac{\sqrt{1-d^2}(\mathrm{acos}(d) - \varphi_0)}{\sum_j ||q_j||^2} q_i, \quad (i = 1 \sim 4) , \tag{4.39}$$

where $d = n_1 \cdot n_2$. q_i is the relative coordinate with vertex p_1 as the origin for $\hat{p}_i$ (that is, $\hat{p}_i = p_i - p_1$), then,

$$q_2 = -\frac{\hat{p}_3 \times n_2 + (n_1 \times \hat{p}_3)d}{||\hat{p}_2 \times \hat{p}_3||} - \frac{\hat{p}_4 \times n_1 + (n_2 \times \hat{p}_4)d}{||\hat{p}_2 \times \hat{p}_4||} , \tag{4.40}$$

$$q_3 = \frac{\hat{p}_2 \times n_2 + (n_1 \times \hat{p}_2)d}{||\hat{p}_2 \times \hat{p}_3||} , \tag{4.41}$$

$$q_4 = -\frac{\hat{p}_2 \times n_1 + (n_2 \times \hat{p}_2)d}{||\hat{p}_2 \times \hat{p}_4||} , \tag{4.42}$$

$$q_1 = -q_2 - q_3 - q_4 . \tag{4.43}$$

Other constraints include preserving the volume of the tetrahedron, constraints on the distance between the vertex and the polygon (equivalent to the collision constraint explained in Sect. 4.2.2), penetration/friction constraints used in simulations of granular material like sand, constraints against twisting for representing curl hair or elastic rods, and constraints not only for elastic bodies but also for fluids (this will be explained in Sect. 4.4). Various such constraints have been proposed. Furthermore, in actual simulations, combining multiple constraints allows for the representation of a

Fig. 4.13 Example of curly hair simulation by position-based method[14]

variety of objects. For example, Fig. 4.13 is an example of simulating hair with twists like curly hair by combining constraints against extension and bending/twisting [13].

Although the displacement vector to satisfy the constraint conditions can be calculated by Eq. 4.34, in an object composed of many calculation points, if you calculate Δp_i for each calculation point only with local information, it may satisfy the constraint conditions in some areas, but not in others. To solve this, it is necessary to calculate Δp_i for all calculation points and update the position p_i, repeating this process. The calculation procedure of the position-based method (for one-time step) including this iterative calculation is shown below.

1. Update all calculation point velocities v_i by external force: $v_i \leftarrow v_i + \Delta t w_i f_{ext}$
2. Update the position of all calculation points p_i (store the updated position as the predicted position p_i') : $p_i' \leftarrow p_i + \Delta t v_i$
3. Process collisions, etc. and update the predicted position p_i'
4. Repeat the following process with a specified number of times, or until the constraints are satisfied

   a. Calculate Δp_i from p_i' by Eq. 4.34
   b. Update the predicted position $p_i' : p_i' \leftarrow p_i' + \Delta p_i$

5. Update velocity and position : $v_i \leftarrow \frac{p_i' - p_i}{\Delta t}, \quad p_i \leftarrow p_i'.$

The position-based method first calculates the *predicted position* (steps 1–3), and then iteratively corrects it to satisfy the constraint conditions (step 4), making it a two-step method. Although the position-based method is based on position, the final velocity calculation (step 5) needs to be calculated to represent the movement due to the inertia of the object.

In step 4(b) of the calculation, p_i' is being rewritten as needed. However, the number of constraints related to the calculation point i can be multiple, so p_i' can be updated multiple times within one iteration. In that case, the numerical calculation method that uses the updated p_i' due to another constraint at the time of updating for a certain constraint is called the *Gauss-Seidel method*. It is known that the Gauss-Seidel method can speed up convergence in iterative methods, but on the other hand, there are problems such as the solution oscillating when trying to handle multiple constraints with different optimal points at once, and parallelization is difficult because of sequential rewriting. In cases where there are problems, it is good to take a method that takes the average of the position correction amounts for all the constraint conditions related to the calculation point p_i within that one iteration (this is called the *Jacobi method*). In this case, for each calculation point i, the position correction is,

$$\Delta p_i = \frac{1}{n_i} \sum_j \Delta p_j . \tag{4.44}$$

p'_i can be updated only once in one iteration. Here, n_i is the number of constraint conditions related to the calculation point i, and Δp_j is the position correction for those constraint conditions. The Jacobi method requires a larger number of iterations to converge compared to the Gauss-Seidel method (depending on the problem, it can be about twice as much), but it has the feature of being parallelizable. So that, there is a possibility that the total calculation time can be reduced by using GPU, etc. Also, even if there are multiple constraint conditions, it is possible to calculate stably without oscillation. If you want to speed up convergence while maintaining the parallelism of the Jacobi method, you should use the *SOR* (Successive Over-Relaxation) method, which multiplies the right side of Eq. 4.44 by the acceleration relaxation coefficient $\omega \in [1, 2]$ [15]. However, depending on the setting of the acceleration relaxation coefficient, convergence may be slower, so you need to find the appropriate value by trial and error.

In mechanical simulation methods, the *stiffness* of the elastic body was controlled using Young's modulus, spring constant, etc., How should it be controlled when using the position-based method? For example, in the case of the stretching constraint, if the iterative process is performed until the constraint conditions are completely satisfied, it will return to its original length in one step, simulating a very hard object. On the other hand, if the number of iterations is small, depending on the number of calculation points, there may be parts that do not return to their original length, resulting in reproducing a soft elastic body. Although it is somewhat controllable by changing the number of iterations, it is difficult to control each object as it also changes depending on the number of calculation points, and the relationship with physical parameters is unknown. One method is to update the predicted position p' by the position correction amount in step 4(b), as $p'_i \leftarrow p'_i + k\Delta p_i$, where the stiffness coefficient $k \in [0, 1]$ is used [16]. If k is fixed during iteration, the stiffness will still depend on the number of iterations. So $k' = 1 - (1 - k)^{1/n_s}$ (n_s is the number of iterations) is used instead of k. This method can express stiffness without depending on the number of iterations, but the relationship with physical parameters is still unknown. If you want to use physical parameters, you need to use XPBD [17] or PD (Projective Dynamics) [18]. XPBD is a method that reflects physical parameters by solving a linear system related to the change amount $\Delta\lambda$ of λ derived based on the motion equation and the position correction amount Δp, PD is a method that combines not only local constraint iteration but also global optimization that solves the energy minimization problem.

4.4 Fluid Simulation

4.4.1 Properties of Fluids and Navier-Stokes Equations

Rigid and elastic bodies have their original shapes, and their behavior is simulated based on these shapes, but in the real world, there are also objects whose shapes do not remain and constantly change in complex ways. This is a *fluid*. Fluids, such as air and water, are familiar to us, and when creating CG animation, they are necessary to reproduce effects such as smoke, flames, explosions, or to reproduce water animations, such as shower, river flow, and sea wave.

Elastic bodies have a clear property of trying to return to their original shape, and various equations were made based on this, but what about fluids? They do not maintain their original shape, but the fluid has several unique properties, and it is possible to formulate them based on these properties. Using these formulas, it is possible to represent them in physics simulations.

Fluids can be described by Newton's motion equation (Eq. 4.18) explained in Sect. 4.3.2 as a basis. However, fluids like water and air are different from solids such as rigid bodies and elastic bodies. It is difficult to define as a single object. Liquids like water do not have an original shape, and separation and combination due to flow are always occurring. Furthermore, it is difficult to define clear boundaries for gases like air. Therefore, it is also difficult to define the mass m of an object based on its shape (position). So, if the shape is always changing, the amount of time change in shape, that is, the velocity v is used as a parameter instead of position, and the density ρ, which is the mass per unit volume, is used instead of mass to rewrite Newton's motion equation.

$$\rho \frac{\partial v}{\partial t} + f(v) = f_{ext} .\qquad (4.45)$$

The v here represents a velocity field, which is a distribution of velocities throughout the entire computational space, rather than the velocity at a certain point. We need to consider what to do with the internal force $f(v)$, just like when dealing with elastic bodies. Below, we will explain the properties of fluids and the internal force terms based on those properties.

Advection

Advection of a fluid is the movement of the fluid at its own speed. This may sound straightforward, but it is necessary to clearly formulate the velocity change associated with the local position change of the fluid, unlike solids, which can clearly define the movement (position change) of the entire shape in the motion equation, because fluids have a motion equation related to velocity change (if you approximate the fluid as a collection of moving objects like the particle method described later, you don't need to consider this term).

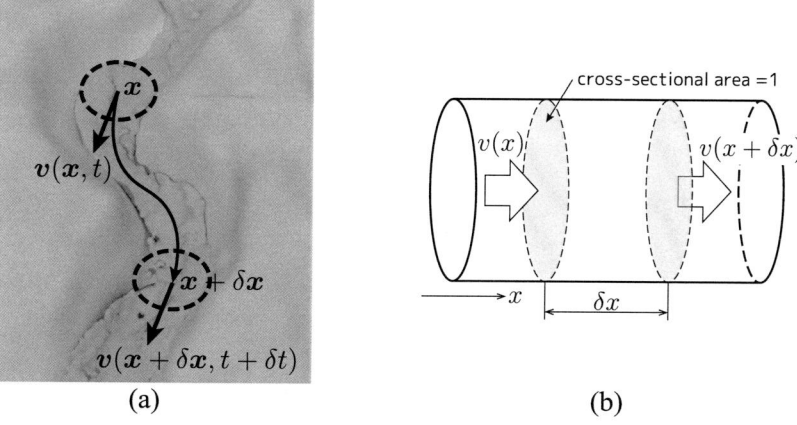

Fig. 4.14 Advection and incompressibility of fluid

As shown in Fig. 4.14a, a local area in the fluid moves at its own velocity $v(x, t)$, from position x to $x + \delta x$. Then the velocity v carried by the lump of fluid also moves from x to $x + \delta x$, so if the velocity after moving is $v(x + \delta x, t + \delta t)$, its acceleration a is

$$a = \frac{\delta v}{\delta t} = \frac{v(x + \delta x, t + \delta t) - v(x, t)}{\delta t} . \tag{4.46}$$

In this case, the velocity field after advection, $v(x + \delta x, t + \delta t)$, becomes an unknown. If we take a total differential of δv with respect to position and time, we can get $\delta v = \frac{\partial v}{\partial t}\delta t + \frac{\partial v}{\partial x}\delta x$. By dividing both sides by δt, setting $\frac{\delta x}{\delta t} = v$, and introducing the gradient operator ∇, we can obtain the following formula.

$$a = \frac{\partial v}{\partial t} + (v \cdot \nabla)v . \tag{4.47}$$

$(v \cdot \nabla)v$ is called the advection term, and by multiplying it by ρ, it can be included in the internal force $f(v)$ of Eq. 4.45, allowing us to simulate the advection of the fluid.

Incompressibility

Mass conservation is a fundamental property of all objects in the real world and is also a property of fluids. On the other hand, *volume conservation* is not necessarily always satisfied. If we assume that the density ρ is constant, we can say that there is volume conservation, but in reality, if a large pressure is applied to the fluid or if the flow speed exceeds the speed of sound, its volume changes and the fluid compresses. Such a state of fluid is called a *compressible fluid*. On the other hand, since it is almost never the case that the flow speed exceeds the speed of sound in our daily lives, it is no problem to consider that the fluid is almost incompressible, that is, it has volume conservation, and such a fluid is called an *incompressible fluid*. The fluids dealt with in CG animation (smoke, flames, water flow, etc.) are almost always incompressible, and it is necessary to incorporate incompressibility as a property of the fluid into the motion equation. (Note that there are cases where it is treated as a compressible fluid in explosions, etc.).

As shown in Fig. 4.14b, consider a case where a fluid is flowing in the x-axis direction inside a circular tube with a cross-sectional area of 1. The density change $\delta\rho$ of the fluid between a cross-sectional position x and $x + \delta x$ during the time δt is derived from the difference in the amount of fluid passing through each cross-section during δt,

$$\delta\rho = \frac{\rho(x + \delta x)v(x + \delta x)\delta t - \rho(x)v(x)\delta t}{\delta x \cdot 1} . \tag{4.48}$$

The denominator is the volume of the region. Dividing both sides by δt and taking the limit as $\delta t \to 0, \delta x \to 0$,

$$\frac{\partial\rho}{\partial t} = \frac{\partial(\rho v)}{\partial x} = \rho\frac{\partial v}{\partial x} + v\frac{\partial\rho}{\partial x} . \tag{4.49}$$

Equation 4.49 represents the change in density. Considering similarly in a three-dimensional region including the y, z directions. In incompressible fluid, it can be assumed that the density does not change either temporally or spatially ($\partial\rho/\partial t = 0$ and $\partial\rho/\partial x = 0$),

$$\nabla \cdot v = 0 . \tag{4.50}$$

Equation 4.50 is called the *equation of continuity*. It represents the incompressibility of the fluid (the flow rate entering a certain region is equal to the flow rate leaving). The equation of continuity is not an equation for the time change of velocity, unlike the advection term, therefore it cannot be directly incorporated into the equation of motion. In the example of the circular tube in Fig. 4.14b, if you consider the force applied according to the difference in pressure p on the two cross-sections instead of ρv, you can derive the relationship $\rho\frac{\partial v}{\partial t} = -\frac{\partial p}{\partial x}$ (the minus sign on the right side is because the pressure decreases as the velocity increases according to Bernoulli's theorem). This can be extended to three dimensions to obtain an equation for the time change (acceleration) of velocity.

$$a = \frac{\partial v}{\partial t} = -\frac{1}{\rho}\nabla p . \tag{4.51}$$

The right side of Eq. 4.51, $-\frac{1}{\rho}\nabla p$, is called the pressure term. It represents the incompressibility of the fluid together with the equation of continuity in Eq. 4.50.

Equation 4.51 includes not only velocity but also pressure p, therefore, the actual problem when calculating is how to determine the pressure p. Let's try to transform Eq. 4.51 using the continuity equation. If you discretize the time derivative of Eq. 4.51 with the forward Euler method (time step width Δt) and multiply both sides by ∇ from the left, it can be transformed,

$$\frac{\nabla \cdot \boldsymbol{v}^{n+1} - \nabla \cdot \boldsymbol{v}^n}{\Delta t} = -\nabla \left(\frac{1}{\rho} \nabla p \right) . \tag{4.52}$$

If the continuity equation is satisfied at the next step $n + 1$, it is represented $\nabla \cdot \boldsymbol{v}^{n+1} = 0$, and the following equation can be obtained.

$$\nabla \left(\frac{1}{\rho} \nabla p \right) = \frac{1}{\Delta t} \nabla \cdot \boldsymbol{v}^n . \tag{4.53}$$

Equation 4.53 is called the *pressure Poisson equation*. By using the pressure p used in this equation to update the velocity in Eq. 4.51, it is possible to satisfy incompressibility. Note that this is not the only way to determine the pressure. In the SPH method explained in Sect. 4.4.3, the ideal gas state equation or the Tait equation is used.

Viscosity

Although not as much as elastic bodies, viscous fluids like cream and butter make a force to maintain their original shape to some extent. In reality, it's not trying to maintain its original shape, a force works to make the velocity of the fluid constant in the direction of the vertical cross-section to the flow (shear direction). This is called *viscosity*. The force due to viscosity is thought to be generated by the frictional force within the fluid. If its magnitude is expressed as stress σ_{visc}, it is proportional to the velocity gradient between fluids from Newton's law of viscosity. Since the velocity gradient is $\nabla \cdot \boldsymbol{v}$, if you put this relationship into an equation,

$$\sigma_{visc} = \mu \nabla \cdot \boldsymbol{v} , \tag{4.54}$$

where μ is a proportional constant and is called the viscosity coefficient. Note that here we simply used the velocity gradient $\nabla \cdot \boldsymbol{v}$. Especially when simulating a fluid with high viscosity, like an elastic body, using Eq. 4.22, we can also use the relationship between strain and deformation gradient as shown in Sect. 4.3.2. Similarly to when we derived the pressure term in Eq. 4.51, if we consider the force applied to the cross-section, we can get the following equation.

$$\boldsymbol{a} = \frac{\partial \boldsymbol{v}}{\partial t} = \frac{\mu}{\rho} \nabla (\nabla \cdot \boldsymbol{v}) = \nu \nabla^2 \boldsymbol{v} , \tag{4.55}$$

where $\nu = \frac{\mu}{\rho}$ is called the kinematic viscosity coefficient. Equation 4.55 is called the viscosity term and represents the viscosity of the fluid.

Navier-Stokes Equations

By introducing the right-hand side of Eqs. 4.47, 4.51, and 4.55 into the internal force term $\boldsymbol{f}(\boldsymbol{v})$ of Eq. 4.45, we can obtain the governing equations for incompressible viscous fluids.

$$\frac{\partial \boldsymbol{v}}{\partial t} + (\boldsymbol{v} \cdot \nabla)\boldsymbol{v} = -\frac{1}{\rho} \nabla p + \nu \nabla^2 \boldsymbol{v} + \frac{\boldsymbol{f}_{ext}}{\rho} . \tag{4.56}$$

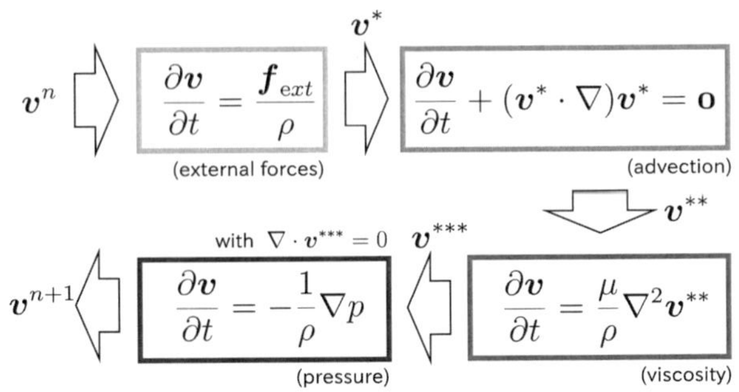

Fig. 4.15 Procedure to solve
the Navier-Stokes equations
by splitting technique

$$\boldsymbol{v}^n \Rightarrow \boxed{\frac{\partial \boldsymbol{v}}{\partial t} = \frac{\boldsymbol{f}_{ext}}{\rho}} \Rightarrow \boxed{\frac{\partial \boldsymbol{v}}{\partial t} + (\boldsymbol{v}^* \cdot \nabla)\boldsymbol{v}^* = \boldsymbol{0}}$$

(external forces)   (advection)

$$\boldsymbol{v}^{n+1} \Leftarrow \boxed{\frac{\partial \boldsymbol{v}}{\partial t} = -\frac{1}{\rho}\nabla p} \underset{\text{with } \nabla \cdot \boldsymbol{v}^{***} = 0}{\overset{\boldsymbol{v}^{***}}{\Leftarrow}} \boxed{\frac{\partial \boldsymbol{v}}{\partial t} = \frac{\mu}{\rho}\nabla^2 \boldsymbol{v}^{**}}$$

(pressure)   (viscosity)

Equation 4.56 is called the *Navier-Stokes equation*. Note that when simulating incompressible fluids, use it with the continuity equation (Eq. 4.50). In that case, the continuity equation represents mass conservation, and Eq. 4.56 represents momentum conservation, and these two equations are often referred to as the Navier-Stokes equations.

The Navier-Stokes equation is a nonlinear partial differential equation. The existence and smoothness of mathematical solutions have not been proven as of the time of writing this book. Therefore, it is necessary to discretize it to solve the equation, as we have explained so far. Even when discretizing, there are many terms to calculate, it is difficult to solve all at once. Instead of solving all the terms at once, a technique called *splitting*, which solves the problem separately in order, is used (see Fig. 4.15). In this technique, first solve the external force term. The resulting velocity field is used as an intermediate velocity field to solve the advection term. Using the velocity field after solving the advection term to solve the viscosity term, then the pressure term. The specific calculation method for each term varies depending on the discretization method, which we will explain in the following sections along with the actual example of the discretization method.

External Forces

In Eq. 4.56, external forces are represented as one term $\boldsymbol{f}_{ext}$, but in reality, various external forces act on the fluid. Many forces are internal but are treated as external forces for computational purposes. Here, we briefly introduce what kind of external forces are considered in the CG field.

Gravity   The most intuitive external force is *gravity*. On Earth, gravity acts downward on objects, and this force is almost the same regardless of location. When applied to fluid simulation, if the y-axis direction is vertical, the effect of gravity acceleration $\boldsymbol{g} = (0, -g, 0)^T$ is added to the external force as $\boldsymbol{f}_{gravity} = \rho\boldsymbol{g}$ (g is about $9.80665[m/s^2]$. If assuming a zero-gravity space, $g = 0$).

Buoyancy   When fluids of different temperatures are placed in the same space, the fluid with a higher temperature increases in volume due to Boyle's law, and as a result, it moves upward due to the difference in density. The force that acts at this time is called *buoyancy*. Buoyancy arises due to the temperature difference with the surroundings, so if you simulate the temperature T and the resulting density change, you can calculate it. But in actual CG simulations, instead of the simulation of density change, $f_{buoyancy} = -\beta(T - T_{amb})g$ is often used to express the buoyancy force due to the assumption of incompressibility. The ambient temperature T_{amb} can be determined by simply fixing it to a certain value, or by using the average temperature of the surroundings.

Turbulence   Fluids are classified into *laminar flow* and *turbulent flow* depending on the state of the flow. Laminar flow is a flow in which the velocity field changes smoothly when the flow speed is relatively low, while turbulent flow, as the name suggests, is a very disturbed and irregular flow. Various causes of turbulence are considered, but basically, it is caused by the forces within the fluid, so if the Navier-Stokes equations can be solved without error, it is possible to reproduce everything from laminar flow to turbulent flow. However, in practice, due to numerical errors during calculation, the fluid velocity changes smoothly in the shear direction, just like the viscous term (it is called a numerical diffusion). A commonly used method in the CG field to solve this problem is a technique called Vorticity Confinement [19].

Using the *vorticity* $\zeta = \nabla \times v$ and the normal vector $N = \nabla||\zeta||$ that indicates the direction of the center of the vortex, the method gives the influence of turbulence as an external force $f_{vc} = \rho(\hat{N} \times \zeta)$ ($\hat{N}$ is the unit vector of N). This method is based on the idea that turbulence is caused by many vortices, and it artificially emphasizes the vortices that were lost due to numerical diffusion. It can be applied as an external force and the calculation is relatively easy. However, the vorticity Confinement has the problem of emphasizing vortices even where it should not become turbulent. To solve this problem, a method using particles representing the vortices that form the basis of turbulence [20] and a method detecting where it should become turbulent using wavelet transformations [21] have also been proposed.

Surface tension   Liquids like water have a clear boundary between the gas layer or different liquids that are hard to mix. A force works to minimize the area of the liquid surface due to the inhomogeneity of intermolecular forces at this boundary. This is called a *surface tension*. Since the surface tension is a force due to intermolecular forces, it can be said to be an internal force, but it is often treated as an external force because its influence can be calculated from the curvature of the liquid surface. There are also methods to reproduce the force corresponding to the intermolecular force as the interparticle force in the particle method described later [22]. When expressing the surface tension acting on the liquid surface as an external force, if the surface curvature is κ and the surface normal is n, it is expressed as $f_{st} = \sigma \kappa n$ (where σ is the tension coefficient).

4.4.2 Grid/Mesh-Based Method

In order to calculate the behavior of fluids based on Eq. 4.56 on a computer, it is necessary to discretize the computational space and make it possible to calculate time integration and spatial gradients. While the time integration is explained in Sect. 4.2, it is necessary to discretize the spatial gradient and solve it numerically because the governing equations of fluids contain many spatial gradients.

Unlike solids, fluids like smoke do not have a clear shape. Therefore, calculation points must be placed to cover all areas where fluid can exist. Depending on how these calculation points are placed, fluid discretization methods are classified into *Eulerian methods* and *Lagrangian methods* (there are also hybrid methods of both, and that will be introduced in Sect. 4.4.4).

The Eulerian method is a method of fixing calculation points in space. As shown in Fig. 4.16, the Eulerian method is the method of dividing the domain and discretizing the spatial gradient using the center points or boundary points, or the integral of the domain volume. The calculation points cover the entire computational space where fluid can exist. In the Eulerian method, the calculation points are basically fixed in space (there is also a method to move the calculation points according to the deformation of the object, in which case it is called the *ALE method* (Arbitrary Lagrangian and Eulerian method)). The method of dividing into a grid as shown in Fig. 4.16 is called the *grid-based method*, and the method using a mesh such as tetrahedra is called the *mesh-based method*.

In the grid method, the entire computational space is divided into square grids. In the case of simulating a liquid and not calculating the air layer, grid cells where no liquid exists may be skipped in the calculation. In that case, for the grid cells corresponding to the liquid surface, free surface boundary conditions are imposed, or the velocity of the surface grid cells is extrapolated to the cells corresponding to the air layer. In the case of simulating a two-phase fluid including the air layer, methods such as using jump boundary conditions that smoothly change in both the air layer and the liquid layer [23], or using a function that smoothly changes between the two phases and simulating simultaneously using a high-order interpolation method [24] are used. Below, we will explain the case of simulating only one phase of fluid with a square grid.

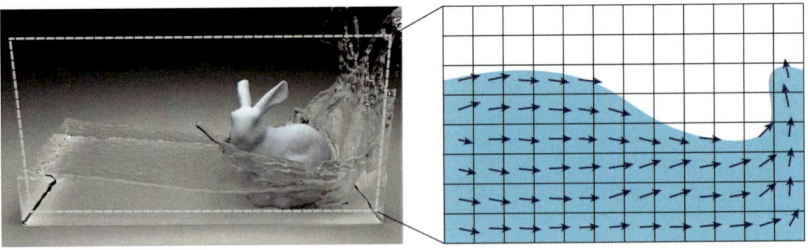

Fig. 4.16 Grid division

When the three-dimensional simulation space is discretized by a square grid, the physical quantity at each cell is expressed as $\phi(i, j, k)$. i, j, k are the grid positions (indices) along each axis when the grid is divided in the x, y, z directions. Assuming that $\phi(i, j, k)$ is stored at the center of each grid cell, it means that physical quantities are not defined at places other than the cell center. Therefore, when the value at a position other than the discrete point is required in the semi-Lagrangian method described later, interpolation methods such as linear interpolation are used. If the number of grid divisions in the x, y, z axis directions is n_x, n_y, n_z respectively, the physical quantity of the entire space is represented by $n_x n_y n_z$ values. The larger these numbers, the higher the computational accuracy and the finer the representation, but on the other hand, the higher the computational cost. In order to solve the trade-off between computational cost and accuracy, adaptive methods such as octrees [25] are used, or methods such as deforming the mesh to fit the boundary in the mesh-based method [26] are taken. Note that both of these have the disadvantage that parallel computation becomes difficult due to the complexity of the data structure and processing.

When performing fluid simulation with the grid-based method, it is necessary to approximate the Navier-Stokes equation using physical quantities at discrete points defined in the grids. What is needed at this time is the discretization of time integration and the gradient of physical quantities $\nabla\phi$. The former, time integration, is omitted here as it was explained in Sect. 4.2. The simplest method to discretize the gradient of physical quantities with the grid-based method is to use the *finite difference method*. When the width of each cell is h, the x direction gradient of the physical quantity ϕ at cell (i, j, k) can be discretized as follows.

$$\frac{\partial \phi}{\partial x} \approx \frac{\phi(i+1, j, k) - \phi(i-1, j, k)}{2h} . \tag{4.57}$$

Equation 4.57 is called the *central difference method*. In the case of second-order differentiation, we can consider it as taking the gradient of the gradient value $\frac{\partial^2 \phi}{\partial x^2} = \frac{\partial}{\partial x}\left(\frac{\partial \phi}{\partial x}\right)$. The gradient at the midpoint (cell boundary) between cells is represented by the central difference.

$$\begin{aligned}\phi(i+1/2, j, k) &= \frac{\phi(i+1,j,k)-\phi(i,j,k)}{h} , \\ \phi(i-1/2, j, k) &= \frac{\phi(i,j,k)-\phi(i-1,j,k)}{h} .\end{aligned} \tag{4.58}$$

Then, by taking further the central difference, we can bet

$$\frac{\partial^2 \phi}{\partial x^2} \approx \frac{\phi(i+1, j, k) - 2\phi(i, j) + \phi(i-1, j, k)}{h^2} . \tag{4.59}$$

In addition to the finite difference method, there are also methods such as the *finite volume method* that use integration, and the finite element method using the approximation function introduced in Sect. 4.3.2.

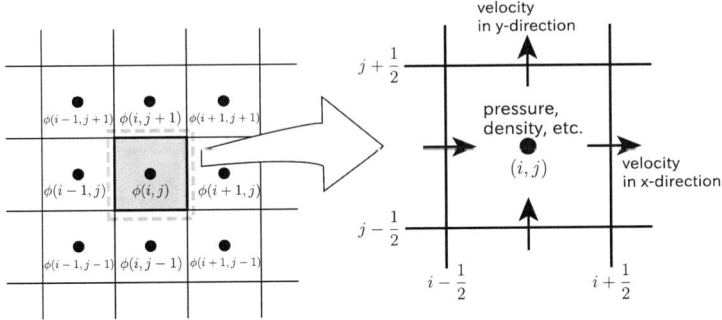

Fig. 4.17 Grid index and staggered grid

A problem with discretizing the first-order derivative using the central difference method is that it does not use the value of its own cell in the calculation of the gradient, and there is no exchange of values between odd-numbered and even-numbered cells, which can result in artifacts that resemble a striped pattern. This is a problem in terms of calculation accuracy, but it also is a significant visual problem when used in CG representation. The *staggered grid* is used to solve this problem. As shown in Fig. 4.17, scalar values such as pressure, and density are stored in the cell center, and the velocity vector is stored at the cell boundary. In the Navier-Stokes equation, the gradient must be calculated for the advection term, the pressure term, and the viscosity term. There is no need to explicitly discretize the gradient when calculating the advection term using the semi-Lagrangian method mentioned later, and the viscosity term is a second-order derivative, so a discretization formula that includes their cell, like Eq. 4.59, can be used. Therefore, the problem is the pressure term, and in the calculation of the pressure term, the velocity is updated by the gradient of the pressure, which is a scalar value, and when using the Poisson equation of pressure in Eq. 4.53, the pressure is determined by the gradient of the velocity. Therefore, by shifting the definition position of scalar values such as pressure and the velocity vector by half a cell, for example, the velocity gradient at the cell center can be discretized by the central difference.

$$\left. \frac{\partial \boldsymbol{v}}{\partial x} \right|_{(i,j,k)} \approx \frac{\boldsymbol{v}(i + \frac{1}{2}, j, k) - \boldsymbol{v}(i - \frac{1}{2}, j, k)}{h}. \tag{4.60}$$

In this case, the processing does not split into odd-numbered/even-numbered cells, so artifacts can be prevented.

I will explain how to solve the Navier-Stokes equation on a square grid using the central difference method as an example. As mentioned earlier, the Navier-Stokes equation is divided into the equation for each term and solved as shown in Fig. 4.15, and the intermediate velocity obtained when each term is solved is represented as $\boldsymbol{v}^*$.

However, the external force term is simply integrated over time using the forward Euler method, so it is omitted, and the explanation starts from the state where the first intermediate velocity v^* is obtained.

First, we explain the *semi-Lagrangian method*, which is used in most cases in the CG field to discretize and solve the advection term using a grid-based method. If we extract only the advection term and set the remaining terms to 0, $\frac{\partial v}{\partial t} + (v^* \cdot \nabla)v^* = 0$ is obtained. In this equation, the term $(v^* \cdot \nabla)v^*$ is nonlinear, and if it is discretized and solved as it is by the difference method, it becomes computationally unstable, and the result tends to diverge. The meaning of the advection term is "the velocity field moves at its speed". Therefore, if we denote the physical quantity containing the velocity at point x at time t as $\phi(x, t)$, and assume that the velocity at that point does not change during the time step width Δt, we can consider that the physical quantity at position $x - v\Delta t$ at time $t - \Delta t$ has flowed to the point x. Therefore, the advection term can be calculated as

$$\phi(x, t) = \phi(x - v\Delta t, t - \Delta t) . \tag{4.61}$$

The advection equation can be derived by Taylor expansion of this equation. When updating the physical quantity $\phi(i, j, k)$ stored in a cell, calculate the position $(x - u\Delta t, y - v\Delta t, z - w\Delta t)$ backtraced using the velocity $v(i, j, k) = (u, v, w)$ from the cell position (x, y, z), and update the value of cell (i, j, k) with the value at $(x - u\Delta t, y - v\Delta t, z - w\Delta t)$. Interpolation methods such as linear interpolation are used to calculate the physical quantity ϕ at that position. Note that the accuracy can greatly change depending on the method of interpolation. Especially when using linear interpolation, a phenomenon called numerical diffusion, where the change in value becomes smooth, is likely to occur. Therefore, methods such as the ENO method and WENO method [27] that perform higher order polynomial interpolation, the BFECC method [28] that corrects the interpolated value, and the CIP method [29] that uses not only the value but also its gradient value for interpolation are often used. Moreover, the semi-Lagrangian method is not a method that satisfies mass conservation/volume conservation, so there may be a loss of physical quantity due to advection. If you want to solve this, it is good to use a conservative semi-Lagrangian method [30].

Next, we denote the velocity obtained by solving the advection term as v^{**} and then explain the method of discretizing and solving the viscosity term using central differences. The viscosity term is a term composed of second-order spatial derivatives, and the discretization formula by the central difference shown in Eq. 4.59 can be used. In the case of three dimensions, assuming that the time derivative is discretized by the forward Euler method, we can obtain the following equation.

$$\begin{aligned}v^{***}_{i,j,k} = v^{**}_{i,j,k} + \nu \tfrac{\Delta t}{h^2}(v^{**}_{i+1,j,k} + v^{**}_{i-1,j,k} + v^{**}_{i,j+1,k} + v^{**}_{i,j-1,k} \\ + v^{**}_{i,j,k+1} + v^{**}_{i,j,k-1} - 6v^{**}_{i,j,k})\end{aligned} \tag{4.62}$$

The viscosity term is also nonlinear, so if the value of the kinematic viscosity coefficient v is large, the calculation becomes unstable. In that case, the part of the right-hand side $-6v_{i,j,k}^{**}$, is treated as $-6v_{i,j,k}^{***}$, and as an implicit method, a method of solving the linear system with the conjugate gradient method or iterative method is used [31].

For the final pressure term, if the pressure p can be calculated, all that remains is to calculate the gradient of the pressure with the central difference, but the method to obtain this pressure p becomes a problem. As mentioned before, it is necessary to solve the Poisson equation for pressure, Eq. 4.53, and this can be discretized with the central difference and solved just like the viscosity term. However, unlike the viscosity term, it is an equation that includes the second-order spatial derivative of the unknown pressure p, and solving it explicitly with the forward Euler method tends to be computationally unstable. Therefore, it is necessary to discretize $\nabla^2 p$ (in the case of constant density ρ) or $\nabla \cdot v^{***}$ with central differences, etc., and solve it with an implicit method or iterative method. This is the reason why the calculation of the pressure term to satisfy incompressibility is the most computationally costly in fluid simulation by the grid method, and various methods are being studied to speed up and stabilize this.

Boundary conditions

In the explanations so far, we have mainly used the values of adjacent cells to discretize the gradient ∇, but when the space is divided into cells, at the cells at both ends, there are directions where there are no adjacent cells, and special processing is required in these cases. To avoid such special processing, a method is adopted to place *boundary cells* as shown in Fig. 4.18a. In the calculation of the Navier-Stokes equations, only the values of the fluid cells inside excluding the boundary cells are calculated, and the values of the boundary cells are calculated using the values of the fluid cells adjacent to them. By doing so, there is no need for endpoint processing.

The way to determine the value of the boundary cell is called a *boundary condition*, and it is classified into two types: *Dirichlet boundary condition* and *Neumann boundary condition*. The Dirichlet condition is a method of directly specifying the value that the boundary cell should take, and is used for wall boundary conditions, etc. Assuming a wall as a boundary and assuming no friction at the boundary, the velocity

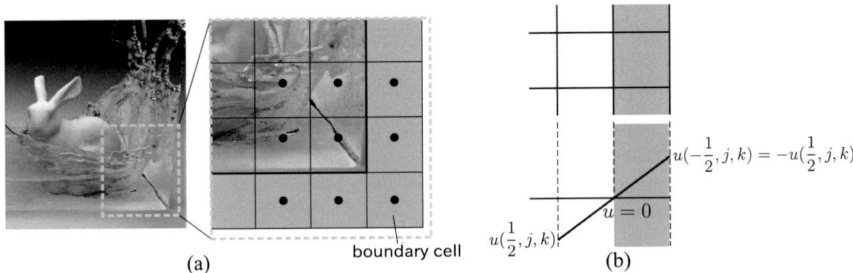

(a)   boundary cell   (b)

Fig. 4.18 Boundary cell (left) and Neumann boundary condition (right)

in the normal direction n of the wall surface becomes 0 unless the wall surface moves, so the boundary condition equation becomes $v \cdot n = 0$. In the case of the grid-based method, it is sufficient to make the component perpendicular to the wall surface 0, so if it is in the x direction, make $u(1, j, k)$ and $u(n_x, j, k)$ ($j = 1 \sim n_y$) to 0. In the case of a staggered grid, the velocity corresponding to the wall surface $u(1/2, j, k)$ is 0, and the velocity of $u(-1/2, j, k)$ corresponding to the inside of the boundary cell is set to $u(-1/2, j, k) = -u(+1/2, j, k)$ so that the velocity distribution in the x direction is exactly 0 at the wall surface as shown in Fig. 4.18b.

The Neumann boundary condition is a method of specifying the condition to be taken at the boundary as a gradient value, not specifying a value, and in fluid simulation, it corresponds to inflow/outflow conditions, etc. If the inflow velocity is v_{in}, the boundary condition can be expressed as $v \cdot n = v_{in} \cdot n$. Unlike the wall boundary condition, this does not mean that the velocity becomes 0 at the boundary. It indicates that it becomes a certain constant velocity. In addition to the inflow/outflow boundary conditions, when a part of a large space is cut out and used as a calculation space, etc., the fluid can freely input and output, or it can be used for cyclic boundary conditions where the fluid that comes out from the left end flows in from the right end.

Example of simulation by grid-based method

As an example of simulation by the grid-based method, we will introduce the simulation of smoke and liquid. Smoke is a phenomenon that occurs when fine particles such as water vapor and soot are advected by the flow of air, and in addition to the density ρ of the air, the density ρ_s of the smoke is defined as a physical quantity on the grid. The simulation can be performed by solving the following smoke density advection equation using methods such as the semi-Lagrangian method.

$$\frac{\partial \rho_s}{\partial t} + (v \cdot \nabla)\rho_s = S , \tag{4.63}$$

where S represents the source of the smoke. Solve the Navier-Stokes equation by the method mentioned above, update the velocity field v, then, the density ρ_s of the smoke is updated according to Eq. 4.63 in a step-by-step manner for each time step. In the case of smoke, it is important to add turbulence, which was explained in the external force term of the Navier-Stokes equation, to improve realism. An example of a smoke simulation using the grid-based method is shown in Fig. 4.19.

In the CG field, in addition to smoke, fluids such as water are also the subject of simulation. Unlike smoke, liquids hardly change their density internally, and have a clear boundary (free surface) with the air layer. At this boundary, light refracts and reflects, so when rendering in CG, it is important what boundary shape it has. Therefore, it is necessary to represent the boundary shape with some function and represent the shape change with the advection equation. For this reason, the *level set method* is often used in the CG field. The level set method is a method of tracking the surface shape by defining a level set function φ that takes a value of 0 at the

Fig. 4.19 Smoke simulation

free surface, a negative value inside the liquid, and a positive value outside. The φ is advected with the following advection equation.

$$\frac{\partial \varphi}{\partial t} + (\boldsymbol{v} \cdot \nabla)\varphi = 0 . \tag{4.64}$$

A commonly used level set function φ is the signed distance field. Using the signed distance field, the distance to the boundary can be clearly determined, and characteristics such as curvature can be accurately determined by the gradient of the distance field. However, when Eq. 4.64 is advected by methods such as the semi-Lagrangian method, the properties of the distance field gradually deteriorate, so it is necessary to periodically update φ to be a signed distance field through a process called re-initialization. For more information on the level set method, please refer to the Refs. [27, 32].

In addition to the level set method, there are also methods such as the VoF method, which uses the volume fraction of the liquid in each cell, and the PIC method, which uses massless particles called marker particles to track the liquid region. The PIC method is a method that uses both particles and grids, and its extended methods will be explained in Sect. 4.4.4.

4.4.3 Particle-Based Methods

In the Eulerian methods explained in Sect. 4.4.2, the calculation points were fixed. However, if you want to simulate the flow, the calculation points do not have to be fixed. For example, when you want to examine the flow of a river, in addition to the method of placing a flow meter or the like at a fixed point in the water, it is also possible to release a large number of floating objects like ping-pong balls from the upstream of the river and observe their movements. Such methods, which do not fix the calculation points but move them along the flow of the fluid, and simulate the

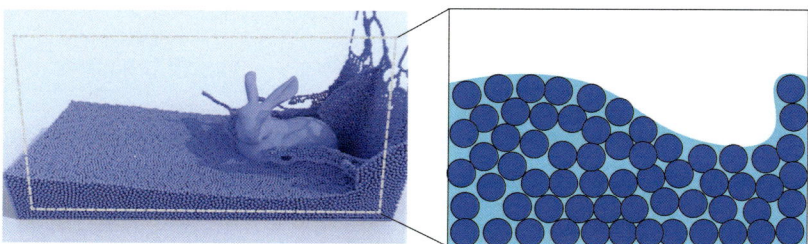

Fig. 4.20 Fluid approximation by particles

flow by their movements, are called Lagrangian methods. Here, we will explain the *particle-based method*, which is representative of the Lagrangian methods.

In the particle-based method, as shown in Fig. 4.20, the fluid (mainly liquid) is discretized as a set of particles, and the movement of the particles determined by the governing equations is considered as the movement/deformation of the fluid. In the particle method, each particle holds parameters of the fluid such as velocity, density, and pressure, and as the particles move, their advection can be considered to be calculated at the same time. Therefore, unlike the grid-based method, there is no need to explicitly calculate the advection term (which is included in particle movement). Among the nonlinear terms in the Navier-Stokes equations, the advection term is known to cause computational instability during discretization calculations. So that, one of the advantages of the particle method is that the advection term can be calculated implicitly (the semi-Lagrangian method is doing similar calculations by backtracing). In the particle-based method, the advection term of Eq. 4.56 is summarized with the time derivative term, and the governing equation of the fluid is often described as,

$$\frac{D\boldsymbol{v}}{Dt} = -\frac{1}{\rho}\nabla p + \nu \nabla^2 \boldsymbol{v} + \frac{\boldsymbol{f}_{ext}}{\rho} , \qquad (4.65)$$

where $D\boldsymbol{v}/Dt = \partial \boldsymbol{v}/\partial t + (\boldsymbol{v} \cdot \nabla)\boldsymbol{v}$, which is called the *material derivative*.

The particle-based method is a type of mesh-free method that does not have a clear adjacency relationship like the grid-based method or the mesh-based method, and it has the feature that it is easy to deal with objects whose topological changes, such as separation and combining of shapes like liquids. On the other hand, as explained in Sect. 4.4.2, it is necessary to use physical quantities of near particles for spatial derivative calculations. It is necessary to find surrounding particles each time by neighborhood search because there is no clear adjacency relationship. The cost of this search becomes a computational bottleneck in the particle-based method, but with the development of GPUs capable of large-scale parallel computation, real-time computation is possible with hundreds of thousands to millions of particles.

In order to simulate the fluid with the particle-based method, we have to consider how to approximate spatial derivatives as in previous sections. Figure 4.21a shows an example of approximating the distribution of a physical quantity ϕ with the amount stored in the nearest neighbor particles when particles are placed in one-dimensional

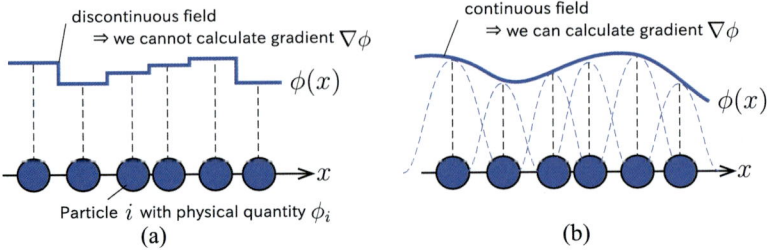

Fig. 4.21 Approximation of the field by particles

space. In this case, the field becomes discontinuous where the nearest neighbor particles switch, and the gradient $\nabla\phi$ cannot be calculated. Therefore, instead of using only one nearest neighbor, consider approximating the physical quantity $\phi(x)$ at position x with the weighted sum of neighboring particles within a certain range from a point x (Fig. 4.21b). If the weight function is a differentiable function including the range boundary, $\phi(x)$ becomes a continuous field, so the gradient $\nabla\phi$ can be calculated. Set the certain range as within the effective radius h, and if the weight function (*kernel function*) that monotonically decreases with the distance from the calculation position x_i is expressed as $W(x - x_i, h)$, the physical quantity $\phi(x_p)$ can be approximated as follows.

$$\phi(x_i) = \sum_{j \in N} V_j \phi_j W(x_j - x_i, h) , \tag{4.66}$$

where V_j is the particle volume, and if the particle mass is m_j and the density is ρ_j, then $V_j = m_j/\rho_j$. N represents the set of neighboring particles within the effective radius h. Equation 4.66 is used to approximate the value of a physical quantity, and there are several methods such as SPH and MPS depending on how to calculate the gradient $\nabla\phi$.

SPH

The *SPH* (Smoothed Particle Hydrodynamics) is a method of approximating the spatial gradient of any physical quantity ϕ by the gradient of the kernel function W. The approximation formula for the gradient is as follows.

$$\nabla\phi(x_i) = \sum_{j \in N} V_j \phi_j \nabla W(x_j - x_i, h) . \tag{4.67}$$

Note that there are some constraints on the kernel function W to make this approximation valid, and it is important to note that not any function can be used for W. First, the kernel function must satisfy normality. If the region within the effective radius h is Ω, then $\int_\Omega W = 1$ must be satisfied. Also, it must be compact support, non-negative, convergent to Dirac's delta, an even function, and smooth. Various kernel functions have been proposed, for example, the Poly6 kernel proposed by

Müller et al. [33], which is often used in the CG field, is defined by the following equation.

$$W_{poly6}(\boldsymbol{r}, h) = \alpha_w \begin{cases} (h^2 - r^2)^3, & 0 \le r \le h , \\ 0, & \text{otherwise} , \end{cases} \tag{4.68}$$

where $\boldsymbol{r}$ is the distance vector between two points, and $r = ||\boldsymbol{r}||$. α_w is a coefficient, and its value can be obtained by mathematically calculating the integral to satisfy $\int_\Omega W = 1$. In the case of the Poly6 kernel, in two dimensions, $\alpha_w = \frac{4}{\pi h^8}$, and in three dimensions, $\alpha_w = \frac{315}{64\pi h^9}$. In addition to this, the spline kernel [34] is also often used in the CG field.

Using Eq. 4.67, the pressure term of the Navier-Stokes equation is approximated as follows.

$$\nabla p_i = \sum_{j \in N} m_j \left(\frac{p_i}{\rho_i^2} + \frac{p_j}{\rho_j^2} \right) \nabla W(\boldsymbol{x}_j - \boldsymbol{x}_i, h) . \tag{4.69}$$

The reason for using $\frac{p_i}{\rho_i^2} + \frac{p_j}{\rho_j^2}$ instead of simply using p_j in the approximation formula is to satisfy computational symmetry (the results of calculations for $i \to j$ and $j \to i$ are the same). It is known that this makes the calculation more stable (there are other ways to calculate the pressure term in the SPH).

The viscosity term, which includes a second-order spatial gradient, can be discretized as follows.

$$\nabla^2 \boldsymbol{v}_i = \sum_{j \in N} m_j \left(\frac{\boldsymbol{v}_j - \boldsymbol{v}_i}{\rho_j} \right) \nabla^2 W(\boldsymbol{x}_j - \boldsymbol{x}_i, h) . \tag{4.70}$$

Various discretization methods have been proposed in addition to Eq. 4.70 for improving stability and simulating high-viscosity fluids. The viscosity term not only represents the viscosity of the fluid but can also stabilize the calculation. Therefore, it is sometimes introduced as an artificial viscosity term for stabilization.

The SPH was originally developed not for fluid simulation, but for astrophysics simulation, and has problems in representing incompressibility. In the original SPH, the pressure p in Eq. 4.69 is calculated using the equation of state of an ideal gas,

$$p_i = k(\rho_i - \rho_0) . \tag{4.71}$$

were, ρ_0 is the rest density set by the user, and k is the gas constant. The density ρ_i is calculated from Eq. 4.66,

$$\rho_i = \sum_{j \in N} m_j W(\boldsymbol{x}_j - \boldsymbol{x}_i, h) . \tag{4.72}$$

By increasing the k in Eq. 4.71, it can satisfy a certain degree of incompressibility, but there is a limit because a large k generates instability in the calculation. Therefore, when simulating a liquid like water, the entire liquid may compress and bounce like rubber.

As a method to solve the incompressibility problem of the SPH, there is *WCSPH* (Weakly Compressible SPH) [35] that uses the following Tait equation instead of Eq. 4.71.

$$p_i = B \left(\left(\frac{\rho_i}{\rho_0} \right)^\gamma - 1 \right) .   \tag{4.73}$$

WCSPH is easy to implement, but it is necessary to make the time step width Δt very small for stable calculation. To solve this problem, PCISPH [36] that iteratively solves the pressure term and IISPH [37] that solves using the implicit method have been proposed. However, these methods increase the calculation cost of the pressure term, and when applied to real-time applications, it is necessary to reduce the number of particles, etc.

For incompressibility, there is also a method called *PBF* (Position-Based Fluid) [38] that uses the position-based method explained in Sect. 4.3.3. The fact that the fluid is incompressible means that the particle density ρ_i does not change from the static density ρ_0, and this is written as a constraint condition,

$$C_i(x_1, ..., x_n) = \frac{\rho_i}{\rho_0} - 1 = 0 ,   \tag{4.74}$$

where n is the number of particles, and x_i represents the position of particle i. The position correction Δx_i of particle i is obtained in the same way as in Sect. 4.3.3,

$$\Delta x_i = \frac{1}{\rho_0} \sum_{j \in N} (\lambda_i + \lambda_j) \nabla W(x_j - x_i, h) ,   \tag{4.75}$$

where $\lambda_i = -\frac{C_i}{\sum_k \|\nabla_{x_k} C_i\|^2 + \varepsilon}$ (ε is a constant to prevent division by zero). ρ_i is calculated by Eq. 4.72. Note that PBF also needs to iterate to satisfy the constraints.

MPS

The *MPS* (Moving Particle Semi-implicit), as its name implies, is a semi-implicit method that solves the pressure term of the Navier-Stokes equation implicitly and solves the rest explicitly. It can be said that this method has advantages in terms of incompressibility compared to the SPH. However, some recent methods such as IISPH, which adopts an implicit method, have been made even in the SPH, It is becoming difficult to distinguish between the two based on the implicit method or not. So, what is the difference between the SPH method and the MPS? A clear difference is how to discretize the gradient $\nabla \phi$. In the MPS, instead of using the gradient of the weight function for gradient calculation, it uses the relative position vector $(x_j - x_i)$ between calculation points i, j,

$$\nabla\phi(\boldsymbol{x}_i) = \frac{d_s}{n_0} \sum_{j\in N, j\neq i} \frac{\phi_j - \phi_i}{||\boldsymbol{x}_j - \boldsymbol{x}_i||^2}(\boldsymbol{x}_j - \boldsymbol{x}_i)W(\boldsymbol{x}_j - \boldsymbol{x}_i, h) , \qquad (4.76)$$

where d_s is the number of dimensions, $d_s = 2$ for 2D, and $d_s = 3$ for 3D. n_i is called particle number density,

$$n_i = \sum_{j\in N, j\neq i} W(\boldsymbol{x}_j - \boldsymbol{x}_i, h) . \qquad (4.77)$$

In Eq. 4.76, n_i is replaced with the standard particle number density n_0 for simplification of calculation. Unlike the SPH, there are no conditions for the kernel function W in the MPS, however it is better to have compact support for computational efficiency.

Boundary particles

Just as boundary grids were set in the grid-based method, boundary processing is also necessary for the particle-based method. As simple boundary treatment, since the motion of the particles represents the behavior of the fluid, the collision response process described in the Sect. 4.2.2 section should be applied between the particles and obstacles such as walls. In many cases, collision response is not a problem, however, when trying to satisfy incompressibility, a phenomenon called particle stacking occurs where the particle distribution near the boundary becomes uneven as shown in Fig. 4.22a. Not only does it destabilize the calculation, but it also creates visual unnaturalness such as creating a void near the boundary.

The non-uniformity of the particle distribution can be caused by the absence of particles inside the boundary due to the collision response, resulting in the density near the boundary is evaluated to be low, and particles are concentrated at the boundary in order to increase the density. The *boundary particle* is used to solve this problem. As shown as the dark particles in Fig. 4.22b, particles are also placed within the boundary. If these particles are used for fluid density calculations, the particles will fill the region within the effective radius even near the boundary, preventing the density from being evaluated as low. This boundary particle is treated as a neighboring particle for liquid particles, but the position of the boundary particle is fixed to the boundary.

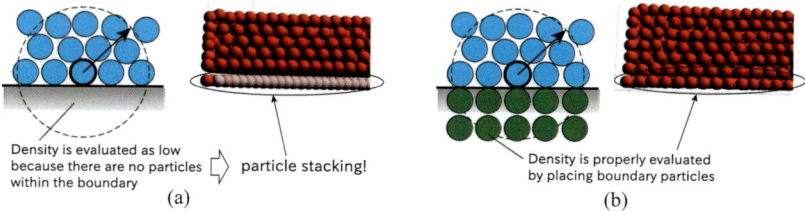

Fig. 4.22 Boundary particles

The problem of the boundary particle is the increased computational cost due to the increase of the number of particles. Considering that particles must fill the effective radius, depending on the settings of the effective radius, particle density, and mass, it is usually necessary to set 2–3 layers of boundary particles. Moreover, if a wall boundary is set around the simulation space, a very large number of boundary particles need to be placed. To reduce the number of boundary particles, methods have been developed such as pre-calculating a virtual volume and increasing the impact of each boundary particle to prevent particle stacking with only one layer [39].

4.4.4 Other Fluid Simulation Methods

Hybrid Methods

The advantage of the particle-based method is that it does not need to explicitly calculate the advection term, but a disadvantage is that it must perform time-consuming neighbor particle searches when reproducing other properties of the fluid, such as incompressibility. On the other hand, grid-based methods can cause numerical diffusion and other errors in the calculation of the advection term, but it is easy to calculate properties such as incompressibility and viscosity because the adjacent grids are fixed. From these considerations, hybrid methods have been proposed that calculate the advection term with the particle-based method and calculate other terms with the grid-based method. These are often used in the CG field.

In the hybrid method, particles are placed within the grid, and the advection term of the Navier-Stokes equation is calculated by just the movement of the particles. The calculation results are projected from the particles to the grid, and the other terms are calculated on the grid side. In a method called *PIC* (Particle-In-Cell), this projection is calculated by a simple weighted average of values. In PIC, the variables of the fluid, such as velocity at the grid calculation points, are determined by the weighted average of the neighboring particles. After calculating the non-advection term on the grid, the particle values are updated by interpolating the values of the grid points containing the particles. In PIC, the use of a weighted average causes numerical diffusion, which can be a problem as it smooths the distribution of values too much. To solve this, instead of simply interpolating and updating the particle velocity, the difference between the velocity before calculating the non-advection term is calculated, and the interpolated value of this difference is added to the current particle velocity to update the value. This method is called *FLIP* (FLuid-Implicit-Particle) [40]. Also, instead of dividing the calculation into advection and non-advection terms, a method that primarily calculates the gradient on the grid and calculates everything else with particles is called *MPM* (Material Point Method), which has been frequently used in recent years for calculations of high-viscosity fluids and elastic bodies where the calculation of deformation gradient is particularly important [41].

Wave simulation using height fields

In real-time applications, simulating large fluid scenes like the ocean with 3D particle-based or grid-based methods is computationally difficult. In such cases, wave simulations using *height field* are often used.

As shown in Fig. 4.23a, if the waves on the liquid surface are represented by a scalar function $f(x)$ for the horizontal axis coordinate x, a two-dimensional wave can be represented by a simple one-dimensional distribution of liquid surface height $h = f(x)$. If this is extended to three dimensions, the three-dimensional surface shape of the liquid can be represented by a two-dimensional height function $h = f(x, y)$. This representation is called a height field. While it cannot represent complex waves such as spray or curling waves, it allows for very fast calculations because it only needs to consider the liquid surface shape represented by a two-dimensional height distribution. Note that a height field only describes the surface shape, and does not consider the behavior inside the liquid.

When simulating fluids, it is important to determine how to define and update the height distribution. If it is a wave that simply moves in one direction, the wave can be modeled using a trigonometric function. By creating a frequency space that adds the characteristics of the wave to Gaussian noise, waves can be generated by inverse Fourier transformation [42]. This method can create large waves very quickly, but it cannot consider the reflection of waves by obstacles or the influence of floating objects. To solve this, methods have been proposed such as using elements (called Wave packets or Wave particles) that carry locally defined waves instead of representing them as one wave overall [43], or using wavelet transformations [44].

There is also a method to simulate the behavior of waves by defining the governing equation that represents the movement of waves and solving it numerically by discretizing it on the height field. The simplest method is to represent the behavior of waves with the wave equation, which is a hyperbolic second-order partial differential equation. If you use the wave equation, you can express the reflection of waves by obstacles and the interference between waves. Also, in the shallow ocean, the speed of waves is affected by the terrain of the seabed, but if you want to consider the influence of this terrain, you can use the *SWE* (Shallow Water Equation) derived from

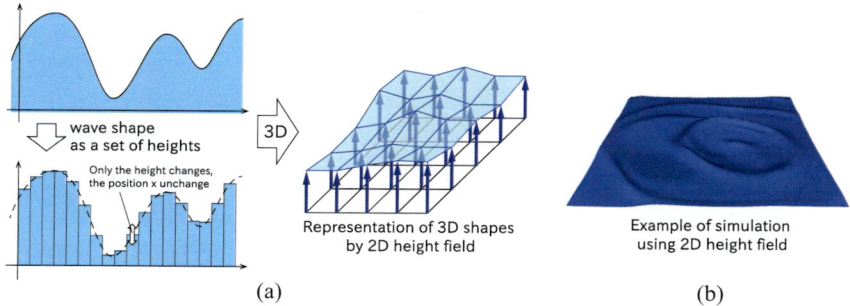

(a)   (b)

Fig. 4.23 Height field representation and wave simulation using it

the Navier-Stokes equation as the governing equation, and calculate the behavior of three-dimensional waves by two-dimensional fluid simulation [45], which is often used in the CG field.

4.5 Other Natural Phenomenon Simulations

In addition to the rigid body, elastic body, and fluid simulations introduced so far, various phenomena can be the subject of physics simulations in the CG field. Here, we will briefly introduce what kind of phenomena there are and how they are simulated.

Fracture simulation

In contrast to elastic deformation, there is plastic deformation that does not return to its original shape after deformation. In reality, like clay, most materials deform as elastic bodies for small deformation, and when they deform beyond a point called the yield point, they no longer completely return to their original shape. Such a body is called an elastoplastic body. When simulating an elastoplastic body, the deformation gradient can be divided into the *elastic deformation gradient* and the *plastic deformation gradient*. For example, by setting a deformation amount at the yield point and considering the excess as plastic deformation, methods such as separating the deformation gradient into two are used.

Even if we assume a rigid body like a rigid body, there are cases where plastic deformation occurs due to the fracture of the object. The destruction and fracture of objects are often used expressions in CG animation. The *fracture simulation* can be divided into two methods: geometric and physical. The former creates a fracture pattern in advance using a geometric method like the Voronoi diagram etc. For example, when a large force is applied, replace it with an object that has already been broken in that pattern, or methods such as generating a separate object along the fracture pattern in real time [46] are taken. This method has a great advantage in terms of calculation cost, however, it is difficult to consider changes in shape after destruction due to differences in the force applied and the shape of the object.

The latter physical method is to calculate deformation using finite element method/boundary element method or MPM, etc. By eigenvalue analysis from the deformation gradient or CDM (Continuum Damage Mechanics), find the direction and amount of deformation where the largest deformation occurs, and then the object is divided into multiple fragments or a fracture surface is created [47–49]. In addition to deformation simulation, fracture analysis is also required. Although it needs a large computation time, it is possible to simulate more realistic destruction.

Simulation of flames and explosions

By adding a governing equation for the temperature to the fluid simulation explained in Sect. 4.4, *fire simulation* also becomes possible. The temperature, like the density of smoke, is advected by the fluid velocity and heat diffuses to the surroundings. If the temperature is T, the governing equation considering heat advection and heat diffusion is

$$\frac{\partial T}{\partial t} + (\boldsymbol{v} \cdot \nabla)T = a\nabla^2 T + E \;, \tag{4.78}$$

where a is a coefficient that represents the ease of heat diffusion (thermal diffusion coefficient), E includes energy providers such as heat input from the outside and heat radiation to the surrounding environment. This equation can be approximated by the semi-Lagrangian method or the difference method, similar to the case of velocity, to simulate temperature changes. Also, buoyancy in the opposite direction of gravity is generated by temperature, so by updating the velocity due to this. It makes it possible to simulate flames that blow upwards [50].

In the case of explosions, they can basically be simulated in the same way as flames, but if you want to reproduce the shock waves that occur when the flow speed becomes very fast, there may be a need for simulation as a compressible fluid, not an incompressible fluid [51]. The simulation methods used for these are often the same as those used for fluids, but if you consider chemical elements (heat generation due to chemical reactions and changes in objects), there may be a need for a different simulation method [52]. Also, while smoke was visualized by the density of soot, flames require visualization by temperature. Since the radiation color due to temperature varies depending on the object, it is necessary to render using distribution functions or lookup tables to correspond temperature and color.

Cloud Simulation

Clouds are created as a collection of fine water droplets when the amount of water vapor in the air exceeds the saturated water vapor amount. They are an important element for improving realism, especially in outdoor scenes in CG animation. Like smoke, by advecting the density of water droplets, it can be combined with fluid simulation [53]. In addition to the flow equation, when simulating the cloud generation process, we need equations for water vapor density q_v and cloud (water droplet) density q_c,

$$\begin{aligned} \frac{\partial q_v}{\partial t} + (\boldsymbol{v} \cdot \nabla)q_v &= -C_c + S_v \;, \\ \frac{\partial q_c}{\partial t} + (\boldsymbol{v} \cdot \nabla)q_c &= C_c \;. \end{aligned} \tag{4.79}$$

By adding and using the cloud density q_c for volume rendering, it becomes possible to simulate including the cloud generation process [54]. In Eq. 4.79, C_c represents the amount of change from water vapor to clouds due to phase transition. It is calculated using the saturation water vapor amount q_s and the conversion rate α_c derived from temperature, etc.: $C_c = \alpha_c(q_v - q_s)$. S_v is the source of water vapor and is set according to the scene.

Sound Simulation

In the simulations introduced so far, we have focused only on the appearance of the phenomenon. But in interactive content such as CG animation and games, the *sound* that accompanies each phenomenon is also an important element for enhancing realism. Many contents use pre-recorded/generated sounds that are played along with the contents/actions, which requires the time and effort to prepare sounds separately. Furthermore, in order to flexibly change sound effects according to the scene, it is necessary to prepare a large number of sounds and assign them to each movement. If sound can also be generated by physics simulation, these efforts can be eliminated by creating sound on the spot according to the scene.

Sound is produced from the vibration of objects, therefore, it is considered that the frequency and amplitude of the vibration correspond to the pitch and volume of the sound. For example, consider the *collision sound* produced by the collision of rigid bodies. The volume of the sound changes with the strength of the collision, but the pitch of the sound is determined by the material and shape of the object (If you think of instruments like a xylophone or a metallophone, it's easy to imagine that the pitch of the sound changes not by how strong you hit it, but by the size of the keys). This frequency unique to the material and shape is called the *resonance frequency*. The sound can be generated by simulation by finding this. If the resonance frequency is ω, the waveform of the sound is expressed by the following equation.

$$x = Ae^{-\beta t} \sin(\omega t) , \tag{4.80}$$

where A is the amplitude, which is calculated from the impact force in the case of collision sound, β is the damping coefficient, which represents the time-dependent attenuation of the generated sound (the attenuation here is the vibration attenuation inside the object, and the attenuation during propagation through the air needs to be considered separately).

In sound simulation, it is necessary to find ω, A, and β in Eq. 4.80. If it is the sound of a rigid body collision, the elastic matrix K, which is determined by the material and shape of the rigid body, can be used to perform modal analysis to find the ω and β of that rigid body (which can be determined from the eigenvalues of K, and there may be multiple depending on the size of K) [55]. Since a rigid body can be assumed to not change its shape, the sound can be calculated from the ω, β that were determined in advance and the impact force obtained during the animation. Even for non-rigid bodies, if the resonant frequency can be determined in the same way, sound can often be calculated. For example, it is known that most of the sound produced by a liquid like water is caused by the vibration of bubbles inside the liquid, and it is possible to simulate the sound of the liquid by determining the resonant frequency of the bubbles using a formula called Minnaert's formula [56].

4.6   Conclusion

In this chapter, we introduced physics simulation technology for creating CG animations. We explained that it is possible to reproduce natural phenomena that are difficult to reproduce by human hands in CG by calculations based on physical laws and discretization methods, and introduced methods for reproducing rigid bodies, elastic bodies, fluids, and other phenomena. In addition to the methods introduced in this chapter, there are also studies on methods to accelerate and refine the results by applying deep learning to the results of physics simulations as learning data, and it is expected that high-precision and high-speed physics simulation technology will continue to develop. Also, although it was omitted in this chapter, there are many studies on methods to add elements of artist control to physics simulations. It is a very challenging problem to realize the movement that people want while not losing the realism of natural phenomena, but by realizing it, physics simulation technology can be made more user-friendly, and it is expected to develop as a technology that not only experts but anyone can use in the future.

References

1. John C. Platt and Alan H. Barr, "Constraints Methods for Flexible Models", SIGGRAPH Comput. Graph., 22, pp.279–288, 1988.
2. Rachel Weinstein, Joseph Teran and Ron Fedkiw, "Dynamic Simulation of Articulated Rigid Bodies with Contact and Collision", IEEE Transactions on Visualization and Computer Graphics, 12, 3, pp.365–374, 2006.
3. Jan Bender, "Impulse-based Dynamic Simulation in Linear Time", Computer Animation and Virtual Worlds, 18, 4-5, pp.225-233, 2007.
4. Tomoya Saida, Makoto Fujisawa, Masahiko Mikawa, "Simulation of Elasto-plastic Bodies Using Slave Particles", Journal of Information Processing Society of Japan, Vol.58, No. 7, pp.1323-1334, 2017.
5. Xavier Provot Institut and Xavier Provot, "Deformation Constraints in a Mass-Spring Model to Describe Rigid Cloth Behavior", In Proceedings of Graphics Interface, pp.147-154, 1996.
6. Andrew Selle, Michael Lentine and Ronald Fedkiw "A Mass Spring Model for Hair Simulation", ACM Transactions on Graphics, 27(3), pp.1-11, 2008.
7. David Baraff and Andrew Witkin, "Large Steps in Cloth Simulation", In Proceedings of SIGGRAPH 1998, pp.43-54, 1998.
8. Eftychios Sifakis and Jernej Barbic, "FEM Simulation of 3D Deformable Solids: A Practitioner's Guide to Theory, Discretization and Model Reduction", ACM SIGGRAPH 2012 Courses, pp.1-50, 2012.
9. Morten Bro-Nielsen and Stephane Cotin, "Real-time Volumetric Deformable Models for Surgery Simulation using Finite Elements and Condensation", Computer Graphics Forum, 15, 3, pp.57-66, 1996.
10. Matthias Müller and Markus Gross, "Interactive Virtual Materials", Proceedings of Graphics Interface 2004, pp.239-246, 2004.
11. Adrien Treuille and Andrew Lewis and Zoran Popović, "Model Reduction for Real-time Fluids", ACM Transactions on Graphics, 25(3), pp.826-834, 2006.
12. Yin Yang, Dingzeyu Li, Weiwei Xu and Yuan Tian, "Expediting Precomputation for Reduced Deformable Simulation", ACM Transactions of Graphics, 34(6), pp.243:1-243:13, 2015.
13. Tassilo Kugelstadt and Elmar Schömer, "Position and Orientation Based Cosserat Rods", Proceedings of the ACM SIGGRAPH/Eurographics Symposium on Computer Animation, pp.169-178, 2016.
14. Hiroshi Demura, Makoto Fujisawa, Masahiko Mikawa, "Simulation of Hair Plastic Deformation Considering Side Chain Bonding", Journal of the Institute of Image Electronics Engineers of Japan, Vol.47, No.4, pp.447-453, 2018.

15. Miles Macklin, Matthias Müller, Nuttapong Chentanez and Tae-Yong Kim, "Unified Particle Physics for Real-time Applications", ACM Transactions of Graphics, 33(4), pp.153:1-153:12, 2014.
16. Matthias Müller, Bruno Heidelberger, Marcus Hennix and John Ratcliff, "Position Based Dynamics", Journal of Visual Communication and Image Representation, 18(2), pp.109-118, 2007.
17. Miles Macklin, Matthias Müller and Nuttapong Chentanez, "XPBD: Position-based Simulation of Compliant Constrained Dynamics", Proceedings of the 9th International Conference on Motion in Games, pp.49-54, 2016.
18. Sofien Bouaziz, Sebastian Martin, Tiantian Liu, Ladislav Kavan and Mark Pauly, "Projective Dynamics: Fusing Constraint Projections for Fast Simulation", ACM Transactions of Graphics, 33(4), pp.154:1-154:11, 2014.
19. Ronald Fedkiw, Jos Stam and Henrik Wann Jensen, "Visual Simulation of Smoke", Proceedings of SIGGRAPH 2001, pp.15-22, 2001.
20. Andrew Selle, Nick Rasmussen and Ronald Fedkiw, "A Vortex Particle Method for Smoke, Water and Explosions", ACM Transactions of Graphics, 24(3), pp.910-914, 2005.
21. Theodore Kim, Nils Thürey, Doug James and Markus Gross, "Wavelet Turbulence for Fluid Simulation", ACM Transactions of Graphics, 27(3), pp.1-6, 2008.
22. Nadir Akinci, Gizem Akinci and Matthias Teschner, "Versatile Surface Tension and Adhesion for SPH Fluids", ACM Transactions of Graphics, 32(6), pp.182:1-182:8, 2013.
23. Ronald Fedkiw, Tariq Aslam, Barry Merriman and Stanley Osher, "A Non-oscillatory Eulerian Approach to Interfaces in Multimaterial Flows (the Ghost Fluid Method)", Journal of Computational Physics, 152(2), pp.457-492, 1999.
24. Makoto Fujisawa and Kenjiro T. Miura, "Animation of Ice Melting Phenomenon Based on Thermodynamics with Thermal Radiation", Proceedings of the 2009 ACM SIGGRAPH/Eurographics Symposium on Computer Animation, pp.209-217, 2009. ACM Transactions on Graphics, 28, 3, pp.40:1-40:6, 2009.
25. Frank Losasso, Frédéric Gibou and Ron Fedkiw, "Simulating Water and Smoke with an Octree Data Structure", ACM Transactions of Graphics, 23(3), pp.457-462, 2004.
26. Bryan E. Feldman, James F. O'Brien and Bryan M. Klingner "Animating Gases with Hybrid Meshes", ACM Transactions of Graphics, 24(3), pp.904-909, 2005.
27. Stanley Osher and Ronald Fedkiw, "Level Set Methods and Dynamic Implicit Surfaces", Springer-Verlag, 2003.
28. ByungMoon Kim, Yingjie Liu, Ignacio Llamas and Jarek Rossignac, "Advections with Significantly Reduced Dissipation and Diffusion", IEEE Transactions on Visualization and Computer Graphics, 13(1), pp.135-144, 2007.
29. Hideaki Takewaki and Takashi Yabe, "The Cubic-interpolated Pseudo Particle (CIP) Method: Application to Nonlinear and Multi-dimensional Hyperbolic Equations", Journal of Computational Physics, 70(2), pp.355-372, 1987.
30. Michael Lentine, Jón Tómas Grétarsson and Ronald Fedkiw, "An Unconditionally Stable Fully Conservative Semi-Lagrangian Method", Journal of Computational Physics, 230(8), pp.2857-2879, 2011.
31. Mark Carlson, Peter J. Mucha, R. Brooks Van Horn III and Greg Turk, "Melting and Flowing", Proceedings of ACM SIGGRAPH/Eurographics Symposium on Computer Animation, pp.167-174, 2002.
32. Douglas Enright, Stephen Marschner and Ronald Fedkiw, "Animation and Rendering of Complex Water Surfaces", ACM Transactions of Graphics, 21(3), pp.736-744, 2002.
33. Matthias Müller, David Charypar and Markus Gross, "Particle-Based Fluid Simulation for Interactive Applications", Proceedings of the 2003 ACM SIGGRAPH/Eurographics Symposium on Computer Animation, pp.154-159, 2003.
34. Joseph J. Monaghan, "Smoothed Particle Hydrodynamics", Annual Review of Astronomy and Astrophysics, 30, pp543-574, 1992.
35. Markus Becker and Matthias Teschner, "Weakly Compressible SPH for Free Surface Flows", Proceedings of the 2007 ACM SIGGRAPH/Eurographics Symposium on Computer Animation, pp.209-217, 2007.

36. Barbara Solenthaler and Renato B. Pajarola, "Predictive-corrective Incompressible SPH", ACM Transactions on Graphics, 28, pp.40:1-40:6, 2009.
37. Markus Ihmsen, Jens Cornelis, Barbara Solenthaler, Christopher Horvath and Matthias Teschner, "Implicit Incompressible SPH", IEEE Transactions on Visualization and Computer Graphics, 20(3), pp.426-435, 2014.
38. Miles Macklin and Matthias Müller, "Position Based Fluids", ACM Transactions of Graphics, 32(4), pp.104:1-104:12, 2013.
39. Nadir Akinci, Markus Ihmsen, Gizem Akinci, Barbara Solenthaler and Matthias Teschner, "Versatile Rigid-fluid Coupling for Incompressible SPH", ACM Transactions of Graphics, 31(4), pp.62:1-62:8, 2012.
40. Yongning Zhu and Robert Bridson, "Animating Sand as a Fluid", ACM Transactions on Graphics, 24(3), pp.965-971, 2005.
41. Alexey Stomakhin, Craig Schroeder, Lawrence Chai, Joseph Teran and Andrew Selle, "A Material Point Method for Snow Simulation", ACM Transactions of Graphics, 32(4), pp.102:1-102:10, 2013.
42. Jerry Tessendorf, "Simulating Ocean Water", SIGGRAPH 1999 course notes, 1999.
43. Cem Yuksel, Donald H. House and John Keyser, "Wave Particles", ACM Transactions on Graphics, 26(3), pp.99:1-99:8, 2007.
44. Stefan Jeschke, Tomáš Skřivan, Matthias Müller-Fischer, Nuttapong Chentanez, Miles Macklin and Chris Wojtan, "Water Surface Wavelets", ACM Transactions on Graphics, 37(4), pp.94:1-94:13, 2018.
45. Anita T. Layton and Michiel van de Panne, "A Numerically Efficient and Stable Algorithm for Animating Water Waves", The Visual Computer, 18(1), pp.41-53, 2002.
46. Matthias Müller, Nuttapong Chentanez and Tae-Yong Kim, "Real Time Dynamic Fracture with Volumetric Approximate Convex Decompositions", ACM Transactions of Graphics, 32(4), pp.115:1-115:10, 2013.
47. James F. O'Brien and Jessica K. Hodgins, "Graphical Modeling and Animation of Brittle Fracture", Proceedings of the 26th Annual Conference on Computer Graphics and Interactive Techniques, pp.137-146, 1999.
48. David Hahn and Chris Wojtan, "Fast Approximations for Boundary Element Based Brittle Fracture Simulation", ACM Transactions of Graphics, 35(4), pp.104:1-104:11, 2016.
49. Joshuah Wolper, Yu Fang, Minchen Li, Jiecong Lu, Ming Gao and Chenfanfu Jiang, "CD-MPM: Continuum Damage Material Point Methods for Dynamic Fracture Animation", ACM Transactions of Graphics, 38(4), pp.119:1-119:15, 2019.
50. Duc Quang Nguyen, Ronald Fedkiw and Henrik Wann Jensen, "Physically Based Modeling and Animation of Fire", ACM Transactions of Graphics, 21(3), pp.721-728, 2002.
51. Nipun Kwatra, Jón T. Grétarsson and Ronald Fedkiw, "Practical Animation of Compressible Flow for Shock Waves and Related Phenomena", Proceedings of the 2010 ACM SIGGRAPH/Eurographics Symposium on Computer Animation, pp.207-215, 2010.
52. Michael B. Nielsen, Morten Bojsen-Hansen, Konstantinos Stamatelos and Robert Bridson, "Physics-Based Combustion Simulation", ACM Transactions of Graphics, 41(5), pp.176:1-176:21, 2022.
53. Ryo Miyazaki, Yoshinori Dobashi and Tomoyuki Nishita, "Simulation of Cumuliform Clouds Based on Computational Fluid Dynamics", Proceedings of the Eurographics 2002 Short Presentations, pp.405-410, 2002.
54. Mark J. Harris, "Real-Time Cloud Simulation and Rendering", ACM SIGGRAPH 2005 Courses, 2005.
55. James F. O'Brien, Chen Shen and Christine M. Gatchalian, "Synthesizing Sounds from Rigid-Body Simulations", Proceedings of the 2002 ACM SIGGRAPH/Eurographics Symposium on Computer Animation, pp.175-181, 2002.
56. Timothy R. Langlois, Changxi Zheng and Doug L. James, "Toward Animating Water with Complex Acoustic Bubbles", ACM Transactions of Graphics, 35(4), pp.95:1-95:13, 2016.

Index

Zeitfracht Medien GmbH
Ferdinand-Jühlke-Straße 7
99095 Erfurt, Deutschland
produktsicherheit@kolibri360.de